We Lived To Tell

POLITICAL PRISON MEMOIRS
OF IRANIAN WOMEN

Azadeh Agah

Sousan Mehr

Shadi Parsi

Library and Archives Canada Cataloguing in Publication

Agah, Azadeh
    We lived to tell : political prison memoirs of Iranian women / Azadeh
Agah, Sousan Mehr and Shadi Parsi.

ISBN 978-1-894692-19-9

    1. Agah, Azadeh. 2. Mehr, Sousan. 3. Parsi, Shadi. 4. Women political
prisoners--Iran--Biography. 5. Political prisoners--Iran--Biography.
6. Women--Iran--Biography. 7. Iran--Politics and government--1979-1997.
I. Mehr, Sousan II. Parsi, Shadi III. Title.

HQ1735.2.Z75A3 2007   365'.45092255   C2007-906200-8

Developmental Editor: Ann Decter
Editor: Rivanne Sandler
Copy Editor: Lisa Foad
Cover Illustration: Azadeh Agah
Cover Design & Inside Photography: Schuster Gindin
Inside Layout: Heather Guylar

Credits:
Excerpt from the poem *Fish* by Ahmad Shamloo translated from Farsi by Sousan
Mehr and Rivanne Sandler. Excerpt from *Haghigha-te sadeh (The Simple Truth)* by M.
Raha translated from Farsi by Azadeh Agah, published by the Independent Iranian
Women's Publication, Hanover, Germany, 1992. Excerpt from Dar Golestaneh by
Sohrab Sepehri, from *Hasht Ketab*, Tahoori Publishers, Tehran, 1984.

McGilligan Books gratefully acknowledges the support of the Ontario Book
Publishing Tax Credit for our publishing program.

We wish to dedicate this book to:

Everyone who has ever fought for justice and human rights, in particular, to our former prison mates, the ones who paid for their beliefs with their lives, and those who survived without compromising their moral standards. We have done our best to give words to our mutual experience.

Our parents and siblings, who were constant sources of hope and love during and after our imprisonment.

A., H., and K., our husbands and best friends, for their tremendous support, love and encouragement.

And to our children, some of whom were put through difficult experiences during our absence from home, and some who were not yet born. Either way, you have lived and coped with the direct or indirect effects of those years. We dedicate this book to you and the next generation, so that you may understand, remember and learn from it.

Contents

Years of Solitude, Years of Defiance: Women Political Prisoners in Iran

SEVERAL YEARS AGO, while visiting the Mona Campus of the University of West Indies in Jamaica, I noticed traces of old aqueducts in a vast open field. I was told these were remnants of a large sugar plantation. The history of colonialism and slavery in that part of the world appeared in front of me. I began to hear the anguish of slaves labouring under scorching heat and dreaming freedom; I heard the sounds of resistance and revolution; the words of Toussaint L'Ouverture, C. L. R. James, Frantz Fanon and Gloria Anzaldúa came alive. How do people deal with monuments of oppression, I wondered. How does the presence of such a relic shape our daily connections to the world around us? Thinking these questions through, my thoughts travelled to another part of the world, to Iran, the country of my birth. A country where I witnessed one of the last revolutions of the 20th century; a country that forced me into exile; a country that I dream of embracing when it is free.

The university where I began teaching in Iran in the fall of 1979 – the first post-Revolution academic year – was located on the slopes of the majestic Alborz mountain in northern Tehran. Adjacent to it was the notorious Evin Prison. Those were joyful days when the prison was liberated by the people, and political prisoners who had survived the brutality of the last Shah of the Pahlavi dynasty left the dungeons as heroes. There was discussion about turning Evin into a university; into a museum; into some kind of an institution to serve people, not suppress them. But the joy was short-lived, and I did not get a chance to fully experience the process of coming to terms with this monument of oppression. Soon, Evin and other prisons throughout the country were filled again, first with the supporters of the Shah's regime and then with the rising dissidents of the Islamic regime. That is what haunted me on the Mona Campus of the University of West Indies in Jamaica. Why can't the course of our histories, with abundant evidence of suppression and extreme brutality, be reversed? Would future generations respond to Guantanamo Bay or Abu-Ghraib prisons the way I did with the sounds and images of slavery? Would they blame us for submitting to the brutality that continues to be inflicted on the souls and bodies of our fellow human beings?

Azadeh Agah, Sousan Mehr, and Shadi Parsi, whose narratives you are about to read, speak so that we remember. Their memorializing of the years of their lives in prison reflects a personal experience with wider political implications. They are engaged in the most human act of coming into terms with prison as a totality and as an institution of oppression. This is the first collection of memoirs in English of women who were political prisoners in the Islamic Republic of Iran, who resisted physical and psychological torture, and survived to tell their stories. Azadeh, Sousan, and Shadi, speak of pain, sorrow, and anger; they also remind us of love, happiness, generosity and forgiveness. They have written these memoirs to put us in touch with the most humane aspects of being human. They are voices of thousands of other women who were incarcerated, many of whom often did not survive. In intricate ways, they invite us into their private lives, private lives that were publicly brutalized. Their tales of years of prison in Evin and elsewhere connect us to an untold history. They depict images and voices of courage, kindness, compassion, betrayal, cowardice, and brutality that stubbornly stay in our head. Azadeh, Sousan, and Shadi's first and final words are *We Lived to Tell*: the title of the book.

Three women, three distinct narrations, form this book. Azadeh, Sousan, and Shadi were political prisoners because they resisted the absolute rule of the Islamic Government. What we understand through their words is that they are secular women with deep yearnings for social justice. They refused to submit, compromise, and be silent. Through the tale of their years in prison, they tell us about a political order, the Islamic Government of Iran, which rules over its own people with an iron fist. Behind the closed doors of prison, an autocratic regime exercises its absolute rule; absolutism with a divine character. The Islamic Government, since coming to power in 1979, has pronounced itself the representative of God on earth. In the 1980s and 1990s, thousands of Iranian political prisoners were subjected to punishment for questioning and confronting its authority and legitimacy and brutally disciplined for disobeying the divine rule of God embodied in the Islamic state. Azadeh, Sousan, and Shadi tell us how state and religion colluded in disciplining their sexuality. They were tortured, denigrated, and vilified for being women and claiming an oppositional space. These women ruptured the boundaries of patriarchal-religious submissiveness, pushed their sexualized bodies into the public sphere and claimed rights. Crossing these boundaries was their crime.

Azadeh, Sousan, and Shadi were sentenced to varying lengths of confinement. Having shared that closed space bonds them together. They differ in social status, education, and age. This unique difference becomes the richness readers experience. In distinct voices, they walk us through long corridors and crammed cells where the best and brightest minds and bodies, like theirs, were viciously tortured. Each narrates vignettes of years of solitude and years of defiance. Each episode depicts a new dimension of life under incarceration: children in prison, relations with loved ones outside, friendships made and broken, moments of deep personal soul-searching on life, death, pain, loneliness, and living beyond captivity. What captured me is their life-wide desire for living and justice. The smell of a flower, the taste of food, celebrating the birthday of a child or an inmate, caring for each other's torture wounds, opening their hearts to each other – these are moments of survival. Two moments, in particular, are deeply troubling for them: one moment is when names of prisoners are being called over the loudspeaker of the prison, when Azadeh, Sousan, and Shadi know that this is the agonizing moment of saying "goodbye" to those who are being called to be executed. How does one say "goodbye" when there is no return? How does one witness such an atrocity and remain silent, these writers ask.

The other troubling moment in prison is the presence of *tavvab*s. The word *tavvab* means repentant; an inmate who has repented her "crime." A *tavvab* is a collaborator or informant. In the Islamic regime, even the universal phenomenon of denouncing self under the condition of incarceration takes a particular religious, political, and ideological form. The state enforces religious morality through the creation of informants. The *tavvab* is a prisoner who is being forced to denounce her politics and be somebody other than herself: an interrogator, a pious woman, a believer, a spy; a *tavvab* is the ears and eyes of her captors, an executor of rules within the cell, an arbitrator among inmates and between inmates and prison guards; truly, a woman who disowns herself and embraces the ideology and politics of her oppressors. To show her religious devotion, she shoots the last shot of executions; she accompanies guards on the streets to identify activists and bring them into captivity. The state captures the body and the soul and combines them into one: *tavvab*. Azadeh, Sousan, and Shadi painfully remember the presence of *tavvab*s in their cells. They tell us about the raging moments of confronting *tavvab*s when they robbed them of the best human qualities: trust, friendship, sharing, support, confidence, and reliance.

In the 1980s, Khomeini and other leaders were engaged in creating new "Muslim" men and women as part of the Islamization of the ancient state system they took over from the monarchs. The phenomenon of *tavvab* is only one element of the theocracy they were building. The prisoner had to be a "Muslim," devoted to Allah who has mandated "his" rule to the Islamic state in Iran – the state dictated self-absorption into beyond self, the means to-be-not-to-be. It is the fanatical creation of new beings for sacrifice; for being to cease. The Islamic Government engaged in systematic annihilation of political prisoners through a process of creating *tavvab*s to demoralize others, to rip prisoners of hope and dreaming life and struggle beyond bars. No wonder, then, that we hear about suicide, psychological disturbances and depression among *tavvab*s, even after release.

The state machinery of *tavvab*-making intentionally wasted the lives of prisoners; life became death and death was the meaning given to life. I know it is not easy to fully grasp the depth of this atrocity. The authors, in profound and reflexive ways, urge us to listen to them and be with them as they speak about their hate and compassion for *tavvab*s. But, we still may ask, what would make a state commit such atrocities? The stories of Azadeh, Sousan, and Shadi are not fiction. They resisted

being molded into their version of "Muslims," resisted giving up "self"
and becoming *tavvab*s.

State Violence: Evin in Iran and Iran as a Larger Prison
The memoirs of Azadeh, Sousan, and Shadi also form a history of a
country going through massive social change. The most important anti-
imperialist revolution of the post-colonial era was taking place in the
already troubled region of the Middle East. The ideological struggle
within prison was replicated outside. The majority of prisoners were
incarcerated because they questioned the legitimacy of the state and its
policy of suppressing what they had fought for and achieved with the
fall of the monarchy: freedom of association, freedom of expression,
freedom of the press. The new rulers soon imposed the veil on women
and gradually created a regime of gender apartheid where women became second-class citizens. No dissenting voice was spared the brutality
of the state: high school and university students, faculty members, and
union activists were targeted. The majority of prisoners in the early years
of the 1980s were, in fact, students, some as young as thirteen and fourteen. Without simplifying a very complicated historical moment when
diverse forces vied for a share of power in politics, for this discussion
we can group the opposing forces into two camps: those who argued
for separation of the state and religion and those who tried to integrate
religion into the state. This political tension has dominated the public
scene of Iran since the establishment of the Islamic Republic. Iranian
women, more specifically, have not ceased for one moment to resist the
unification of the state and religion.

The phenomenon of "political prisoner," that is, one who is incarcerated for her political beliefs or political action, as well as their torture and mistreatment, is often associated with dictatorial regimes. The
torture of prisoners by the United States in the prisons of Abu Ghraib
and Guantanamo Bay has shattered this distinction.[1] Equally revealing
is the justification of torture by some advocates of liberal democracy
who argued that the lesser evil of torture is needed in order to eliminate
the greater evil of terrorism.[2] And when the United States ratified the
United Nations Convention Against Torture and Other Cruel, Inhuman
or Degrading Treatment or Punishment (entered into force on June 26,
1987), it added reservations so numerous that torture can still be legally
perpetrated.[3] If the mistreatment of political prisoners and prisoners

of war is universal, despite the U.N. Convention Against Torture, what distinguishes the cruelty inflicted on prisoners in Iran?[4] Why does Iran refuse to ratify the Convention? Why were women incarcerated in Iran on a large scale for the first time and why did the Islamic regime undertake two massacres of political prisoners in 1982 and 1988? Why were the penal order and its prison networks Islamized? This book will help us find some of the answers.

Behind the prison walls, the Iranian state exercises absolute, unrestrained, and arbitrary power on behalf of Allah. I will try to put these events into the context of what was happening outside the prison walls. When Ayatollah Khomeini replaced the Shah as head of the state in early 1979, he began to lay the foundations of the "Islamic government," a political order which he had formulated in the early 1970s while in exile in Iraq. The slogan was "'Neither the East nor the West, the Islamic Government." In other words, the Islamic order was to be an alternative to both socialism and capitalism. It would be a state that represented the rule of Allah on earth. It was called "the rule of the jurist-theologian" (*velayat-e faqih*) – the governing of the affairs of Muslims on behalf of Allah. Khomeini himself was the first ruler-theologian. This is, to some extent, similar to the governance of Vatican, where religion and politics are merged to constitute the state, a regime that was replaced by early social reforms of the 16th and 17th century and the revolutions of the 18th century in favor of a democratic order based on the separation of state and church. It is important to note that the Islamic theocracy is, in fact, a "capitalist" theocracy where capitalist economy is wedded to religion.

Khomeini inherited the extensive state machinery of the Pahalvi monarchs, which was secular, although it had made extensive compromises with Islam and the religious establishment. The secular patriarchy unleashed extreme repression against women who engaged in the struggle to overthrow the monarchical regime. These women were imprisoned, tortured, and killed in armed struggle by the notorious Organization of State Security and Intelligence, *SAVAK* (its Farsi acronym). Once overthrown, the Shah's secular patriarchy was replaced by Khomini's religious patriarchy.[5]

Khomeini wanted to Islamize both the state and the society. His mission was, therefore, to merge religion and state, and religion involved more than the supremacy of *mosques* and seminaries. Politics, law, society, economy, culture, and everything including the justice system, the penal order, and prisons, had to be Islamized. Such a project could not be implemented by consent: there was extensive popular opposition. Coercion was the main means to the end. The memoirs of Azadeh, Sousan, and Shadi are histories of the struggle between the architects of theocracy and the resistance to it by politically conscious Iranians.

It is important to remember that these memoirs are written and published during the centenary of Iran's Constitutional Revolution, which continued from 1906 to 1911. This was the first major democratic revolution of the non-capitalist world. Genuinely Iranian in origins, it was, in many ways, inspired by the French Revolution of 1789 and the 1905 revolution in neighbouring Russia. The revolutionaries, despite their diverse political persuasions, aimed at the democratization of the state, separation of powers, the formation of a modern justice system, and separation of state and *mosque*. It was also, like the American Revolution of 1776, a national liberation struggle for independence from two colonial powers, Britain and Russia, which had divided the country into two spheres of influence. The significance of this revolution can be gauged in the rise of women as a new social force into the political life of the country. In 1911, when only four states in the world had granted suffrage rights to women, a representative of the new Iranian parliament launched an initiative for granting women's rights. On August 22, 1911, *The London Times* reported from Tehran that, "The supporters of women suffrage should be gratified to learn that even in the midst of Persia's present trials and troubles, where the ex-Shah has raised his standard and civil war is loose, a champion of the women's cause has been found in the Persian Mejliss [Iranian parliament]."

These few references to the beginnings of modern Iranian history give us some clues about the obstacles that the founders of the Islamic theocracy would face almost seventy years later. The number of women participants in the first revolution was indeed small. However, step by step they gained more prominence, and launched their organizations and publications during the numerous struggles that continued until the second revolution of 1979. By 1979, women were a political force to be taken into account by both the outgoing monarchical regime and the incoming Islamic theocracy. There was a sizeable women's intelligentsia, composed of authors, poets, artists, academics, journalists, scientists, and a relatively large professional group including engineers, physicians, judges, parliamentarians, ministers, nurses, pilots, and teachers.

During the revolution, masses of women, like the rest of the population, revolted against the monarchy, but demands for gender equality were not prominent until the fall of the Shah in February 1979. However, when Khomeini replaced the Shah, he was unable to extend his control over much of the population and the country. Non-Persian nationalities such as the Kurds, Baluches, Arabs and Turkmens were demanding autonomy in the new regime. The universities, which had played a decisive role in the revolution, were liberated and were in the hands of leftist students and faculty. The print media also had revolted against the Shah and had no interest in surrendering their hard won independence to the new rulers.

It was not surprising, therefore, that immediately after coming to power, the country's first internal conflict was Khomeini's war against women. He ordered them to put on the *hijab* head cover, and dismissed all women judges because women were not able, according to Islamic law, to judge. Widespread protests against these measures were followed by more coercive campaigns against women and new initiatives for creating a regime of gender apartheid. Soon after this, the air force attacked Kurdistan, and by August the entire army launched a major offensive against the Kurds, and their nationalist movement for autonomy within Iran. At the same time, the print media was suppressed, while broadcast media continued to be a state monopoly, as it had been under the Shah. In April 1980, armed gangs attacked the universities, and closed them down for two years as they embarked on the "Islamic Cultural Revolution." While women, the nationalities and the print media had not been successfully integrated into the new state, the Islamic Cultural Revolution was launched in order to remove the left from the campuses, and launch the project of Islamization of the entire society, beginning with higher education institutions. All of this was followed by a widespread crackdown on the opposition in June 1981. The extensive prison network could hardly cope with the tens of thousands of prisoners arrested at that time. Summary trials and mass executions were one response to the challenge.

Before the prison network was filled with political activists, the Islamic regime had launched a campaign to discredit the left and the secular Islamist. This is not surprising. The secular left, mostly communists and Marxists, had been the main political foe of the monarchical regime. Values of heroism of political prisoners and their invincibility in torture cells dominate Iran's political culture. This tradition of resistance is immortalized in the poem of the prominent poet Ahamd Shamlu. In *Nazli sokhan nagoft* (Nazli did not Utter a Word) Nazli, pseudonym of a real prisoner, is tortured to death but does not surrender to interrogators.

Azadeh, Sousan, and Shadi were in jail during the Iraq-Iran war of 1980-88, which left its imprint on the country and its prisons. Khomeini used the occasion to consolidate his theocracy by, among other things, suppressing any form of dissent. However, the devastations of this war – death, destruction and a failing economy – led to more dissidence throughout Iran. While the resources of the country were mobilized to win the war, the government was also fighting other opposition forces, some of which, including Organization of People's *Mojahedin*, engaged in armed resistance. The number of prisoners soared. At the same time, resistance was on the rise, and by early 1987 there were hunger strikes in some of the prisons. The response was the execution of 20 strikers. Conflicts within the Islamic regime, which consisted of a number of factions, were not subsiding in spite of Khomeini's frequent interventions.

Faced with the prospects of the collapse of the theocratic order, Khomeini declared, in January 1988, a regime of "absolute rule of the jurist-theologian" (*velayat-e motllaqeh-ye faqih*). This upgraded Islamic state was, according to Khomeini, derived from the absolute dominion of the Prophet of God. From now on, any measure in the interests of the state could override Islamic ordinances, including the most important ones such as prayer, fasting and the pilgrimage to Mecca.[6] In other words, loyalty to the state was the only valid measure of Muslimhood. It was clear that Khomeini was responding to two challenges to the stability of the state. One was resolving incessant factional fighting, but the more important concern was to stem any prospect of a popular revolt, that is, revolutionary overthrow of his regime. The new absolutism was, therefore, a final solution for the ongoing crises of the Islamic state: uproot all sources of resistance. The most vulnerable were political prisoners, who included not only the rank and file of the opposition, but also their leaders and cadres. By the summer, the government launched a massive annihilation project known as the "Massacre of 1988" (*Koshtar-e 1367*).[7] Within the course of a few months, thousands of prisoners, who were serving different prison terms, were summarily executed.

The stories of Azadeh, Sousan, and Shadi point to the failure of the Islamic state-building project initiated by Khomeini. If the state was unable to force women into submission in prison, a site of absolute and arbitrary exercise of power, it also failed to construct its ideal "Muslim woman," the active agent of producing and reproducing a regime of gender apartheid. Indeed, the memoirs of other political prisoners, written in Persian and published in the Iranian diaspora, confirm the failure of the state and the invincibility of these women.[8] Outside the prisons, too, women have turned public spaces such as the streets, campuses, the printed and digital page, city parks, sport stadiums, mountains, and highways, into sites of resistance. They have succeeded not only in seriously undermining the theocratic state but also, together with other social movements such as labour and student movements, to raise the spectre of revolution, this time to overthrow the theocratic order.

Tens of thousands of political prisoners were punished for questioning the authority and legitimacy of the state, which was nothing less than "fighting the authority of Allah and the prophet" (*moharebeh ba khoda va rasul-e khoda*). Punishment took a fully religious character. The extensive repertoire of *Shari'a*, the canonical law of Islam, was used. There is, in these memoirs, considerable evidence about the union of state and religion in disciplining women. Without trying to theorize about the gender and religious components of prison and punishment, these memoirs portray a detailed picture of how the Islamic regime of prisons targeted them as women. The religious penal order had devised intricate ways of controlling women's sexuality. For instance, while women's cells were fully segregated from the men's, prison authorities were concerned about the intensive contact of so many inmates within a small space. They were worried about the possibility of same sex relations among the inmates. At the same time, torture, both physical and psychological, was masculinist. Prisoners were tortured not only for opposing the state, but also for doing so as women. During interrogations, most women were accused of getting involved in political activities in order to fulfill their sexual desires through meeting the members of the opposite sex. The prison authorities began a massive public campaign, which portrayed women as "sinners" who had engaged in political opposition to the Islamic state as a venue for sexual gratification. Also, they attempted to discredit political groups, specifically the left, as immoral people who had no "decency" and opposed family values.

They "Lived to Tell," What Shall We Do?

The Islamic regime in Iran has developed and, indeed, has refined an Islamic regime of prison administration, with its own organization of space, techniques of torture, and other punitive technologies and methods. In a preliminary study on disciplining sexuality in prisons of Iran, I have identified four methods: assaulting women's political agency and autonomy; torturing the female body; criminalizing homosexuality; and using rape as torture. By their presence in jail and by not yielding to the absolute power of the state, women political prisoners exposed the solidly masculinist nature of the Islamic regime, its politics and ideology. Three weeks after assuming power, Khomeini dismissed women judges because, according to Islam, women are intellectually and emotionally weak. Every hour and every day, these prisoners challenged the Islamic judicial-political order in its entirety. Khomeini wanted women to play a crucial role in Islamizing state and society by nurturing good Muslim children; these prisoners ruptured the boundaries of patriarchal-religious submissiveness, and offered a secular, radical, and revolutionary alternative to the theocratic order.

The oppression of women in countries that are targeted by the United States is currently used as justification for military or humanitarian intervention. To "free" women of Afghanistan, Iraq, and perhaps soon Iran, these nations are sanctioned and bombed. Azadeh, Sousan, and Shadi's memoirs continue a century of women's struggle in the Middle East. This is a history with abundant evidence of resiliency, courage, and boldness. In this history, the image of passive women of the Middle East is a fantasy created by male-centred colonial powers. The evidence in these memoirs also rejects the claim that women in Iran can be liberated through the military or "humanitarian" intervention of the United States or any other country. The gender balance sheet of the occupation of Iraq and Afghanistan is one of anti-feminism and colonial feminism. *We Lived to Tell* shows that Iranian women themselves are capable of dismantling the patriarchal-capitalist theocracy, a project that has been on the top of their agenda for three decades.

Shahrzad Mojab
August 2007

Endnotes

1   For documentation and analysis of the justification of torture by the United States, see Karen Greenberg and Joshua Dratel (eds.) (2005), *The Torture Papers: The Road to Abu Ghraib*, New York: Cambridge University Press.

2   Michael Ignatieff (2004), *The Lesser Evil: Political Ethics in an Age of Terror*. Princeton University Press.

3   See, e.g., *Human Rights Watch*, "Getting away with torture? Command responsibility for the U.S. abuse of detainees," April 2005, http://www.hrw.org/reports/2005/us0405/index.htm

4   For the text of the United Nations Convention Against Torture and Other Cruel, Inhuman or Degrading Treatment or Punishment, and ratifications of the document, see http://www.ohchr.org/english/law/cat.htm

5   For a historical review of political prisoners in modern Iran see Afshin Matin-Asgari (2006), "Twentieth century Iran's political prisoners," *Middle Eastern Studies*, 42 (5): 689-707.

6   Asghar Schirazi (1988), *The Constitution of Iran: Politics and the State in the Islamic Republic*. Translated by John O'Kane, London: I. B. Tauris Publishers, p. 64.

7   The history of political repression in Iran during the 1980s and 1990s with mass imprisonment, torture, and execution of political prisoners needs to be studied and documented. The field of Iranian Studies, and in particular women's studies, has failed to engage with this topic. There are three scholarly works in English with focus on political prisoners. These are: Darius Rejali (1994), *Torture and Modernity: Self, Society, and State in Modern Iran*, Colorado: Westview Press; Ervand Abrahamian (1999), *Tortured Confession: Prison and Public Recantations in Modern Iran*, Berkeley: The University of California Press; and Reza Afshari (2001), *Human Rights in Iran: The Abuse of Cultural Relativism*, Philadelphia: University of Pennsylvania Press. For a legal human rights analysis of the massacre of 1988, see Kaveh Shahrooz (forthcoming), *With Revolutionary Rage and Rancor: A Report and Preliminary Legal Analysis of the 1988 Massacre of Iran's Political Prisoners*.

8   For a comprehensive list of prison memoirs see the website of my research called *Memories, Memoirs, and the Arts: Women Political Prisoners of Iran* www.utoronto.ca/prisonmemoirs).

Years of Fire and Ash

SOUSAN MEHR

Cyclamens

I HAD BEEN THINKING of him all afternoon and evening. It is impossible not to think of him when it is raining or when I am passing by flower shops and I see the white and mauve cyclamens behind the windows. Davoud used to accompany me on my walk home from university each day. When we would pass the flower shops, we always looked for the two flowers that seemed most like a couple.

Tonight, I'm sad – sad as the night I found out he had married, and that his wife was pregnant and sick. I had been visiting with fellow students at the dormitory. "The poor woman is very sick," they said. We had already split but the news shocked me and on my way home, I felt filled with loneliness. I was confused and couldn't figure out my feelings. I just knew I felt sorry, so sorry. For him? For myself? For what had happened?

I've lived with this sorrow for three years now; I'm used to it. We took separate paths. He didn't very much care about what was happening to the country, about the revolution, about the people. I, on the other hand, had spent my teenage years dreaming of helping my people; I had desperately wished for a revolution. I couldn't possibly feel indifferent about what was happening.

Here at home, the lights are off. I don't feel hungry, just tired and sad. I go to my room. I listen, as usual, to the radio broadcast by the political organization I support. I wonder if another revolution is possible. It's only been a couple of years since the first one occurred; could another happen so quickly? Right now, I'm too exhausted to care. I want to sleep. I brush my teeth without paying attention, and go to bed.

"Where are you?" he asks. His smile is tentative. He is standing in front of the window. The lights flashing behind him prevent me from seeing his face clearly. He always asks me the same question, with an uncertain smile, and I wonder how to answer him.

We are in an art gallery.

He stretches his hands towards me and says, "Come, I found words for this painting."

We had agreed that works of art become alive when they can be described in words. Together, we used to find words for works of art that we saw and music that we heard. We made poems out of them.

His hands are still outstretched.

"No, I have to go," I say. "The gallery will be closing soon."

He says something, but I can't hear him. The distracting sound of tap water drowns out his voice. Disappointed, he puts his hands in his pockets and mumbles. He's trying to tell me something, but the sound of a vacuum cleaner blocks his voice. Where is all the tumult and commotion coming from?

I wake up to the insistent ringing of the doorbell. I hurriedly put on my robe and rush to the yard to open the door in the wall that surrounds the house. The door, however, is already open, and two men are jumping over the wall into the yard. Five or six armed *pasdar*s[1] are in the yard, talking loudly.

One of them grabs my sleeve and drags me inside the house. He fires several questions at me without waiting for answers. "What is your name? Who else is at home?"

---

1   A *pasdar* is a member of the Revolutionary Guard.

The others follow us inside. They are all bearded. They rudely go everywhere in the house. There is no sign of humanity in their eyes or in their manner. They are like hunters.

The *pasdar* clutching my arm says to another, "Check the radio channel. Look for alcohol and matches under her bed. Search the other rooms and the rest of the house." Then he turns to me. "Why are you at home alone? Who are you living with?"

Another questions, "Who was that jumping out the kitchen window?"

"There's no one else at home," I say.

"What's the safety sign[2] for the house?" demands yet another.

"Safety sign?" I pretend not to understand him.

"Don't try to fool me. Tell me what you know, otherwise you'll be beaten all the way from here to Evin."[3]

"Give her to me." A bigger and more impatient guard threatens me brutally.

Finally, the leader pushes me towards the other room. "Go get dressed." To the others, he commands, "Brothers, hurry up. We have lots of work to do."

I take my clothing and go into the bedroom. A *pasdar* comes with me. I don't know what to do – I can't dress in front of him. When he turns his back, I ready myself: pants, shirt, sweater, long coat, scarf and socks. It's mid-September and getting cold. For three days, it has been pouring nonstop. Every now and then the *pasdar* turns and looks me up and down to make sure I'm not hiding anything in my clothing. He asks me a lot of questions. He seems more curious about my life than about my political activities. He thinks it is strange that a single girl is living alone in this house. He wants to know who I live with.

The group leader asks, "Whose motorcycle is this?"

"It belongs to the landlord," I say.

"Lock the rooms," he instructs the *pasdar*s and points to the bedrooms. To me, he says, "Wear your *chador*.[4] And give me your scarf."

---

2   A safety sign is a pre-arranged warning signal for a fellow dissident. It might be a curtain placed in a certain way or something left in a window.

3   Evin is a large prison located in the village of Evin in the north of Tehran, close to the mountains. It was originally built for political prisoners during the time of the last Shah and was used primarily for political dissidents during the 1980s.

4   *Chador* is a veil covering the entire female body.

I pass it to him and wonder what he wants with my scarf. I take a *chador* and put it on. It's not mine and it's too long for me.

One of the *pasdar*s says, "Wear it properly."

I pull it over myself to cover my hair.

The *pasdar* folds my scarf and hands it to me. "Use it as a blindfold."

I close and cover my eyes, and think of the childhood games we used to play with blindfolds.

One *pasdar* tells another, "Have you checked the house escape routes? Lock the rooms. We'll put the landlord and the house under surveillance." Again he asks me, "What's the safety sign for the house?"

I maintain that I know nothing. "What a question! How would I know?"

"Don't raise your voice, you filthy *monafeq*.[5] Soon you'll see how I make you spit out your dirty information."

I'm pushed out of the house. I hear the doors shut with a bang and lock. Someone holding onto a corner of my *chador* drags me. I can only see the ground and my booted feet. I'm pushed towards a car. I feel the neighbours' eyes staring at me through the curtains. I imagine sympathy and fear in their eyes.

I'm scared, but I know where I'm being taken and part of me feels a sense of relief – I'm finally going to be with my friends, the best of people, the dearest.

The car door is opened.

"Get in." A *pasdar* says, but instantly changes his mind: "No, wait, get in from the other side." He drags me to the other side of the car and pushes me into the backseat. I see a pair of feet wearing big brown men's slippers. Both slippers are for the right foot. The feet are bandaged and blotched with blood.

"What happened?" I ask the owner of the feet.

The *pasdar* sitting in the front screams, "Shut up! Don't talk with each other!"

To ease the *pasdar*'s rage, the owner of the feet says, "Yes, brother. Don't worry, this one doesn't have too much to say."

I recognize the voice – it belongs to Sima. Now, I know it is she who

---

5   *Monafeq* means hypocrite; someone who is only pretending to be a true believer.

has betrayed me, but I also know she hasn't made my case worse than it already is.

The *pasdar* asks, "Where's the other one?"

I don't hear any answer.

The *pasdar* yells, "Dirty *monafeq*, I'm asking you, where's the other one?"

"Are you asking me?" I ask.

"Yes you, *kafar*.[6] Where's the other one?"

Sima's heavy silence tells me that the *pasdars* know that two of us live in the house. "I don't know," I say, "She only comes home sometimes."

"When is she supposed to come?"

"I don't know. She doesn't tell when she'll be home."

"What's the safety sign for the house?"

"I don't know," I answer.

"We have the house under surveillance. Don't make your case worse, miserable rat."

I don't know what to do. I try to think fast, weigh my options, the odds. As my roommate and I agreed, she is not to go home if I don't show up on time tomorrow for our appointment. She won't ever return home. I'd better say that we don't have a safety sign. But then, they probably won't believe me. What if they find out that we have another arrangement? I decide it's better to tell them that we have a safety sign.

"The curtain is the safety sign. If it is on the right side, it means that the house is safe to enter." I pray the curtain is on the right side.

"Ah ha!" he says victoriously, "Now you're on the right track."

Suddenly, the car stops and the *pasdars* begin talking. I raise my head to get a look at them. Both have their heads craned out the car windows. I hear some shooting out on the street. One of the *pasdars* hurriedly gets out of the car with his Kalashnikov rifle, and runs. There is a lot of screaming and commotion out there. The driver opens the door and stretches his body out of the car. I look at Sima seated beside me. She has betrayed all of us. I touch her hand. She shakes her head.

"What should I tell them?"

She shows me her bruised neck, back, and feet.

I ask anxiously again, "What should I tell them?"

The driver turns back towards us. "Quiet. Don't talk."

---

6   *Kafar* is the term for an infidel, or non-believer.

I wait until the driver turns his attention back to the street. I tell the owner of the bloody feet, "If you see our friends, don't show them how badly you've been beaten. Just tell them what they should say."

"You don't know much," she whispers. "Just give them dried-up information."

I can hear her desperate breathing. She used to laugh so loudly. Sometimes she sang for us. She was a funny, lively person. Her current condition pains me and I feel pity for her. I don't have any bitter feelings towards her; I feel forgiveness. Then I think, who am I to forgive someone? I can only forgive her as far as it relates to myself.

The car begins moving again. The *pasdar*s are talking excitedly. "Lousy *kafar*, he thought he could escape!"

"Where did you trap him?"

"At the back of the house. He jumped down from the roof."

He probably broke his leg, I think sadly to myself.

"How many were there?"

"Only one. The other two weren't home."

Again, I feel pained. I know they will beat and torture him until the others are also arrested. God help him.

"We'll find them, all of them! Sons of bitches!"

Sima is moaning quietly.

"We'll be there in a minute," a *pasdar* says to Sima, a reward for her bloodied feet.

They help her out of the car. Her slippers won't stay on and her feet are becoming even more colourful as the bloodstains mix with the brown mud.

One of the *pasdars* tugs my *chador*.

A *pasdar* who is standing by the car door asks, "How many of them have you hunted down?"

"Fourteen, sons of bitches. One of them tried to run. He's there, the one who is limping."

What a commotion! I focus all of my concentration on my sense of hearing. I feel pain in my stomach.

An old woman wearing a long robe over her nightgown and sandals on her feet, is weeping, "I swear to God, I don't know where she is. Why have you brought me here? She hasn't come home for a long time. I haven't heard from her."

She must be my roommate's mother. I wish Sima hadn't known the old woman's address.

I raise my head a bit higher in attempts to look around. I'm surrounded by prisoners. All of us are waiting behind a big gate.

Beside me, someone is moaning, not with pain, but fear. "Oh, my God. I don't know what to do. Oh, my, how can I? Oh, my God!"

From her voice, I sense she may be old and I try to reassure her: "Don't worry, mother. Trust God. God will help you."

She seems to regain control of herself and becomes quiet.

Inside, the hallways are equally as tumultuous and noisy. The *pasdars* and interrogators are busy attempting to interrogate all fourteen of us simultaneously. I raise my head and see Sima spread on the floor as if in prayer. Her lower back, legs, and feet have been whipped so badly that she's not able to sit down properly. I try to talk to her but she doesn't answer me. Her eyes are closed. I wonder if she's afraid, if she's asleep. I raise my head again and see two feet standing in front of me. I feel the weight of eyes upon me.

"Didn't I tell you not to look, *monafeq?*"

"I wasn't looking. I have a headache. I just rearranged my scarf around my head."

"Don't talk nonsense."

"What's so important to look at here, anyway?" My comment is met with a sharp blow and acute pain penetrates my body.

The other *pasdar* says, "That's enough for her, for now. We'll punish her when her turn comes."

One hour, two hours, five hours, I'm not sure how much time has passed.

Every once in a while, an interrogator referred to as Brother Masood asks me various questions.

"Who owns that gun at your place?" he demands this time.

I know he's bluffing. Since my roommate and I last searched her room to find one of her documents, she has only been home once, and she'd brought nothing with her. This stupid question tells me that they don't have any important information about me. I pretend to be a simple, frightened person. "Gun? Oh my, have you found a gun in the house?"

He says curtly, "Think about it. I'll be back again."

But I know very well that they have bigger prey to feast upon – they don't want to waste their time on me. If the *pasdar*s are busy until my morning appointment with my roommate passes, I'll be relieved. The pain in my abdomen is getting worse. I flag a passing *pasdar*, and tell him I need to use the washroom. He calls for another *pasdar* to take me. I tell him that I want to talk to a sister, not a brother.

Without any embarrassment, he asks, "What do you want? Do you need pads?"

"Yes," I say reluctantly. I can't believe one of the very people who segregate men and women, even in buses and universities, has no qualms about invading my privacy. I worry about the unknown dangers that may await me.

"Sit down on this bench and wait," he instructs.

I do as I'm told.

"Keep both feet on the floor!" I hear a *pasdar* yell.

I don't know who he's referring to, or what he means. I listen carefully.

"Hey you! I'm talking to you! Put your leg down!" I realize that it's me he's addressing – I've inadvertently crossed one leg over the other. Even crossing legs is prohibited in their culture.

Questioning

After many tedious and frequent interrogations, I'm finally taken to a cell. I am terribly tired after no sleep. The last words that the interrogator said to me were, "Now go and think it over. I'll call you again tomorrow." In fact, it is tomorrow. A few minutes after entering the cell, I hear the morning *azan*.[7]

A grey army blanket, old and dirty and folded in two, sits in the corner of the cell. A half-full glass of milk, a half-eaten cooked egg, and a pair of torn, bloody socks are also in the cell. After spending so many hours blindfolded, I carefully survey my surroundings and try to take in everything. I think about how the previous occupant was probably whipped so much that she couldn't eat properly. The bloody socks tell me what happened to her feet.

The cell is small; wall-to-wall, I can take only five steps. It has a small metal toilet and sink, and a small, inaccessible window is located

---

7   *Azan* is the call for prayer, three times a day in the Shiite tradition.

on the upper part of one wall. A lamp in a metal grid spreads dull light.

Even though I know that I'll be in jail for a long time, I'm thinking about my ID card, passport, diary, letters, and postcards. I laugh at my silliness. It's not even been twenty-four hours since I've come to Evin and I'm thinking of freedom and ordinary life. Of course, I'll always think about natural life. That's a legitimate right of every human being.

The army blanket is so filthy that I can't make myself sit on it. A thick pipe providing heat runs along one wall at the ground. I wrap myself in my *chador* and lie down close to the pipe.

The cell walls are bloodstained and covered with writing. I'd like to read everything, but I'm so exhausted that I can't. I try to sleep. The interrogator's threat – "Now go and think it over. I'll call you again tomorrow" – repeats itself over and over in my head. I realize from their questions that they don't have anything solid with which to interrogate me. I relax a little, but I'm afraid to fall asleep. I can't keep my eyes open either.

I have to catch the bus. If I miss it, I don't know what I'll do in this dark, deserted land. I'm running, terrified that I'll miss the bus. The bus is moving slowly and I think I can catch it. But as soon as I get close and try to knock on the door, the bus speeds up and drives away.

Horrified, I wake up. My mind has been so active, it seems like I haven't slept at all. There's a commotion in the hallway. A female *pasdar* opens the cell door and gives me tea in a filthy, red plastic cup. I take the cup of tea along with a sugar cube. The tea smells and tastes strange. I move closer to the pipe. They call me for interrogation before I fall asleep again.

"Have you thought it over? Tell me what you know."

"I swear to God, I have nothing to say."

"Where's your roommate?"

"I don't know. She doesn't tell me where she stays when she doesn't come home."

"When was she supposed to be home?"

"I don't know. She never tells me when she will come or go."

He doesn't mention the gun again.

I spend the whole day in a small room, sitting on a chair that has a small desk flap attached to its arm. In front of me is a dirty, pale blue wall; it's so close that I cannot even stretch my legs. I have sharp pains in my back, legs and head. My whole body aches. I'm not hungry, but my stomach burns. I'm exhausted. I'm wearing a blindfold and, under my *chador*, a scarf on my head. Off and on all day, I've been questioned and made to fill out questionnaires. Then I'm abandoned for hours, facing the blue wall.

The commotion in the hallway tells me it's lunchtime. It's a good thing I don't have an appetite; they don't give lunch to people in the interrogation rooms.

It's sunset. I've been interrogated by different *pasdar*s three or four times. I've been consistently threatened with flogging or whipping. One of the interrogators whipped my head, face, lower back, and shoulders with an electrical cable – a piece of metal covered by rubber, about sixty centimetres long and four or five centimetres thick, flexible, yet hard enough to be painful. I don't have any energy. I feel dizzy. There's pain throughout my whole body, especially in my eyes and head.

I've been forgotten. Seated in the interrogation room, I can hear the sounds of people having dinner in the hallway. Sounds are the only signs of life: the sounds of interrogation, walking, eating, moaning, yelling, fatigue, hunger, weakness and misery.

The door opens and the head interrogator, Masood, and a colleague, enter the room. Masood takes a glance at the questionnaire and papers that I'd filled out during the day and says, "She's written nothing." The two men whisper together. "Get up and go. Think it over. Think it over," I'm told. "Tomorrow, I'll call you again. I have forced others to confess, others much stronger than you. You too, will say what you have to say."

I try to get up. I feel dizzy. I hold the arm of the chair and walk very slowly. I don't want them to see I need help. I don't want their help. Not because I'm too proud, but because I don't trust them. I'm afraid when one of them comes close or touches me.

In the Cell

I enter the cell.

My three cellmates look at me with surprised eyes. We greet each other.

One of them asks, "Didn't they give you a blanket?"

"No."

This cell is too small. It's made to accommodate one person. The prisoner who sleeps close to the toilet can't stretch her legs.

There is writing on the wall that says: "This is Father Taleghani's cell." Father Taleghani was an activist-clergyman who fought with the Shah and was imprisoned for several years by the Shah's intelligence service. He was a leader of the Islamic Revolution. But unlike other clergymen, he was an intellectual. He believed in freedom for all political parties, while the fundamentalist clergymen believe only in *Hezbollah*.[8] For them, anyone else, including me and my friends, are all *kafar* or *monafeq*.

There are bloodstains and several people's handwriting on the walls. Two army blankets are spread on the floor.

One of the cellmates says, "Sit down. Have you eaten?"

"No."

"Here, have my food. I couldn't eat all of it. You'd better hurry up. Soon, they'll come to collect the dishes."

"I don't feel hungry."

"When were you arrested?"

"Last night."

"Have you eaten since then?"

"No, I had a cup of tea."

"So, eat this fast. They may call you again for interrogation."

One of them, who has big, thoughtful eyes, says, "Eat something. But I don't think they will call you for interrogation again until morning." It seems she is more experienced and knows more.

I ask, "Do you have any water?"

I drink some water and eat a few spoons of cold rice coloured with tomato sauce and spices. When the *pasdar* comes to take the dishes, Mahrokh, the experienced one, asks her to give me blankets. The *pasdar* returns with two army blankets. I don't have a toothbrush or anything else. Feeling very sleepy, I lie down.

One of my cellmates says, "Wait until we assign the spots. We don't want to wake you up again."

They talk with each other; I say nothing. I'm so exhausted that I don't care about anything. Finally, they show me my spot.

---

8   *Hezbollah* means Party of God.

I lie down and feel like I'm suffocating. There's not enough air in the cell for four people. I wake up an hour later; the others are also awake. Mahrokh is reading the *Qur'an*[9] while the two others talk. I tell them that I have to use the toilet; and am told of the procedure: "When someone wants to use the toilet, the others turn their backs to her. If you want to be more comfortable, you can cover your body, including your face, with your *chador*, so you have privacy."

They can see how bewildered I am. "Don't worry. We're used to it. All of us are in the same situation. Under these circumstances, this is the best way." They do their best to make me feel comfortable. I've travelled a lot and I'm adaptable. But tonight, it takes a long time before I use the toilet and relieve my stomach ache.

Worried and fearful, I wait the entire day to be called for interrogation, but nothing happens. I'm glad. The time for my appointment with my roommate has passed. I'm anxious, however – if they're not calling me for interrogation, it could mean that she's been arrested.

"Don't be silly," I say to myself. "They don't have a clue. If I don't show up, she won't go home." I try to soothe myself with these thoughts, but worry that she wasn't able to find anywhere else to stay and that she had to go home. The anxiety is causing diarrhea. I'm ashamed to bother my cellmates on the very first day of my confinement. I hold myself in so much that by the time I use the toilet, I'm in pain.

One of my cellmates, Shery, is eighteen or nineteen years old. She was arrested on the same day as me, but was taken to the cell a few hours before myself. She's an uncomplicated and cheerful girl who talks and laughs incessantly, as if she doesn't realize what is waiting for her. Zohreh, fifteen or sixteen, is quiet and talks only when she has to. I can feel that she's worried and wants to say something to myself and Shery. Mahrokh is tall. Her eyes are fearful and she talks cautiously. In the morning, she says, "They bring us breakfast. In Evin, no one starves, and some other things that are said about this place are a bunch of lies."

I realize very quickly that she is a *tavvab*[10] or pretending to be one. We have to be careful about what we say in front of her. I wonder why she's not more careful about hiding the fact that she's a *tavaab*

---

9   The *Qur'an* (Koran) is the Holy Book of Islam.
10 *Tavvab* means a repentant sinner. *Tavvab*s were prisoners who were used by prison authorities as informants.

from Shery and I. Is she trying to help us? I try to understand. I realize how complex human behaviour becomes in such a difficult situation.

After breakfast, a *pasdar* knocks on the door. Mahrokh quickly goes to the cell window and is told to prepare for interrogation. She looks nervous. Her large eyes become even wider with fear. She tries to be alert and careful. It's clear that she's been called for interrogation many times because she knows how to get ready fast. She puts on her *chador*, her blindfold, and her sandals.

Once Mahrookh leaves the cell, Zohreh says, "You'd better know that everything we say and do is reported by Mahrokh. Be careful. Don't whisper, even when the others are praying. And tell nobody what I told you."

I talk to Shery and find out that Sima was also the one to betray her. "Is your interrogation over?" I ask.

"No. My interrogator has told me, 'Go and think it over, I'll call you tomorrow.' And he will call me!" she says with a laugh.

I'm wondering why she's not worried, why she's laughing! She notices my questioning look and becomes serious. With worry in her eyes, she says, "I don't have anything to tell them." She stares at nothing in particular.

"Me, neither. I don't have anything to tell them."

Shery and I read the writing on the walls. One of them is a beautiful poem by Ahmad Shamloo:[11]

I don't suppose
my heart was ever
warm and red
like this before.
I sense that
in the worst moments of this black, death-feeding repast
a thousand thousand well-springs of sunlight,
stemming from certitude,
well up in my heart.
I sense, further, that

---

11 *Fish* is a 1959 poem by Ahmad Shamloo (1925-2000), renowned Iranian poet, lexicographer, writer, and anti-government activist.

in every nook and cranny of this salt barrenness of despair
a thousand thousand joy forests,
stemming from the soil,
are suddenly springing.
Oh, lost certitude, oh, sea-creature
fleeing in the concentric,
shivering,
mirroring pools,
I am the clear pool:
mesmerized by love,
search out a path for me
among the mirror pools.
I don't think
my hand was ever
strong and alive
like this, before.
I sense that
at the flow of blood-red tears in my eyes
a duskless sun pours forth a song.
I sense that
in my every vein,
in time with my every heart beat,
the warning bell of a departing caravan tolls.
She, bare, came
one evening
through the door
like the soul of water.
At her breast
two fish
In her hand a mirror
Her wet hair,
moss fragrance, intertwined moss.
On the threshold of despair,
I bellowed: Ah, oh retrieved certitude.
I won't put you again aside.

Another section of the wall notes a daily schedule of how to spend
time in the cell. Another piece of writing consists of a few dates and

a time written in front of each date, mostly around sunset. In front of each date there's also a number.

I am about to ask Zohreh the meaning of these numbers when the door opens and Mahrokh steps in. Her face is contorted into a fake smile. Her eyes are even bigger, as if she has seen a terrifying scene.

I ask her the name of her interrogator.

She looks at me, shocked. I realize I'm not supposed to ask. However, she answers, "Brother Masood."

"He has interrogated me, too. Did he tell you when he'll call me?"

"No," she answers shortly.

"Did he ask you about me?"

"He did. He asked me what were you and Shery talking about."

"Well, what did you tell him?"

She smiles self-assuredly and says, "Well, of course, I told him what you talked about."

Shery and I exchange a look. I'm glad I don't know Shery and haven't talked to her much.

It's almost sunset. The melancholy sound of *azan* grips my heart. Zohreh and Mahrokh get ready to pray. Shery sleeps a lot. Mahrokh tells her to get up so that she and Zohreh have enough space to spread out their prayer mat. Mahrokh starts to pray. Zohreh is doing her ablutions. *Azan* is almost over when we hear the sound of gunshots. Mahrokh stays bent down on the floor in her prayer position. Zohreh shows me her fingers, counting the number of gunshots, and then points to the writings on the wall: the date, the time and the numbers. I realize that each gunshot is an execution. The numbers represent the dates and times of the excecution and how many were executed. I want to write tonight's number on the wall but I don't have anything with which to write. They've confiscated my purse. I try to remember the date, time and number, in case I find a pen later on.

I look at Mahrokh, still prostrating. She's wrapped herself in her *chador* and her shoulders are trembling. She cries quietly. We listen to the gunshots in silence. For a few minutes, the barrage of fire stops. It's followed by a series of single gunshots. Now all of us are counting. Zohreh, Shery and I show each other the numbers with our fingers. Mahrokh is still crying in her prayer position. Zohreh, wearing her scarf and *chador*, spreads her prayer mat and starts her prayers. Shery and I look at each other in silence.

When they finish their prayers, Mahrokh's eyes are red and watery. "May your prayers be accepted," Zohreh tells her.

"May God accept them," Mahrokh answers.

These words feel strange to me, as though I am back at my grandmother's mourning ceremony.

"Did you hear the gunshots?" I ask Mahrokh.

"No. Well, yes. There was some noise. But I'm so absorbed in talking to my God that I'm not aware of my surroundings." She steals a look from me with a false smile on her face. All of us know she's lying.

"Why did you cry so much? Your eyes are red."

"It's good to cry when you're in a prostrate position. It purifies your heart."

The complexity of relationships in prison is more apparent moment by moment. We've barely finished the bread, butter and watery jam that is our supper when Shery and I are called for interrogation. We are both kept in the same room. Masood enters and says, "Did you think it over?"

We are quiet.

As he leaves the room, he says, "I'll be back soon."

A few minutes later, Masood takes Shery to another room, and another interrogator, Akbar enters the room and sits in front of me. I can see his legs and part of his body. There's something on the table and he thumbs through it – a notebook or a file. As he flips the pages, he mumbles. I raise my head a little and see some postcards that I had brought back from Italy, most of them bought in the churches I'd visited in Rome. One of them is a painting by Michelangelo called *The Creation of Adam*: it depicts two naked men, their hands stretched towards one other lovingly. When he sees this one, his mumbling gets louder. I'm sure he takes them for pornography and if not, he pretends to anyway, as proof that we are filthy people.

"That's it," he says. "Their team houses[12] are like pleasure houses." And again he starts mumbling. This time he's looking at a picture of Greek gods and goddesses; a woman with a very delicate lace dress is flying. He gives me a piece of paper and pen and says, "Write it down. Write your confessions." He pronounces "confessions" as if he is sure I'm morally corrupt.

---

12 Team houses are clandestine living quarters where activists also planned and
  organized.

I write: "I felt sympathy for the friends of prisoners and I let them hide in my house so they wouldn't get arrested." I know it seems ridiculous. Do they believe me? I'm not living with my family – despite the fact that most single girls in Iran do before marriage – because I want to help political activists. I have to find another reason.

He takes the paper from me. His first question is why I'm not living with my family.

"We set off for Tehran after the war between Iran and Iraq started," I say. "My parents live with my brother and his wife. I couldn't get along with my sister-in-law, plus my workplace is far from my parent's house, so I decided to live by myself."

Suddenly, I have a shooting pain in my heart. I remember I lied and told my family that I was living with my friend, Narguess. My friendship with Narguess goes all the way back to high school. She is married and has two children. My family believed me, because they knew how close we were. Now I'm worried – if my family is investigated, they might mention her name and then she might be in danger, too. The *pasdars* might think that I lied to my family. Sima knows Narguess; she's her contact with our organization.

Narguess and her husband were arrested once when Narguess was pregnant with her second child. Narguess was released because the interrogators couldn't find anything against her. Her husband confirmed that Narguess wasn't aware of his political activities. Now, Narguess' second child would be two or three months old. She lives with her sister because her husband is still in jail. If the interrogators find out that Narguess is not living in her own house and that her husband is in jail, things will be more complicated. My family knows the full names of Narguess and her husband. That's enough for the interrogators to find her name among those who've been fingerprinted. I have to think about it. I am worried about Narguess.

The interrogator leaves the room with the photos and postcards. I know he will show these items to the others, to make them into an immoral offence.

The interrogator enters the room along with Masood. Masood looks at my paper and says, "Take her to the basement, she should be beaten."

The interrogator says, "Get up." He is holding a pencil and tells me to hold the other end of it, so that he can lead me towards the hallway.

"Wait here. Soon, it's your turn," he says and leaves me standing in a corner.

I raise my head and see Sima sitting on the floor, not with a *manteau*,[13] but with a *chador* and blindfold. She's leaning on her hand. If my family mentions Narguess and the interrogator asks Sima about her as a result, Sima might think I've said something about Narguess and she may also say something about her. I take advantage of the opportunity and speak to Sima. "Don't say anything about Narguess. Even if they ask about her, say nothing."

I want to explain more when a *pasdar* comes close to me and asks, "What were you talking about?"

"I'm sorry brother; I was praying. I did it loudly unintentionally."

He believes me.

I think it's three or four hours since I've been waiting in the hallway. There's the sound of screaming from one of the interrogating rooms. Other than that, the hallway seems quiet. It is they've forgotten me. The screaming subsides.

I'm waiting for my torture in silence and darkness. I feel very sleepy. I sit down and lean my head on the wall. After a while, I become aware of two interrogators talking.

"Why is she here?"

"She's supposed to go to the basement."

They whisper and one of them comes over to me and says, "Get up and go to your cell. Think it over. I'll call you tomorrow."

I'm so happy, it's as if I'm going to paradise. I hear the sound of running and commotion. One of the interrogators yells, "Prepare the clinic! He's taken cyanide." That's why I wasn't taken to the basement. They needed the torture beds[14] for the newcomers.

My cellmates are asleep. I lie down in my spot, and wake up with the morning *azan*. I feel like I've slept only a few minutes.

After morning prayers, my cellmates ask, "What happened?"

"Nothing, nothing happened." And I sleep again. They wake me for

13 A *manteau* is a long coat worn by females to cover the body.
14 Torture beds are metal beds without mattresses used to flog face-down prisoners. Their hands are tied to the head of the bed and their feet to the foot of the bed.

breakfast and tea. Between sleep and a cup of tea saturated with cam-phor,[15] I don't know which to choose. I prefer sleep; I'm so exhausted. I wake up horrified. It's nine in the morning. Everybody is quiet. I get up and fold the blanket; I want to cry. I look at my cellmates and control my tears. I wash my face and hide the tears in my eyes and on my cheeks, with water. In a corner of the cell, my roommates have set aside a cup of cold tea, a few cubes of sugar, and a piece of bread and cheese for me. I haven't yet finished my breakfast when someone pounds on the cell door. My heart starts racing in my chest but they don't want me for interrogation. One of *tavvab*s who works in the ward asks us if we need any clothes. Mahrokh speaks for me, "Yes, sister. This one is a new-comer. She has nothing with her."

The *tavaab* gives us a few pieces of clothing and says, "Take what you need, then I'll come and collect the rest."

I take a shirt and a skirt and I ask, "Whose clothes are these?"

With their eyes full of sadness, Mahrokh and Zohreh say, "They probably belonged to those who have been executed."

I talk to the skirt in my hands. "Surely you belonged to a tall slim girl. You've witnessed her being tortured. I'll keep you with me for the rest of my life. I promise I won't turn my back on your owner's pain."

A Bird in a Trap

It's been a few days since I brushed my teeth.

Mahrokh says, "There's a used toothbrush. If you wash it with sav-lon[16] you can use it."

I feel sick using another person's toothbrush, but I don't have any choice.

Around noon, they call us for showers. I don't have anything except the shirt and skirt given to me. Shery is in the same situation. Mahrokh and Zohreh consult about what we should use as a towel.

Before we can figure something out, however, there is a knock at the door, and I'm called for interrogation. My heart pounds in my chest like a bird captured in a trap. They will surely flog me this time.

---

15 Camphor was given daily to prisoners in food or tea, to keep them calm and blunt sexual desire. With camphor added, food never tasted the same.
16 Savlon is a liquid disinfectant, normally used in hospitals.

They take me to an interrogation room where an interrogator is
waiting. As soon as he sees me, he rudely says, "Sit down." He puts a
paper in front of me and says, "Write down anything you know, including the names of all the *monafeq* you know."

"I've written everything I know. I have nothing more to write
about."

Masood, who has apparently been in the room all this time, asks,
"Who is Narguess?"

I begin to cry. "I swear to God, she hasn't done anything. She's a
friend of mine from high school."

I see Masood's hands waving, as if to say, "It's not worth it, let it
go." Sima has been so cooperative with them that they don't need me.
They are aware that I don't know anything more than they already know.
Masood leaves the room. The other interrogator says, "Write down what
you just said."

In the afternoon, I'm taken to my cell. The small window on the
cell door is open and we take turns looking out through the window
and describing what is going on in the hallway. A few hours later, I see
Narguess' three-year-old daughter playing in the hall. So, Narguess is
here. I wonder if it was my warning to Sima that brought Narguess
here. An individual who can't tolerate torture cannot trust others to be
strong. Who knows? Perhaps she betrayed Narguess under torture before I even said anything.

After a few hours, one of our cellmates says, "Someone is back
from interrogation. It seems like she's been flogged."

I go to the window and see Narguess, a pair of plastic men's sandals
in her hand. She's been whipped and can't wear the sandals. The *tavvab*
who works in the ward is taking her to a cell. When they are about to
pass by my cell, they pause – the ward *tavvab* has been called back to
the main hallway. There's no one in the corridor except Narguess. She's
standing in front of my cell but I can't talk to her because of Mahrokh.
I give a hint to Zohreh, who picks up on it immediately and calls out my
name, her voice louder than usual. Narguess turns her head and sees me
through the small window. Now, she knows I'm here. She can use me as
dried-up information.

It's been a few days since Shery and myself have been called for
interrogation. I haven't seen Narguess going for interrogation, either.
Narguess' daughter sometimes plays in the hallway and I tell her stories

through the cell window. I make a small basket for her out of plastic bread bags.

One day, the ward *tavvab* asks me, "Why do you talk to this child? Do you know her?"

"She wants me to tell her stories."

Now, whenever Narguess' daughter is playing in the hallway, the *tavvab* closes our cell window. I hear the child standing in front of our cell, calling "Auntie, Auntie." I love her very much but I can't answer her. She is upset and my heart is broken. I hear the *tavvab* give her some snacks and tell her not to talk to us.

The days and nights pass slowly. Zohreh sleeps most of the day. Sometimes I do, too. Not moving around enough has made us sick. We all feel down and ill, bored and worried. The cell is too small for four people. We cannot walk or do any physical exercise. Mahrokh is still called for interrogation occasionally. We mostly sleep or talk about our lives before prison. Since I'm older than the others, I have more to say. Sometimes, when I'm narrating parts of my life, I feel like I'm reading a book. I've never talked about or thought of my life in this way. Now that I'm not living a normal life, I feel like I'm talking about someone else.

My cellmates like to listen to my stories. They are young and naïve, and it seems like instead of living and experimenting with their own lives, they are living and learning through mine.

Tonight, I'm feeling very sad, and I also have a toothache. Mahrokh and Zohreh are trying to cheer me up. Zohreh is telling jokes and we're laughing loudly until suddenly, someone bangs harshly on the cell door.

Mahrokh gets worried. She jumps up to the small opening in the cell door and says: "Yes, brother?"

The guard says: "Are you having a party? Shame on you. Our volunteers are killed in the war and by your friends, and you are laughing at our martyrs."

Mahrokh says she's sorry and he leaves. Mahrokh is frightened. We're all shocked. What does our laughter have to do with their martyrs? The logic behind this idea makes us laugh even more, but we control ourselves. They don't want to see any sign of happiness in us; they want us to suffer all the time. Zohreh is trying to make a joke out of it. Still, Mahrokh is worried. Although she seems to be one of the *tavvab*s, she always steps up for us. She speaks up when we need something, gives us all the information she has when she comes back from interrogations.

She tells us about the number of people she thinks have been recently arrested, including their names, if she can remember. She tells us what she knows about the personalities of the interrogators: the ones who are calm and the ones who aren't, and those who are better to turn to for our needs.

"Talk about your life," Zohreh asks me. "Not only will you forget your pain, we will also be entertained."

I'm trying to remember a part of my life that isn't sad but I can't; I can only remember the night that my classmates told me the news about him.

The Mermaid's Red Shoes

"On my way home from the dormitory in the dark early hours after sunset, a light rain was falling. When I passed the bridge, the calm river was receiving the cloud's tears. Where was my little mermaid? He promised to keep the little mermaid's red shoes safely in a box until the spell was over."

"What do you mean?" asks Shery.

"I wrote a poem about a little mermaid who was under a spell, and her red shoes symbolized my heart. When he read the poem, he promised to take care of the red shoes while she was under the spell."

"Oh, my, then what happened?" asks Zohreh.

"I couldn't believe he had reached such a decision so soon. I was still suffering, with hundreds of unresolved questions in my mind, and he had already married. His wife was pregnant and sick. I felt so sorry for him and I wished him happiness. After we broke up, all of his actions were hasty and unwise. He wasn't true to his pain or mine.

"When I arrived home that night, the rain was heavier and it had gotten windy. In the outside hallway, a white pigeon lay half-dead on the floor. Poor thing; it wasn't able to withstand the storm. I took the pigeon into my room and put it on a towel. I stared at the wounded bird and cried, 'If you were happy, I would be able to say *adieu*, farewell. But now I will always think of you. You've left me a legacy of pain and guilt.'"

"This is so sad," says Zohreh. "It sounds like fiction, not real life. Did you ever see him again?"

"Yes, after a year he came back to the university. I was taking my final courses. I needed two elective credits and had chosen library science. He had just completed a master's degree in this field, and guess what? He was the teacher for my course.

"Oh, my God," says Mahrokh. "What did you do?"

"I dropped the course and when we saw each other in the corridors, we barely said hello. Then the universities closed because of the Cultural Revolution.[17] And then there was the war. I never saw or heard of him again. I went to another city and worked for one year, and then I went to Tehran."

"By the way, what date is it today?" Shery asks. None of us know. Mahrokh guesses that it must be the end of September.

"Oh, my God, what am I going to do with this pain?" I moan to myself. It is midnight or later; my cellmates are asleep. I can't calm myself; this toothache is so painful.

Mahrokh hears me breathing abnormally and asks, "What's the matter? What's wrong with you?"

"It's my tooth. I'm in such pain – I can't sleep."

Mahrokh knocks on the cell door. No response. She knocks harder a few more times and finally the ward *tavvab* wakes up and comes to our cell door. "I'm sorry to bother you, sister, but one of us is in pain with a toothache."

The *tavvab* leaves and returns with two painkillers. She says that I'll have to wait until morning to see a doctor.

The painkiller helps me for only half an hour. I'm in such pain, and I have no room to walk or move – I can't even whine or cry because I don't want to bother my sleeping cellmates.

I think of my parents; they wouldn't leave me to suffer. Silently, I cry into the night and try to console myself. Wouldn't it be worse if I were in the basement, tied to a torture bed, being whipped by interrogators? These thoughts keep me busy but the pain is severe. I take the second painkiller but this does not affect me much at all. I'm so tired and weak. Even my ears are paining me now. I have never suffered so much from loneliness.

17 The Cultural Revolution began with the government of the Islamic Republic closing higher educational institutions to purge them of un-Islamic elements. The universities in Iran were closed from 1980–1982.

Finally, the sounds of morning life begin to hum in the corridors. It's time for the morning prayer. One by one, my cellmates wake up.

"Oh, my God, look at you!" Shery says. "You are so pale."

"You should have woken me," says Mahrokh.

"But what could you do?" I ask.

"I could at least talk to you, or ask for more painkillers."

Zohreh stares at me with sympathy in her eyes and surprisingly, I feel a bit better – or rather, I feel less pain.

I ask the *tavvab* to send me to the prison clinic. She says she'll try and gives me another pill, but I've had too many painkillers on an empty stomach and now my belly is aching, as well. Breakfast arrives but I cannot eat. I feel so weak. I drink my tea with sugar very cautiously. Although I'm cold, I'm sweating. It's now ten in the morning and I'm still in pain. A knock on the door startles me. I'm sure it's for me to go to the doctor, but in fact, it's an interrogation call for Mahrokh.

I'm angry and feel as though I'm going to lose control. "Why don't you take me to the doctor? I've been in pain for more than twelve hours."

The guard asks me some questions and says I'll be taken to the doctor soon. Finally, I'm called to go to the prison clinic.

The dentist is a young woman with sad eyes. Once she begins checking my teeth, the guard who is with us takes leave, telling her to call him when she is done. While she works, I look out the only window that the room has. I can see the sunny blue sky. It must be very nice out. A bird holding a tiny piece of wood in its beak flies toward the top of the window. I cannot see where it is going, but I can imagine it's making a nest. I see the bird fly back again, another small piece of wood in its mouth.

"Is there a forest behind this window?" I ask the dentist.

She looks at me cautiously and replies very shortly, "I don't know." Then, when she sees the confusion in my eyes, she softens. "I am a prisoner like you. I don't know what is behind this window."

I gasp. Suddenly I feel joyful. No, I am not out there; I'm imprisoned in this mournful house. But outside, life is going on! Birds are making nests, flowers are growing, and breezes are blowing. Life is going on.

A Phone Call

"I wish I had my purse with me. I have a pen and some paper in it," I think out loud.

"You can ask them," says Mahrokh. "They might give it to you."

She is called for interrogation. When the guard comes to take her, I ask him for my purse. He says that I'll get it back when I'm transferred to the public ward. I don't miss the opportunity to ask him, "When will I be transferred?"

"When your interrogation is over."

That tells me nothing.

Soon after, the ward *tavvab* knocks on the door and calls me for interrogation.

Again, I am in a room all by myself. Now what? What do they want from me? The same interrogator who has asked me hundreds of questions before comes in and asks once again about my roommate.

"I do not know. Believe me, I don't know."

"Why should I believe you?"

"For safety reasons, she would never tell me where she stayed."

"Then why didn't she go to your house? Did you change the safety sign?"

"No, I didn't touch anything. Maybe one of the neighbours saw her on the street and told her that I was arrested."

Although he tries to control himself, he is very angry and says furiously, "You stupid double-crosser! Do you think people will help you? Everyone is with us. They know what you do in your team houses. They know girls and boys do whatever they want in those houses. They know your friends are committing adultery there. When I send you for *ta'zir*[18] you will see how people help you!" He leaves the room.

How can an individual be so stupid? Why would activists put their lives in danger for the reasons he said? Do these interrogators really believe what they say, or this is just a way to threaten me? Although I'm worried that he will send me to the torture room, deep in my heart I feel glad, thinking of how angry he got over the possibility of people helping us.

Five minutes later, the lead interrogator enters the room and says, "You are stupid! You are making the situation worse for yourself. Your

18 *Ta'zir* is religious punishment, usually flogging.

roommate has already been arrested and told us everything. We only want to know how much of a betrayer you are."

I know he is bluffing. I keep quiet.

He gives me a pen and paper and tells me to write down everything.

"I don't have anything more to write. I've already written everything."

"Okay, write it again."

When I finish writing, he reads it right away and starts to talk, trying to convince me that the activists are bad and immoral, fighting a revolution willed by God.

I listen and do not argue at all. I know it's useless. "Now go to your cell", he says. "You will choose God's way when you stay here for many years."

It's morning again, and today it's our turn to shower. While we are waiting for the *tavvab* to call us, I get summoned to interrogation. This time, a very young man with an accent from my hometown takes me to a large cell that has no roof. A very dirty carpet is spread out on the floor and there are two telephones on it. He asks me my home phone number and dials. When the phone starts to ring, he gives me the receiver, then picks up the other receiver and covers the speaker with his hand.

My father picks up the phone.

"Hello," I say, and cannot talk anymore: the lump in my throat won't let me.

"Hello? Hello?" my father responds. Although I do not answer, he doesn't hang up. It seems he knows that this is a special call. Finally, he says, "Is that you, Sousan?"

"Yes, Dad, it's me. Please don't worry. I'm okay."

"Are you in prison?"

"Yes."

"Which one?"

"I'm in Evin."

"This is a mistake. When will they let you go?"

"I don't know yet. Please send me some clothes, a toothbrush and some—"

He doesn't let me finish. "Why do you need these things? Aren't you coming home soon?"

"I don't know. I don't think so."

He's silent. I can visualize his pain and sorrow in the lines under his eyes and around his mouth. Finally, he says, "Talk to your mom."

I can imagine my mom's face on the other side of the line. Although she has heard the conversation with my dad, she asks me the same questions.

"I am in Ward 209, Mom. Please send me some clothes."

"Why do you need clothes? Aren't you coming home?"

"Not yet. Don't worry. I'm okay. Believe me, I'm okay. I'll see you soon." I know I'm lying but I cannot tell them the truth. I have to keep them hopeful.

The guard tells me to finish the call.

"Mom, I have to go. Don't worry, okay?"

She cannot answer.

My father says, "Okay, take good care of yourself. We will do whatever we can to get you released. We are praying for you."

I am hopeless. I know they cannot do anything to get me out of prison. I'm also sad and excited. It's been a month since I last heard my parents' voices. I feel close to them, to their kindness and support, to normal life. I know how far away it is. I cannot control my tears.

Snowflakes Falling

From the cell's small window, I can see the snowflakes sadly fluttering down. Mahrokh, Zohreh, Shery and myself are all called for interrogation. We are worried and curious, until the guard tells us to pack our belongings.

"Oh, my God," says Mahrokh. "They are sending us to the public ward."

I'm so happy. Finally, I'm going to be with my friends, the ones who I love more than anyone else in the world, the ones who understand me more than anyone else. A guard gives me my purse. I check it; nothing has been touched except my ID card, my phonebook, and some papers.

There are many other prisoners in the hallway with us. I look for Narguess and find her easily because her older daughter keeps talking and asking questions. I get closer to her and we say hello to one another. The guards and the *tavvab*s yell at us to keep quiet. One of them says, "You are all going to the same place. You can talk there as much as you want."

On the way to the public ward, I help Narguess with her children. Her older daughter still remembers me and calls me "Auntie" right away. We're shuffled into a room where four or five female guards yell and try to keep us quiet and lined up. They question us one by one, and send each of us to a different ward, either upstairs or downstairs.

I have a very bad headache and I ask one of the guards if I can remove my blindfold.

"Why?"

"I have a headache."

"Oooooh, she has a headache! Ooooooooh, are you listening sisters? This sweetie has a headache!"

They all laugh out loud and another guard says, "This headache is nothing; you will have much more pain in the future."

It's Narguess' turn; I'm next to her and I'm praying that the guard sends us to the same ward.

"Do you know each other?"

"I was just helping her with her children," I reply.

She takes this answer as a no and sends us to the lower floor. I am in Room Three and Narguess is in Room Four.

In the Public Ward

Our friends! Great! It's so good to be with friends. I'm happy and sad. I always loved being with my friends; they are the best people, and now I am with them.

Feeling curious and excited, I go down the stairs of the public ward. Finally, I have access to this secret world. But I also feel depressed, knowing, as I go down these stairs, that when I'll be able to walk back up them is not in my hands. I don't know how long these stairs will keep me from freedom and ordinary life.

Narguess and I carry our bags and her children. We enter a hall, part of which is under the stairs. There's a big door that opens to a yard and further down, another door on the left: it leads to the public ward hallway, which is lined with rooms. A few people are walking in the hall. They're curious and watch us discreetly. One or two of them have a row of prayer beads in their hands and whisper prayers quietly to themselves. I tell Narguess that I'll see her later and stop at the threshold of Room Three.

"Hey guys, here's a newcomer." I hear voices from the corners of the room. I smile and greet them in a friendly way. Some of them answer my greeting. They are all wearing dark clothes; some of them have scarves on. Most of them look sad and worried. Some of them look at me with contempt; others look on with sympathy. Some of the younger ones look less sad.

One of them asks, "Are you a student or do you work?"

Another one says, "Obviously, she works."

"Why were you arrested?"

"I helped the activists."

"When were you arrested?"

Before I get a chance to answer, one of them says, "Leave her alone. Don't interrogate her."

I don't mind answering questions. But a very young girl with braids gets close to me and says, "Tell them that you've already been interrogated and have your sentence." She leads me to two other girls and says, "Put your bag here."

Faces and looks tell me that I should be vigilant. Something in the atmosphere doesn't seem friendly. Feeling hurt, I let myself be led by my guide. She says, "They will tell you where and how to put your things."

Shirin and Ashraf introduce themselves. Shirin is about eighteen or nineteen years old. She looks nervous and restless. Her short hair is curly and dark brown. Dark eyes glow against the fair skin of her face. Ashraf is older and looks more experienced. Her long, light hair is carefully brushed back into a ponytail. She is tall and beautiful. They both try to be helpful to me. We talk a little and they teach me the most basic rules of the public ward.

"Where's the washroom?" I ask.

Shirin smiles and says, "At the curve of Rosewater Valley."

"Where? What do you mean?"

"Let's go, I'll show you where the washrooms and showers are."

We walk toward the intersection of the two hallways. I can tell that we're getting close to the washrooms from the bad smell. Now I realize why the intersection of the hallways is called Rosewater Valley. There's a long line for the washroom. Some inmates show their urgent need to use the washroom. I start to go back towards the room.

"Why are you going back?" Shirin asks. "Don't you need to use the washroom?"

"Yes, but I can wait until there is no line."

Shirin laughs. "It never gets less busy here. There is always a long line. If you need to go to the washroom, you always have to wait in the line."

I get in the line. There are women and girls of different ages, from young teenagers to grandmothers. Finally, it's my turn. Behind me, there is someone whose need is more urgent than my own, so I let her go ahead of me. She's reluctant, but accepts.

Some of the inmates in line look at me in surprise and one of them ridicules, "She's new."

I decide that even when I settle down and get used to the routine, I'm going to keep on being polite. I'll keep my humanity in every way. Being a human doesn't only mean enduring torture.

I've been in the public ward a few hours. All the inmates are strangers to me and I feel terribly lonely. All of them behave carefully with newcomers. The atmosphere is strained. Around ninety people are living in this room like sardines in a tin, but there's a distance between everyone. It might be because all of them have been under interrogation and don't want to talk about their previous activities to each other. We all have secrets. Plus, some of these women are *tavvab*s.

The young girl who introduced me to Shirin and Ashraf approaches me with both of them in tow. Shirin says, "She's the room representative. She's been chosen by the ward office."

Her name is Sepideh. She is solemn and looks mature for her age. She's kind to me.

Shirin says, "Our representative is nice. She's not like the others."

I ask, "What do you mean?"

"You'll find out later."

Since I've entered the ward, I have heard that several times.

I go to Narguess' room. She is settled in a corner of the room with her children, talking to a young woman. After we exchange introductions, the young woman asks me, "When were you arrested?" When she hears my answer, she cheerfully says, "Oh, so you are the one."

Narguess and I look at her puzzled, waiting for an explanation.

"I recognized you from your voice," she says. "You're the one who calmed me down when I was so nervous the very first night of our arrest. We were arrested on the same day."

So, the woman I had spoken to that day wasn't an old woman after all. She was young with a voice a little weak for her age. We hug each other. We exchange looks and silently make an agreement not to let anyone find out that our arrests are connected. I might have connections with people I don't know personally.

At lunchtime, everybody has to eat in their rooms, so I return to mine. Two workers take big, heavy pots of food to each room. I learn that each day, four of us are room workers. It will soon be my turn to take care of dividing the allotted food and cleaning the room. Dividing the food is a very hard task because there is not enough food for ninety people; each share is so small that mistakes are absolutely unacceptable.

Lunch is rice mixed with lentils. Shirin and Ashraf ask me to sit next to them. Trying to be friendly, I ask Sepideh to join us. She politely declines.

Shirin and Ashraf's body language tells me I have done something odd. I look at them questioningly. Shirin explains that people come together for daily activities based on their political parties and beliefs.

"What you mean?" I ask.

"I mean Sepideh will only sit next to other *tavvab*s. Soon they will try to bring you into their group. The *sar-e moze'-is*[19] will try to do the same thing. You have to be careful."

"Well, what are the two of you?" I ask.

"We are neither."

"Then what are you?" I ask again.

Ashraf answers, "We are ourselves. I don't like any of them."

"I hate them," adds Shirin.

"Who is 'them'?" I ask.

---

19 A *sar-e moze'-i* is a person who openly stands their ground.

"I hate *tavvab*s; whatever we do and say is reported to the office by them. You have to be careful with your relationships. You show your beliefs by choosing who you spend your time with or talk to."

"That is so stupid."

"Unfortunately that's the way it is," says Ashraf, sadly.

Mahrokh and Shery have been sent to another ward, but Zohreh is in Room One. I see her in the line for the washroom. She whispers, "You know we have to be careful about what we say and who we talk to; whatever we do is reported to the office. There is a record of everything we do in the ward. It's on our file for the court. They will judge and sentence us based on it."

"But this is very stupid," I say. "How can they decide on my life and destiny based on what *tavvab*s say? They might lie or be mistaken. Plus, I might like to make friends with someone who doesn't necessarily have the same beliefs as I do. What kind of deal is this?"

"This is what it is," she says. "Be careful, soon we will be called to the court for our trial."

In the hall, under the stairs, I'm crying bitterly. This is a corner where Often, I can sit all by myself. What happened to the best people in the world? What happened to my dearest friends? How can they betray each other? I cannot get some of the spiteful looks of my cellmates out of my mind. How much have they been tortured to reach this point? I don't hate them, but I do not respect them either.

"Why are you sitting here? Why are you crying?" Shirin says. "Come on, let's go to our room!"

A woman approaches me cautiously and stands behind me in line. She smiles; I smile. She obviously wants to talk to me. I make it easier for her and ask, "What room are you in?"

"Room Two," she answers. "You are in Room Three, aren't you?"

"Yes, I am."

"Your friend, the one that has two children, she is in Room Four, isn't she?"

"Yes."

Now it's very clear that she wants to talk about Narguess. "You know, I've seen her before."

I grow worried; this woman might be a *tavvab* with some information about Narguess' activities. I try to stay calm. "Oh, have you? Where?"

"I've seen her here before, when she was pregnant. We were in the same cell the first time she was arrested."

"Oh, I see."

"You know," she says. "There is something I want to tell you. Your friend should be very careful. Lajevardi[20] announced once that whoever is arrested twice will be executed."

"What you mean? Even if they haven't committed something to deserve such a harsh conviction?"

"Yes, their major crime is fooling the guards."

"Okay, thank you for letting me know. I'll talk to her."

Visiting Day

Narguess is crying softly, with deep sadness. Tomorrow is visiting day, and it marks our first visit with our families. Everybody's happy and excited except for Narguess – she has been told that she has to give her three-year-old child to her family. She can only keep the little one, who is now five months old. Although she knows it's better for her daughter to go out and lead a normal life, it's very hard for her to separate from her child. It's not a good time to talk to her about what I've heard.

Finally, it's morning. After breakfast they will start calling us, group by group, to another building to visit our parents. I'll be so happy to see my parents but I know how hard it will be for them to see me behind glass windows and have to talk to me through the telephone set, knowing that what we say will be monitored by the guards. How hard it will be for them to leave me behind bars and go home without me after the mere ten minutes we are given to visit. I have to be strong and pretend that things are not as bad as they think. I wish I could tell them that the hardest thing for me in this hell is the existence of *tavvab*s.

Everybody's excited. Although the water is icy cold, some prisoners are taking cold showers to look fresh. Some are brushing their hair

---

20 Asadolah Lajevardi was the Director of Prisons during this time. His office was in Evin. A fanatic hardliner, his edicts and opinions carried weight beyond the jurisdiction of Director. He was later assassinated by a member of the *Mojahedin-e Khalq*.

carefully, although it will be covered by a scarf or *maqna'eh*.[21] Most of us are embarrassed and troubled about how to answer our parents' endless questions. We don't want them to suffer but we cannot really lie much either. They know we are not being pampered in a hotel.

Names are read in alphabetical order. My turn will be in the early afternoon. Narguess' last name starts with the same letter as mine, so we are both anxiously awaiting our turns.

She has washed her children's faces and keeps talking to her three-year-old, trying to prepare her for their separation and explaining that she should be brave and make it easier for her grandma to take care of her. "You know sweetheart, I don't know when we will see each other again, but I promise I will try my best to come to you as soon as I can. Even though we are not with each other, you will always be in my mind and my heart."

"Is baby coming to Grandma's too?"

"No, your little sister has to stay with me for a while longer because she is so small, not as grown-up as you. You are a big girl now. I'm sure when you miss Mommy you can hug Grandma. She is very nice and loves you so much."

"When are you coming home?"

"Soon sweetheart, soon." I have never seen Narguess' face like this. She is not crying, but is consumed with sorrow. How am I going to tell her what I know?

My name is called. I'm trying to keep myself calm and in good spirits. We go to the ward office, and are then taken to another building in a minibus. Before entering the visiting hall, they tell us to take our blindfolds off and hide them.

We are standing behind the windows, ready and waiting for our parents to enter the hall on the other side. Suddenly, parents enter the hall running, trying to reach their children as soon as they can. My parents are the last to enter. They look confused and lost. It's their first time and they are shocked by the brutality of the *pasdar*s' attitude.

I smile and pick up the telephone receiver.

They stare at me, searching my face for answers to their questions. They want to make sure I am healthy. They are looking for torture scars. I point to the receiver on their side and ask them to pick it up.

---

21 A *maqna'eh* is a long scarf that is slipped over the head to cover the neck, chest, chin, and part of the forehead. It is sewed tight at the front.

My father does so as if it were something dirty. All his instincts are against the situation in which he is trapped.

"Hello, how are you?" I say.

"Hello, sweetheart, how are you?"

"I'm okay."

"Can you show me your feet?"

"No, Dad, but believe me, I'm okay," I say, and jump a few times to prove that my feet are fine.

My mom is quiet. She is also staring at me.

I look at her and smile.

She takes the receiver and asks, "When are you coming home?"

"I do not know yet."

"When will you know?" Her voice has changed. She is trying to hold back her tears.

"Maybe next time I can answer you. First, I have to be tried. I haven't been called to court for my trial yet."

She regains control of herself and thoughtfully keeps asking me questions.

I ask them about my sister, brothers and relatives, trying to relieve the bitterness of this visit until the *pasdar*s announce that visiting time is over.

Before she hangs up, my mom seems to remember something very important, and gives me some advice: "Just try to keep your dignity. Never do anything to harm people. Be nice to *everybody*," she emphasizes. "Everybody."

I assure her I will and say goodbye, giving them hope that we will see each other again next month.

My mom's face, advising me to keep my dignity, is carved in my mind. What would a *tavvab*'s parents do if they knew what she was doing in Evin?

Almost a month has passed. In one week, it will be time for our next family visit. Narguess knows about the possibility of her execution. She is calm, but she is losing weight.

The loudspeaker calls some names for interrogation, including Narguess and I. Everybody is guessing that we are going to the court for sentencing. A friend tells me, "Say the same things you said in your interrogations. Act simple and do not argue in court. If they say there is

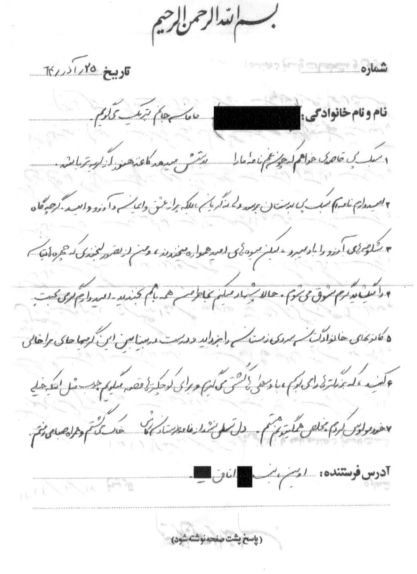

A Mother's Day letter from prison, and response.

بسم الله الرحمن الرحیم

تاریخ ۱۳۶۴/۱۰/۱۷   شماره

نسبت پاسخ دهنده نامه با زندانی: ████████ (مادر)

۱ با این دختر ███████ ...... طبقه و دانش ... با خط ... یافت ..... یا بری حتی گریه ...... خطبه ...... گرفت

۲ نگفته بود ... هم بهم خورد .... ها آزاد شید ..... دیده درست ..... از ..... نه ... از یک تکه ...

۳ خانواده که دختران گری دینه بریم خانواد... عمرد... و اگهکم تک باریش ... ت ..... تفصیل ..... بار ...

۴ پرسیده دیگی چرا داشته باشد بینه دختر سرو نروز خانواد... چگونه ایست ..... دارند ..... میشن

۵ پرسیده بود من ..... با ..... حوایت ..... از ..... نیست ..... از سیدی محبوب

۶ صورت ..... دارکری آراسته ست ..... تیریف ..... شرح داره ██████ ...... از هگ ... نرخ گذشت

۷ آنها سرباز ██████ ...... سربه ۴ و جهل و ..... نگیرات ...... میام ..... ایستادی با حنا
عکس ..... به ای ... همراه خواهر ... ب ..... حصرا... برای آزاد ..... دعا کرد .. مستری می حم

آدرس و مشخصات پاسخ دهنده:

anything more than what you have done, do not accept it. Sometimes it helps." I listen carefully and repeat the same advice to Narguess.

A *pasdar* tells me to enter a room. As I enter, a voice commands, "Take off your blindfold."

The court looks just like the interrogation rooms, tiny with bare walls. There is a small desk in the room and a cleric is sitting behind it. The judge tells me to sit on the chair in front of the desk. He is an old man with a big, black turban on his head. He has mean blue eyes. He starts reading my charges.

I tell him that I felt pity for activists because they were in danger.

"Didn't you feel pity for our martyrs?" he roars. "You said 'my ass' to our martyrs?"

I'm shocked. I wasn't expecting this type of language from a religious cleric in a court.

He notices me momentarily shiver and suddenly changes his language; he tries to convert me to the true religion.

I keep quiet and pretend to listen carefully. Everything and everybody is ridiculous. I won't get into any discussions or arguments.

After he finishes his speech, he moves his hand in disgust and tells me to leave.

Narguess and I are sitting next to her sleeping baby daughter near some other inmates. We speak quietly.

"The judge read many charges that I have never committed," she says. "Obviously, my file was prepared in such a way as to lead the judge to sentence me to death. I didn't accept any of the charges and told him that all those addresses that are supposed to be the organization's team houses are in fact, my relatives' addresses. The judge was surprised and said he will look into it."

"So," I say, "There is still hope."

She smiles bitterly. "Only God knows what will happen. There are some people who want my execution, including the Executioner.[22] What can a judge do if he is sure that I'm lying?" She stares off into space for awhile. "I'm only worried for my daughters."

I don't know what to say, however, I hear myself respond. "I'm sure everything will be all right."

---

22 The Executioner of Evin is the name given to Lajevardi, the Director of Prisons, by the prisoners.

A Small Mirror

I wake up with an endless thirst. Trying to remember where I am and why I'm here. I review my dream. I'd been in prison for a long time. A small mirror was found. After years of being in jail, where mirrors are forbidden, everybody was excited to look at themselves. When my turn came, I anxiously held the mirror up to my face. I was much older and all of my hair was grey.

I get up, navigate through the narrow spaces between the sleeping bodies, and go to the other corner of the room, where I drink some water. Upon my return, I find I've lost my spot. The sleeping spaces are so narrow that if one or two people in the row move onto their backs, there is no more room for people who have left their spot. I have to wake a couple of them to make room for myself.

During breakfast, I'm telling Shirin and Ashraf about my dream when the loudspeaker calls my name to the administrative building. Everybody guesses that I'm being called to receive my sentence. Some are wishing me luck. I'm wondering why Narguess has not been called. Is this a good or a bad sign? I don't want to believe anything will happen to Narguess, and try to believe that everything will be all right – but I don't know on what grounds I can still have even a bit of hope.

A group of us are in line. One by one, we are called to enter a room to receive and sign for our sentence. People have been predicting, according to similar cases, that my sentence will be between two and four years. I'm surprised to find out I'm sentenced to stay in this hell for eight years. The day will indeed come when I will see my hair turn grey in jail.

A Sky Framed With Barbed Wire

"I think your friend Narguess will be released soon," Ashraf says with a delighted smile.

"You think so? Why?"

"Only two groups do not get a sentence: those who get out of this hell for execution or freedom," she explains.

I feel dizzy for a few seconds; everything goes blurry but I control

myself quickly. We cannot reveal our fear. If the *tavvab*s learn about
Narguess, they will compete with each other to spy on her and report
to the *pasdar*s.

After a few months of silence, Narguess is suddenly called for interrogation. I run to her. "What do you think it is?"

"I do not know; I only know that I'm not going for execution because they let me have my child with me. Before they execute me, they
will force me to send my daughter to my family."

"You are right, but even if they force you to send her out, it does
not necessarily mean you will be executed. They are forcing all mothers
to send their children out. They only let mothers keep their children if
there's no one outside who can take care of them."

Narguess tells me how to take care of her daughter in her absence
and walks to the ward office. My eyes follow her. Is this the last time I
will see her? No, impossible. Nobody has heard of such a case before.[23]
I calm myself. But are there really any rules here? Anything can happen
here, for any reason, or no reason at all – anything.

Narguess' body language tells me that disaster has arrived. She tries to
smile in front of the others and pretend that everything is okay. Her face
is flushed and her eyes are wide. She is nervous. I know she is gathering
all her energy for the upcoming event. I have to wait until she does not
have everybody's attention.

"They let me talk to my mom and my sister," she answers a couple
of curious inmates who want to know why she was called for interrogation. "I'm sending my daughter to my mom. You know, I'm happy about
that. It's better for her to be out there. With or without me, she needs
to have a normal life."

My heart beats fast and suddenly it seems to stop. This last sentence
has double meaning.

Narguess looks at me, trying to tell me something.

I feel like crying, yelling, screaming; I feel like exploding. But I cannot even cry. Suddenly my feeling changes: it can't be. She has definitely
been threatened, but this is their routine, not necessarily the truth. There
is still hope. Of course they wouldn't tell her if they were reviewing her
case to reduce her charges.

---

23 Narguess has been in prison twice and, according to Lajevardi's edict, should be
     executed. But there is no established precedent for second incarcerations.

"Don't try to give me hope," she says.

Everybody's asleep. Her daughter, too. We are sitting in a corner in the hallway next to the washroom. All the rooms, even the corridors, are covered with sleeping inmates. There is only a small space next to the washroom that is reserved for those who need to use the washroom during the night. The strong odour of the toilets keeps people away and gives Narguess and me a small space to talk privately.

"I'm ready as long as I know someone will take good care of my children," she explains.

"I'm not trying to give you false hope. I'm happy you are ready, and don't worry, your sister and mother will take care of the children. Your husband's parents are there for them, too. Now, tell me what happened."

"They took me to another section. An interrogator that I didn't know asked me questions about some addresses that were mentioned in my file. In the court, they accused me of going to all of these addresses that were known team houses of the organization. I denied this and explained that they were all addresses of my family and relatives. Then he threatened that they would execute me because I was lying. He did not believe me."

"Well, they never believe us, but they might do some investigating," I answer.

"But you know, I heard something that surprised me," she continues. "In the few minutes that we were alone in a room, one of the prisoners told me that there is a kind of fight between two groups of *pasdar*s that are from different parties. Recently, in order to disgrace one another, one group began reviewing some files that have been under the investigation of the other group. Anyway, they all hate us. It doesn't matter which group, they are united against us."

"What about your daughter?"

"He said I have to give her to my family. They cannot keep her here when I'm gone."

Her name is Sousan, just like me. She is, at most, twenty years old. People who know her better say that she has always been very quiet, but she broke down when a very close friend of hers was executed. I don't know if it is because we both have the same name or because of her situation, but I keep thinking of her and observing her. I try to help her. I wash her clothes; I even wash her in the shower. She is so depressed that she doesn't eat properly. I usually feed her. She has become my responsibility. People are used to it now. Whenever they think she needs something, they ask me to do it. She's like a younger sister I have to take care of, a silent friend. I'm sure she feels the same way and needs my care and attention.

I'm reading the newspaper. First, I usually check the obituary section. I'm always worried that someone dear to me might have passed away. Parents usually don't tell their children about the deaths of family and friends. They try not to give us bad news, so we have to find out from the newspaper. Sousan is next to me. Without looking at the newspaper, she whispers something about death. I cannot understand what she is saying but since she was transferred to our ward, it's the first time she has spoken. It sounds more like thinking aloud than talking.

I try to talk to her. "Do you want me to read the newspaper to you?"

Silence.

"Is there any name that you want me to check for you?"

Silence.

"Fortunately there aren't many names on this page. And no one from my family or friends."

Silence. She turns to me. She doesn't look at me but I feel she is aware of me. Two teardrops roll down her cheeks. She remains within her unshakable silence. I wipe her cheeks and talk to her, but she is not with me anymore. She is somewhere far away.

Mina is in the yard, sitting in a corner next to her daughter, Assal. Narguess and I are taking a walk; Narguess is carrying her daughter.

"Let's sit somewhere. My back is hurting," Narguess suggests.

We approach Mina and Assal and sit near them. Narguess' daughter is asleep. Assal is on a blanket spread out on the ground. Narguess turns her face towards Mina to ask if she can lay her sleeping daughter next to Assal, but stops suddenly.

Mina is staring at Assal. She is paying absolutely no attention to her environment. She is drowned in her own thoughts. Staring at her daughter, she is crying and crying; there is not even one small movement in her face or body. Tears are the only sign of life in her. A statue with tears.

We stay quiet. Time passes; Mina's tears are endless, as are her silence and stiffness. Mina's husband was executed when she was pregnant. She had also been taken for execution, but before it began, her husband revealed that she was pregnant. Her execution was postponed because of her pregnancy, but recently, she'd been told to send her daughter out to her family.

Narguess is still holding her sleeping daughter. Two mothers, awaiting execution, saying farewell to their children under a sky framed in barbed wire. The sun begins to set and darkness covers the trembling lives and resisting souls. I will write about this one day, I think to myself. This is not a myth or a legend; this is true and one day, I will record it all.

Mina and Narguess give their daughters to their families. What is next?

Shadi

Shadi is sitting in the hallway in a corner. She is busy writing in her notebook. Lately, she looks lonely and cries a lot. She hasn't been called for interrogation recently, so I can't assume she's upset about new charges. Maybe one of her friends or family members has recently been executed, or maybe separation from a good friend is bothering her. The deep sorrow in her big eyes draws me to her. "Hi."

"Hi," she answers and holds her notebook in her arms against her chest.

"Your eyes are filled with tears so often lately, and you're alone most of time!" I say.

She bends her head and keeps quiet for a few seconds. Then she says, "Sometimes loneliness is better than being with others."

"You're right, there are moments when it feels as though nobody can understand you, that a poem has more to say to you than people."

"Do you like poetry, too?" she asks.

"Oh yes, I can't bear life without poetry and literature."

"Do you write poems yourself?"

"Yes, I do, sometimes. How about you?"

"Me, too, sometimes I write poems," she replies.

Shadi and I are walking in the yard. She's talking about a failed friendship. She isn't telling me what really happened, she's just talking about her feelings. I don't ask what happened, not only for the sake of safety, but because I know it doesn't change anything – what counts is the broken heart. A friendship is a treasure, a relief, and a solace. It's a shelter for the lonely, disconsolate and disheveled souls of prisoners.

When you can't decide very simple, basic matters in your daily life, when you are entirely controlled and forced to be an obedient robot, the only way to stay alive, to save your life and your humanity, is to spread your love. Prison cannot tolerate spirited people. Prison is harder on kind hearts that only obey the rule of love and humanity.

Shadi gives me a poem she has written, called *The Five Seasons*. This is my reply to her:

You will begin the fifth season
with the torrent of your tears
raining down on the parched fields.

You will tie your "ink-stained fingers"
to the innocent perseverance of each stem
under the attack of the wind.

And the devastating wind
will bind
your delicate colourful dress
to the wings of storm-struck birds
in the unknown alleys of night.

The fifth, season of love;
fluid message of rocks, threat of termination.
But those looks,
mysterious looks of affinity,
carry the fragrant breeze of flowers
celebrating the immortal fountain of love
each Spring.

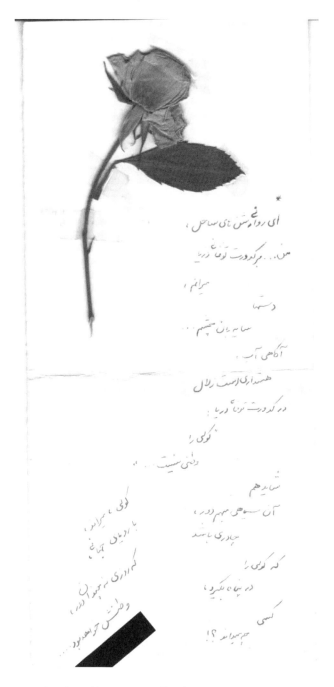

On the day of her release, Shadi wrote this for Sousan.

In the fifth season,
you'll be alone,
observing the metamorphosis of your inner butterfly.
The cool gust of wind in your hair
will write the rule of solitude
as patient as History,
since the cloak of friendship
fits this injured body no more.

Sara

Her hair is red. Her innocent face is calm. Sara is called along with some other inmates and we all know they are going to be executed. She doesn't want to take anything with her; she wants to leave her belongings for others to use. But this is not allowed. She packs some pieces she thinks are less useful, wears her *chador* and walks toward the hall under the stairs.

We are all around her, trying to hug her for the last time. She cries and smiles simultaneously. Like an excited bride leaving her family to go on to her new life, she hugs each of us. Carefree, flying like a feather blown by a gentle breeze. Her spirit overshadows the fact that she is going towards death. She walks lightly, lighter than a ballerina dancing to romantic music. This dance is immortal, endless.

When she hugs me, although she smiles and looks deeply in my eyes, I realize she is not with us. The great mystery of death is dragging her away.

Mina and Narguess

Mina is called to the ward office where she is told to pack her belongings. There is a commotion in the ward. Has she been called for execution? Recently, her father, who is a physician, was trying to transfer her from Evin to his hometown prison. Apparently, there the father could do something to save her life, or perhaps even rescue her from prison. We don't know where she is going. Her face remains as proud as it always is, under all circumstances. Without hope or wish for any sign of pity from those she considers enemies, she shows she is ready for any consequence of her activities. It has been almost ten months since Narguess went to her last interrogation, and about nine months since her second daughter left.

"Narguess," I say, "Last night I had a strange dream. I dreamt that we were children in our hometown. Near the school we used to go to, there was a railway. A train conductor let us play on his train. Suddenly, the train whistled and the conductor announced that the train was leaving. All of the children playing in the train station, including you and me, tried to get on the train before it started moving. I jumped up and was sure that you were there. The train started moving. I was happy that I could get a seat by the window. I turned happily towards you, but you weren't there. You could not get onto the train but I was happy. I wasn't sad that you weren't there."

She smiles. "Well, this is about our separation. We might not be together anymore."

I know what she means. "Then why wasn't I sad? I was happy."

"Well, I don't know. Maybe it's a transfer between wards. It's about one year that we've been here. Many people have been transferred."

"No, this cannot be the answer," I say. We both keep quiet, drowned in our thoughts.

It's a sad morning. Last year, around this time, I was arrested. The weather is getting cold. A few days have passed since the day I had that dream and nothing has happened. After all, it was just a dream.

Then, the loudspeaker starts crackling. We all listen. "People whose names I read should get ready to go to the O*tagh-e Azadi*."[24] We listen carefully. We want to know who is getting out of hell.

Suddenly, I hear Narguess' name. I jump up. I ask all the people around me if they have heard the same name. I can't believe my own ears. Yes, she is on the list. The fight between the two parties has turned into a miracle that saves her life.

---

24 *Otagh-e Azadi* means Freedom Room, which was an office in Evin where prisoners were taken before their release.

A Flyaway

It's been a few months since Narguess was released. I'm walking in the yard. It's the beginning of spring and the weather is nice and mild. A gentle breeze is caressing my face. Some birds are sitting on the barbed wires. "Beautiful birds, don't be silly," I say to myself. "Use your freedom and go to my hometown. Fly over the river and rest on the trees of the small islands, rest on the bridge." I'm thinking of the bridge we used to pass to go to university. Davoud and I had a game that we usually played on the bridge. He would make a phrase out of a word that I chose. Then I would continue, adding my phrase. We would take turns adding phrases until we reached the other side of the bridge. Our poem, story or joke would fly away, while the joy of creating something together would stay with us.

"Whenever you walk in the yard by yourself, you look like you're not in this world. Where are you? Why are you so sad?" Ashraf asks. She will be released in one month. Her fiancé is waiting for her. They will get married soon.

I don't want to make her sad with my memories. "It's nothing," I answer. "So, when do you think you'll get married?"

"I don't know yet. I need some time to find myself again."

We walk together silently for a while. I review the past; she reviews the future. The time in the yard is over. We have to go inside the ward.

It is around ten o'clock in the morning. The only newspaper in the room is being passed among ninety people. I trade the pages I have with someone else. I start reading the obituary section. A familiar name catches my eye and then I see another condolence message from the staff and students of the university we used to go to. There is no doubt. This is Davoud. The announcement clearly mentions his first and last name. I'm shocked. How could it be possible? What happened to him? I am confused and sad.

"Hey, Sousan. Sousan? I'm talking to you? Are you okay? Are you okay?" Shirin is asking me questions nonstop.

I get up and go towards the washroom, hoping to be alone at least for a couple of minutes. Some people are in line. I go to the hallway under the stairs and sit in a corner, hold my head in my arms on my knees, and try to concentrate, understand, absorb, accept and believe the reality. Life sometimes takes such phenomenally strange turns. He wouldn't risk his life for any belief. He wouldn't go near danger. And yet now, he is gone, and I am alive.

I'm confused and can't figure out my feelings. I just know I'm sorry, so sorry. For him? For myself? For how things turned out?

"Where are you?" he asks. His smile is tentative. He is standing in front of the window. The lights flashing behind him prevent me from seeing his face clearly. He always asks me the same question, with an uncertain smile, and I wonder what to answer him. He stretches his hands towards me and says, "Come."

"No, I have to go," I say. "They will be closing soon." He says something, but I can't hear him. The disturbing sound of tap water drowns out his voice. Disappointed, he puts his hands in his pockets and mumbles. He's trying to tell me something, but the sound of a vacuum cleaner blocks his voice. Where is all the tumult and commotion coming from?

Shirin is calling me over and over. "Sousan! Sousan! What's wrong with you? Hey, do you hear me? That's enough! Get up. We have to pack our belongings. There is a transfer to another ward. You are on the list."

As Long as There are Poppies

AZADEH AGAH

The Cell

I KNEW HER GREEN EYES; they told me something, but I couldn't put my finger on it. I looked at her questioningly, but said nothing. She had a half smile on her lips, the kind you flash when you don't want to give away a secret. Was it for my benefit? I said hello to her and the other three women seated in the tiny space. They responded with a faint chorus of hellos.

To break the silence, I introduced myself, without referring to anyone's name. Green Eyes took the initiative of introducing herself and the others. I realized why the eyes looked so familiar: they belonged to an old acquaintance from university years. She was unrecognizable now.

Drastic weight loss had left her very thin, almost like the images in news reports of famine, and her green eyes were listless and tinged not merely with sadness, but deep disappointment. She had recognized me but said nothing, for fear of giving away my identity. She was surprised to see me there, I would later find out. She thought I would surely have been out of the country by then.

When the Islamic government began cracking down on dissidents, many intellectuals sought refuge from the repression exercised by the Khomeini regime by fleeing to Western countries. Thousands were arrested inside Iran and imprisoned and executed at will. The war between Iran and Iraq had closed the country's international ports and borders, which kept many people from leaving. The only way out of the country was to be smuggled by human traffickers who charged a hefty sum of money and couldn't guarantee a safe journey. But there were also those who refused to leave the country to the Islamic regime and took the risk of staying and fighting for their beliefs.

The evening that the *pasdar*s came to arrest us, we had a few friends over for dinner. The doorbell rang and, without looking to see who was there, I opened the door. I was suddenly faced with several men armed with Kalashnikovs, and a fellow whose head was covered with a brown bag bearing two eyeholes. I screamed and called for my husband, who hastily ran to see what was wrong. One of the guests and my daughter also heard my cry and followed. My daughter tried to touch the machine guns, thinking they were toys, but I pulled her aside and held her back. When the *pasdar*s told us to cover up and go with them, we asked to see the warrant for our arrest. One of the *pasdar*s pulled out a piece of paper and showed it to me. On the warrant were only our first names.

I objected. "Do you know how many Azadeh's live in this town?"

"Why do you think we've brought along this man?" The guard pointed to the tall fellow with the hood on his head.

My husband, daughter, and myself got into a car with three *pasdar*s. Another car, carrying the tall hooded fellow and several more guards, followed. We were told to put our heads on our laps and refrain from speaking to each other. After a long ride on the expressway, we descended down a very steep road. I realized we must be going to Evin Prison.

Evin is the name of an old village located on the foot of a mountain in the northwest of Tehran. When the Shah had this prison built in the 1960s, Evin was still considered to be outside the city limits of Tehran.

But when we were taken there, the village had turned into a relatively prosperous residential area, though remnants of the village were still present.

Upon arrival at Evin Prison, the car stopped in front of a large metal door. The guards showed their slip of paper and were handed a couple of filthy, black blindfolds. We put them on reluctantly. The driver drove deeper inside the Evin compound and stopped in front of a building. I later realized that the building was Ward 209, the most dreaded section of Evin Prison.

Green Eyes looked worriedly at me and the little girl I was carrying in my arms. She offered me room to sit down on the dark, coarse, military blanket serving as a floor cover. The cell was very small, perhaps two by one and a half metres. On one wall, there was a sink, and next to it, a metal one-piece toilet without a lid. These cells had been made during the Shah's rule[25] for the purpose of solitary confinement. During the Islamic regime, they were utilized for detainees under interrogation. Overpopulation of the prisons forced the prison administration to put five or more prisoners in every solitary cell.

On the wall facing the door, was a picture of the Almighty Leader, Ayatollah Khomeini:[26] he gazed at us with piercing eyes. Underneath was the heating unit, which emitted very little warmth, but its pipes allowed us to hear sounds from the surrounding cells. On the ceiling of the cell, there was a painted glass window, which we could not reach by hand. To open it, we had to climb on each other's shoulders or poke at it with a long object. At night, when the prison was quiet, we could hear, through the half-open window, the conversations of the guards keeping watch on the roof. In the early hours of the morning, we also heard the barrage of executioners, gunfire. We could tell how many were executed by counting the number of single shots fired to their heads to finish them off.

On the iron door of the cell, there were two windows: a square one on top with bars, which opened and shut from the outside and served as a look-in for the guards, and a rectangular one at the bottom, through which they pushed in our plates of food. The rectangular opening could

---

25 Shah Mohammad Reza Pahlavi ruled from 1941 until the Islamic Revolution of 1979.

26 Ayatollah Khomeini was the first Supreme Leader of the Islamic Republic of Iran, February 1979-June 1989.

be pushed open from the inside. Through it, we could summon the guards by extending out a long piece of cardboard. Or, we could spy on the events taking place in the narrow corridor that separated the rows of cells from each other.

The floor of the cell was made of wood. Each prisoner was given one or two military blankets of coarse, dark wool that smelled like sheep and sweat. One served as a mattress, the other as a cover. But every time a new inmate walked in, it took the guards awhile to update the number of blankets, and in the meantime, prisoners had to share what was available.

That night, the women accommodated me by sharing their blankets and red plastic cups which had been discoloured by frequent use. Fortunately, at the time of my arrest, I had worn my long woolen coat, so I was able to use it as cover. There was room only for everyone to sleep on their sides, and Green Eyes made sure she slept next to me. When everyone was asleep, she put her mouth to my ear and started whispering in such a low voice that I could barely hear. She told me what was going on in the prison and what I needed to know to be able to survive. She also updated me about old comrades: those who were still alive, those who had been executed or killed under torture, and those few who were now collaborating with the prison authorities. In particular, she warned me against sharing information with other prisoners, for one could never be sure if they were *tavvab*s or not. Thus, the best policy was to avoid sharing sensitive information with anyone.

That night, I didn't sleep at all. My daughter was ill and kept tossing and turning, and I couldn't stop listening to the unfriendly sounds coming from the other side of the walls – guards speaking to one another on the roof, toilets flushing in adjacent cells, the footsteps of men going about in the main corridor of the ward, a prisoner chanting the *Qur'an* in a loud voice. My cellmates later told me that the man reciting the *Qur'an* was the leader of a leftist group that had split from an Islamic guerrilla organization before the Revolution. He had "repented" and embraced Islam once more. Was he doing this to save his skin or had he truly changed his mind? One could never be sure. He was executed before he had a chance to explain.

Even though it was winter, I was gasping for air. My body felt hot and turbulent. I kept reviewing my past activities, weighing them with the Islamists' yardstick. I could imagine receiving anything from a death sentence to freedom, depending on what I was accused of. I knew they would come for me early in the morning. I was arrested at night and when I got to Evin, the principal interrogators had already left for the day. Someone asked me a few questions and hit me a few times on the head and back to let me know I was in the notorious Evin Prison. I guess he needed to make the "right" first impression. So I knew I would be summoned first thing in the morning and I was preparing my replies.

As soon as the sunlight shone in through the open crack of the window, I got up, washed my face with the frigid tap water, brushed my teeth with my fingers, and sat to wait. I hadn't been allowed to take anything from home – no toothbrush, change of clothes or undergarments. The only thing I had brought along was a small bag, full of diapers and baby formula, for my two-year-old child. Pretty soon, I thought to myself, I am going to stink.

Soon, everyone was awake. I heard footsteps in the corridor. The girls said, "Tea," and their faces lit up. I thought about how, in difficult situations, even unimportant things can make you happy. In anticipation, we lined up our plastic cups and waited for the female *pasdar* to reach our cell. Finally, she knocked at the door and asked for the cups. One by one, our cups were filled with tea that smelled of camphor. I could smell the camphor because I was new to prison. The others drank their tea without complaining about the scent. Some bread and a tiny piece of feta cheese completed our breakfast.

Before I got to finish my tea, there was another knock on the door. This time, they called my name. The moment I was dreading had arrived. I got up and, in anticipation of being beaten, put on my long woolen coat and covered my head with a large shawl that I had worn from home. I looked for something to wear on my feet. The night before, the guard had taken away my shoes. This was one method of making sure that prisoners would be spotted if they tried to run away. One of the girls offered me her slippers. I felt really stupid wearing a woolen coat with a pair of plastic slippers, but there was nothing normal or logical about this place. I borrowed a cellmate's blindfold and was ready to go. The women accepted the responsibility of my daughter for the time I would be absent. The youngest member of the cell, a fourteen-year-old child, had already established a nice relationship with my daughter.

The female guard led me to the main corridor, where I stood against the wall, waiting. Then someone called my name and asked me to follow him into a small interrogation room. He ordered me to sit on a chair, the type used in schools, with a small desk flap for writing. He put a pad of paper in front of me and asked me to write down "everything" I knew. When he realized I wasn't writing anything, he asked if I was deaf. I automatically raised my head to look at the person asking me the question, and was hit on the head with the folder that he had in his hand. He said, "Don't try to look at me, or I'll have you flogged in the basement."

I calmly explained that it was an automatic reflex and that I hadn't meant to look at him. I also added that I didn't understand what he meant by "everything." He left me to sit and began speaking to another man who was being interrogated in the same room. I recognized the voice. He was the man who had led the guards to our home. I knew that the interrogator had placed us in the same room to manipulate me. He had already broken this fellow, and wanted to show him off to me to make me capitulate, too. After some time, he re-approached me and wrote down a question on my pad. He told me to answer the question in writing and to sign the page when I was done. Then he continued to carry on friendly conversation with the other fellow, for my benefit.

Each time my answer was not what he wanted to hear, he showered me with profanities and called me a double-dealing infidel. When my replies made him angry, he hit me on the head and left me to sweat in silence in anticipation of more misery to come.

By the time it was noon, I felt really hungry. I realized I hadn't eaten for twenty-four hours – since yesterday's lunch. I felt quite weak for lack of food and sleep. A guard was distributing lunch to everyone in the corridor. I could smell the rice and lentils, a popular dish within modest Iranian households. I happened to like this dish and I could feel my mouth watering. The server finally reached our room and handed me a plate full of rice. I quickly ate several spoonfuls, as if someone was going to take the food away from me. I was unable to finish my plate of rice. I needed something with which to wash it down. When the server returned to collect my plate, I raised my head a bit and asked for a glass of water. Unlike the interrogator, the server didn't object. He was an old man with curly grey hair and sunburnt skin. He didn't have a mean look on his face like the rest of them. I detected an Azari[27] accent. He said he would come back with water in a little while. My mouth was so dry I

---

27 Azari is the language of the people of the northwest province of Azarbaijan.

could hardly talk. I was hoping he would come with the glass of water before the interrogator returned.

I felt bored. I had been sitting for so many hours with nothing to do. Why was I sitting there doodling my thumbs? But that was the idea. They wanted to scare you with the anticipation of pain and torture. Hours went by and nothing happened. I listened to guards making angry comments about us. They called us spoiled brats with full stomachs. At times, I could hear a hand cutting the air to slap a prisoner in the face. I wondered if the blindfolded man I had seen earlier in the main corridor was still there. He had been crawling on his knees. His complexion was pale and his feet were bandaged. He must have been subjected to *ta'zir*, the flogging of the soles of the victim's feet, I had thought to myself.

I heard a woman moaning with pain. I guessed she must have been tortured and lost her mind, because between the moaning, she sang a song from the pre-revolutionary times – totally the wrong thing to do, under the circumstances. The guards told her to shut up or they would take her to the basement, hinting at more torture. But she heard nothing. She continued singing and moaning. Then they dragged her away and I didn't hear her anymore. It was only later that I learned the significance of the word basement. In the basement of Evin Prison, interrogators tortured prisoners to extract information.

Finally, the day was over and a guard brought me back to my cell. My cellmates were eager to find out how it went. They were relieved when I returned on my feet rather than crawling on my knees. In fact, I had no critical information for the interrogators to extract, which spared me the trip to the basement that day. Those who had experienced flogging on the soles of their feet spoke of an excruciating pain, comparable to nothing. One of my cellmates had two horrifying brown scars on the soles of her feet that resembled cobwebs with hollow centres.

I felt so much safer being back with other prisoners. I hugged my daughter and tried to comfort her. It was like I had returned home to family members. One of the girls handed me a cup of sweetened water. The women routinely did this for cellmates who had been called to interrogation. They used part of their sugar ration to make me *sharbat*,[28] which was the only luxury they could afford to offer me. They took turns asking me questions and giving me advice on how to handle the

---

28 *Sharbat* is water mixed with something to make it sweet.

next session. I was exhausted and sleepy, but could not relax until the interrogations were over. That night, we had bread, carrot jam, and a small piece of butter for dinner. At ten o'clock, the lights were turned off and we had to sleep.

Another restless night awaited me. My daughter, running a fever, was extremely warm to the touch. I was very worried for her and there was nothing I could do until the next morning. My husband, who had also been arrested, was another source of anxiety. I tried to prepare for the next day, aware that next time I might not be so lucky. I was glad that it was winter and that I had heavy clothes on. Would the cable coming down across my back feel any less painful? I was preoccupied with these thoughts when I heard a guard on the roof calling others to morning prayer. I knew I had missed the chance to sleep for another night.

I felt sick to my stomach. My insides were in turmoil. My mouth was dry, and the metallic taste of anxiety was on my tongue. I was dying for a few of hours of sleep, but I felt too alert – my racing thoughts made me incapable of slowing down. I hated the dark and couldn't wait for my cellmates to awaken. When one of the women finally moved, I began talking to her right away, lest she go back to sleep and leave me alone with my morbid thoughts.

A new day brought the same breakfast and the same procedures, taking turns to use the toilet and the faucet. I had become constipated, not able to respond to nature's call in front of four other women. They tried to accommodate me by turning towards the wall when I wanted to use the toilet, but I was still unable to relax. I didn't have a toothbrush and after three days, this also bothered me. One of my cellmates pointed to an old toothbrush and suggested I use it. It was under the sink, left over from a previous prisoner. The thought of putting someone else's toothbrush – which had been sitting on the floor for God knows how many days – in my mouth, made me nauseous. Another suggested I disinfect the toothbrush and use it. We had been given Dettol to disinfect the toilet and the sink everyday. I could use some of it to do the same with the toothbrush. I filled one of the plastic cups with disinfectant and water and placed the old toothbrush in the solution. I had also worn the same clothes and underwear for three nights and days. I was itching all over, and I smelled of sweat. A cellmate offered me a new pair of underwear, which she had recently received from home. That was the most generous gift anyone could have given me. I washed the used pair and left it to dry for the next day. Another woman offered me a shirt so I could wash my pullover and hang it to dry. We had made a clothesline by weaving together the strips of plastic in which our daily rations of bread were wrapped. One end was tied to the bars of the cell door window and the other, to the pipe of the heating unit. With help of my cellmates, I was beginning to look and feel halfway decent.

Days went by, but no one came for me. Everyday I woke up thinking, today is the day, but nothing happened. My cellmates said that some interrogators do this to break prisoners. In the cases of prisoners with no time-sensitive information, interrogators believed that the longer the wait, the wearier prisoners would become and soon volunteer everything they knew. Every day that went by was a day that would not be counted in my future sentence. In this period, the duration of imprisonment officially began with the date of trial. I had not yet been tried.

Green Eyes had already been tried but hadn't received her sentence, which meant she had been sentenced to death. Those prisoners who had a death sentence did not officially know about it until the day of execution, at which time they and all of their belongings were called to the guards' room. In the public wards, all the prisoners knew the routine of the prison. When an inmate was called with all of her belongings, prisoners would come out of their rooms to say goodbye and see her to the ward door one last time. But Green Eyes never left the cell for the public ward.

With every passing day, I despaired more about getting out of Evin any time soon. I had managed to get my daughter out of Evin after a few days; I sent her to my parents. But that added other worries. Would they be able to take care of her? Would she be psychologically scarred as a result of the trauma she had endured? Was she feeling better from her illness? I had no way of knowing the answers to any of these questions. I still didn't have visitation rights with my family members because I was officially under interrogation. On visiting days, I had nothing to look forward to, except the tales my cellmates brought back from their visits. They returned with glowing eyes and rosy cheeks, excited from having seen their loved ones, and told me of what they had heard. Prisoners were allowed to receive a relatively small sum of money from their family members to be able to buy necessary goods from the prison store. There was, however, no store as such. A list of available goods would circulate every two to three months and prisoners ordered what they needed. Still, that didn't mean one received everything one ordered.

Given the fact that Iran was in the midst of a bloody war with Iraq, some goods were rationed even in the society at large. Obviously, prisoners were not on a top priority list to receive those scarce goods. What prisoners ordered, however, could not exactly be called luxury goods. Rather, they were bare necessities, such as sanitary napkins, toothbrushes, facial tissues, shampoo, underwear, hand cream – things that should have been provided by the prison itself. Prison food was deficient in many nutrients, and there was little in the way of fruits and vegetables. We were not, however, able to order these, and had to manage with what little was provided with prison food every now and then.

Prison authorities thought of us as godless creatures who did not deserve to live like human beings. They often said things like, "You should be grateful we don't let you starve to death." Every morning, they distributed the daily ration of bread and sugar to our cells: three sugar cubes per person and a package of flat bread to be split among cell occupants. Sometimes, the bread was really uncooked on the edges, and we discarded it to avoid an upset stomach. However, if they saw the discarded segments in our trash (which they collected and carefully inspected), they punished us by withholding our ration of bread for one day. In order to avoid this punishment, we learned to place the pieces of bread on the heating unit and not eat it until it was bone dry. Since we had our bread ration for the day, we could consume it whenever we wanted, even as a snack in between meals. We called the small pieces of dried bread "prison biscuits," and at times, with a little imagination, they even tasted like biscuits. The sugar rations went into a jar from which we only took what we absolutely needed. We saved the rest for emergency situations: prisoners returning from interrogations and floggings, incidences of low blood sugar, or a cellmate's birthday. Aside from the daily ration of sugar cubes, the only other sweets provided were dates and carrot jam which were served with butter and bread, as part of our meal. Once in a while, we had the luxury of getting one, or half of one, very small, sour orange per person. In the summer, large, seedy cucumbers and rotten grapes replaced the orange. Our diet was far from balanced. There were few dairy products offered. Aside from the tiny piece of feta cheese provided at breakfast, we had no other source of calcium. To compensate for this, we ground the shells of our rations of boiled eggs and mixed it with our meals. One night a week, we had soup for dinner, which we jokingly called the "weekly report" because the soup was composed of the remnants of every meal we had eaten during the previous week.

We had our daily routine, which we diligently followed. Before breakfast, we took turns washing up with the cold tap water. Then we collected the blankets and folded them into long, narrow stacks, to be used as "sofas." We had a square piece of plastic that served as a table-cloth. After breakfast, we took turns exercising while others sat patiently on the folded blankets and talked. One of our exercises was to simply walk forward and backward; this was to avoid making too many turns in the small space. Then there was jumping up and down to help with circulation, and at the end, some stretching. This took up to an hour and a half, depending on how many of us took part in the daily exercises. Then, there was a period of time spent on personal chores, from washing clothes to clipping our nails. If we had the official daily newspaper (the issue from the previous day), someone read it aloud for everyone to listen. Occasionally, we got our hands on the crossword puzzle, which was extremely popular with the prisoners. The first cell to receive the paper usually kept the crossword. Since we had no paper or pencil, we used safety pins to punch in the letters.

Lunch was served after the noon prayer. Once again, the plastic cloth was spread on the floor; plates were extended out of the rectangular opening in the door and returned with food. Before the guard reached our cell, however, we engaged in a guessing game in attempts to predict what we were having for lunch. Often, we were right. We had come to recognize the awful smell of each routine dish being served week after week. After lunch, we observed an hour of silence to allow for relaxation and meditation. During this period, each individual engaged in reviewing their prospects and contemplating strategies for coping with the situation at hand. In the afternoon, we had storytelling, "movie" going, or "travelling" sessions. If a prisoner had read an interesting novel, she would recount it to the others in detail, using vivid descriptions and acting out the exciting passages. If we decided to go to the movies, the routine was the same, with one difference – those who had most recently come to prison were more often asked to talk about films that they had seen. Travelling sessions were the most exciting for younger cellmates who had not travelled far and preferred to listen to those who had been to more interesting places.

Dinner followed the evening prayer. The routine was the same as lunch, except the meals were lighter and often cold. They included such dishes as bread, butter and jam; bread, butter and dates; bread, potato and a hard-boiled egg; and, of course, the "weekly report" soup. After dinner, everyone engaged in different activities, such as mending clothes, washing dishes and cleaning up to prepare the "beds." Everyday, one of the women was responsible for cleaning up the cell.

Since there was very little room, shorter cellmates slept in the space by the toilet, about a metre and a half in length. The person who slept next to the wall had the best spot in the cell, for she benefited from the cool privacy of the wall, and was able to avoid the exhaled air from the individual sleeping a couple of inches away. Those sleeping in the middle had the worst of it: if they wanted to turn over, they had to sit up to make the turn, in order not to awaken their cellmates.

As darkness fell, silence enveloped the block of cells, and prisoners whispered in order not to be heard. If a guard heard voices from a cell, he would bang on the door and threaten us with flogging. This, however, did not prevent us from making jokes out of the situation and laughing heartily. We tried not to concentrate on outside noises so we could relax and fall asleep. Those of us who had problems sleeping would ask the guard for a sleeping pill, which she provided with permission from "Doctor" Salman (it was well-known among prisoners that he was just a member of the Revolutionary Guard and had no degree in the field of medicine). There was no information about the brand or dosage of the medication. For all we knew, he could be giving us poison. When "Doctor" Salman visited the cells, he had a hood on his head which, resembling the hoods worn by the members of the Ku Klux Klan, prevented us from seeing his face.

If a prisoner was ill, she had to wait until morning to tell the guards, and even then, it would take a few days, weeks even, before she was able to make a visit to the prison clinic. The procedure for seeing a real doctor – often an inmate who happened to be a physician and who had been ordered to work for free – was to get on the list the guards circulated every once in a while. Depending on what type of ailment you were suffering from (whether you needed a specialist, a dentist or a general practitioner) you had to wait one to several months to see a doctor. There were some exceptions to this rule, such as an inmate brutally tortured and in danger of dying before having confessed all of his or her information, a woman giving birth to a child, or suicide attempts. In the event that an interrogator went too far with a prisoner under torture and he or she could not be saved, documents indicating that the prisoner had gone to court and received a death sentence were cooked up. The interrogators always had the cooperation and backing of the court judges working there. This situation made the interrogators powerful and capable of doing whatever they wished with the inmates.

After a few months in the cell, I had grown so fond of my cellmates that I wished I could stay there until I was sentenced. I had a feeling of security among them, which I knew I would not enjoy in the public ward. But my wish did not come true. One morning, a guard knocked on the cell door and called my name. I was to be ready with all of my belongings, to be transferred to the public ward. Since I didn't have much to gather, I spent the time saying goodbye to my cellmates. As I followed the guard to my new destination, I tried to prepare myself for the new ward, the new cellmates, and how I would behave among them. By now, I was an experienced prisoner and had learned how to survive.

Later, I saw three of my old cellmates in the public ward, but regretfully, I never saw Green Eyes again. She never made it out of Evin Prison alive.

Life in the Public Ward

In the public wards of Evin Prison, there were three roughly distinguishable categories of prisoners. The *tavvab*s – fewest in number – were prisoners who collaborated with the prison officials to various degrees. A limited number would take part in executions and the interrogation of newly arrested prisoners, but more commonly, they would spy on cellmates and function as room and ward representatives. The second group, which was by far the largest, included prisoners who had decided to do their time in a dignified manner and leave the prison alive. These inmates generally abided by the prison rules and regulations, but did not collaborate with the interrogators and the guards. In the third category, were those who were unrelenting in their beliefs, uncompromising in their attitudes, and openly intolerant of the harsh rules and regulations imposed by prison officials. They were called *sar-e moze'-i*. A *sar-e moze'-i* held to his or her political and ideological convictions, or was simply unwilling to follow regulations that opposed the principles of human rights. This category of prisoners was also limited in number. Obviously, the distinctions between the three groups were not rigid and often some people vacillated back and forth between the groups. The *sar-e moze'-i* were loathed by the *tavvab*s and respected or tolerated by the mainstream group. The attitude of the prison authorities toward them, however, was one of distrust, hatred and vengeance.

During the time I spent in Ward 209 I had heard stories from a cellmate about the kind of atmosphere that reigned over the public wards. She had advised me to make sure I wasn't branded one way or another and to be careful how I approached the prisoners in various groups.

The day I was transferred from the solitary ward to the public ward, a guard banged on the cell door and asked me to be ready as soon as possible with all my belongings. I hastily grabbed my prized possessions, including my second-hand toothbrush and the few items of clothing I had borrowed since my arrest, and said farewell to my cellmates. This was always one of the most difficult things to do in prison. Outside prison, one never spends twenty-four hours a day with anyone, not even family members. But in prison, you are in constant contact with a group of individuals, with whom you either develop very close bonds of friendship, try to coexist with, or ignore altogether. When I realized I was going to leave the cell, I was happy to be going to the public ward, where I could exercise and move about. But I also knew this could be the last time I would lay eyes on the four women with whom I had spent so much time in a tiny cell. They might not all make it out of prison alive.

The guard returned and told me to exit the cell and stand facing the wall in the long corridor. I hated that corridor. All the interrogation rooms opened into this narrow hallway, spilling out the familiar sounds of prisoners under torture. I stood there for several hours before I managed to attract the attention of a male guard, who finally asked me to follow him. By then, I was aching all over as a result of standing in one spot for so long. I regretted having had to stand in the corridor, when I could have spent that time with my cellmates. The guard walked very fast and it was difficult to keep up after having been deprived of movement for so many months. With the dark blindfold over my eyes, I felt so disoriented that I had to extend my arms out in front of me for balance.

We finally made it to the ward entrance, which was nothing but a thick, dark, filthy curtain. Inside, there was a small room belonging to the guards who were responsible for the ward. The female ward attendant took charge of me. After a few questions, she assigned me to one of the rooms on the lower level. I still didn't know which ward I was in. All I knew was that there were four public wards that, built during the Shah's regime, housed women. The men's quarters were in a newly constructed building called *Amuzeshgah*.[29] I was so eager to finally see the public ward that as soon as the attendant told me to go inside, I ran down the stairs and into the ward.

Ward 246 (also known as Ward Three) consisted of two levels, each administered separately by the same female guards. Both levels were located underground, and each consisted of three wings circling a small paved courtyard. Below the flight of stairs descending from the guards' room, there was a hall that led to the courtyard, the "library,"[30] and the prisoners' quarters. The latter section was separated from the hall by iron bars that were kept closed most of the time, especially at night.

---

29 *Amuzeshgah* literally means place of learning.
30 The "library" was a small room exclusively for the *tavvabs,* who used it for everything but reading books.

The hall was used for group prayers on special occasions, for gatherings to hear prison announcements, and by *tavvab*s at will. Inside the lower ward, there were two narrow L-shaped corridors, with a water cooler at the junction of the two. The bathroom was at the end of the first corridor and the toilets were at the entrance to the second. There were four small rooms along the first short corridor and three larger ones along the second, longer corridor.

The minute I stepped inside the ward, I heard voices whispering, "*jadidi, jadidi.*"[31] Upon entering the room to which I was assigned, what caught my attention was the sheer number of people sitting around the room watching television or chatting. There were over ninety people living in a room that measured twelve by eighteen feet. One of the *tavvab*s, who also served as the room representative (without having been elected to the position by the prisoners), came forward and asked me my name and my political affiliation. I answered. Then she assigned me a hook on the wall to hang my belongings and a spot on the floor to sleep on at night. She also mentioned that this was "bath night."

In the solitary cell, we could only shower once a week – during the day on Fridays. Three at a time, we were sent to the tiny bathroom and given fifteen minutes to shower. We had to take turns using the shower and never managed to finish in the time allotted. The guard would continually come to the window, which opened from the outside, and urge us to stop wasting all that water and finish up quickly. We didn't even have privacy in the bathroom. Once, while I was waiting for my turn to use the shower, I watched, in amazement, as a male guard opened the small window and quickly closed it when he realized he had been noticed.

In the public ward, showering began in the evening and went on till the early hours of the morning. Those who were on the priority list (older inmates, mothers with small children, those who were ill, and women who had finished their menstrual cycle and needed to purify themselves to be able to pray again), took up most of the early hours, when the water was warm or, at least, acceptably warm. As time passed, the water gradually cooled off and showering became a kind of torture. The person in charge of bathing at the ward level was a *tavvab*. There was also an inmate in every room, who made up the shower list and

---

31 *Jadidi* means newcomer (i.e. to the prison).

gave it to the person in charge of the ward. Twice a week, they stayed awake all night to send prisoners to the shower room in groups of four or five. Since our bathing time was so short, there were ten or twelve people in the shower at any given time. There were four shower stalls in the bathroom. The women took turns soaking and washing themselves. At times, the sewage system backed up and we ended up showering ankle-deep in dirty water. Because there was no privacy, women bathed in their underwear.

I had been under the impression that in the public ward, each room stocked some items of necessity for those poor souls who, like me, came to the ward with almost nothing. I asked the woman in charge of emergency goods for a hairbrush, a new toothbrush, some shampoo and a bar of soap. She regretfully informed me that supplies had dried up: there was nothing left to dispense. I jokingly said, "Then you don't need to wake me up, because I have nothing to wash myself with." The prison policy was to provide each woman with a bar of soap and a box of sanitary napkins per month. But I had entered the ward in the evening and rations were not always delivered on time. I had to borrow every item from other women, including sanitary pads. The supply of sanitary pads was sufficient for prisoners only because many women stopped menstruating as a consequence of ingesting camphor with daily meals. Those who no longer had periods donated their ration of pads to those who menstruated more often than once a month.

That night, a young woman in her twenties, whose bed was next to mine on the floor, overheard my conversation with the woman in charge of emergency supplies, and offered to lend me her shampoo, soap and hairbrush. This was the beginning of a solid friendship during my stay in that ward. One thing we learned to count on while in Evin was the generosity of other inmates. If it weren't for that, many of us would have had a hard time surviving our prison terms.

I was awakened around two in the morning and sent to the shower room. I was in great need of a nice, hot shower, but all I got was a lukewarm trickle of water, which occasionally came to a halt at the worst times. On one occasion, the water stopped running while I was waiting my turn to rinse the lather off my head and face – the burning sensation in my eyes was unbearable. That we had to go back to bed with wet hair, and endure the freezing temperature of the room, added insult to injury.

I was new to the room and had only received two military blankets, one serving as a mattress and the other as a cover. The ward was below ground level and the floor was made of concrete, covered only by a thin, worn out carpet. Imagine the discomfort of sleeping on a blanket all night long. Those who had spent more time in Evin had asked their families to bring them good blankets from home. But I hadn't been allowed family visits and had to live with the two coarse military blankets I had been allotted, and use my items of clothing as a pillow.

My first night in the public ward was not a happy one, but I got to make the acquaintances of some of the women in the room. The same three categories that existed in the ward were present here. I was still under scrutiny by all groups; they wanted to "classify" me and adapt their behaviour toward me accordingly. Gradually, inmates from different political inclinations came forward and asked me questions, to which I provided cautious replies. Despite my diligent efforts in camouflaging my sentiments, that night I was pretty much "discovered" by the various groups in the room. They all decided to leave me be for the time being.

The next morning, I learned of another inconvenience: there were only six toilets for over three hundred inmates. When I tried to use the washroom, I realized there was a long line in the short corridor of the L-shaped ward. While I stood in line, I met more prisoners from other rooms, all of whom were curious to get to know me. A middle-aged woman, who later became a good friend of mine, asked, "What brings you here?"

My reply was cautious. "The same reason that has brought the others." I guess I still had the look of a novice, which caught everyone's attention.

While I waited my turn, I noticed that some women went directly to the head of the line, said something, and then disappeared inside the washrooms. When I expressed surprise at this behaviour, someone explained that these were prisoners who suffered from digestive track diseases, kidney problems, and incontinence brought about by excessive torture. When I finally managed to get to the toilet, I felt relief and excitement at having some privacy. But no sooner had I entertained this thought, when someone began banging on the door, shouting, "Number Three [referring to the last of the three toilets on the right hand side of the washroom], hurry up, there's a line here!" Then and there, I knew that there was no such thing as privacy in prison. Nonetheless, this system certainly beat going to the toilet with four other people sitting around in the solitary confinement cell.

After washing up, it was time for breakfast. The women who were responsible for the day's chores brought in a large container of camphor-scented tea, and a plate bearing a piece of cheese that measured about four by four by two inches, and a bunch of machine-made *taftoon*[32] bread. Each prisoner also received three sugar cubes with which to sweeten their tea. By the time the cube of cheese was meticulously divided into some ninety transparent pieces with the help of a string of sewing thread, the tea was lukewarm and the smell of camphor, even stronger.

Some days, butter and carrot jam replaced the cheese as our morning meal. Women often exchanged their rations with one another. Those who disliked cheese offered their share to the ones who disliked butter and jam, and vice versa. Since I liked both cheese and jam, I didn't participate in the barter. But sugar was nothing to be taken lightly. We had a woman in her thirties who had low blood sugar and couldn't live on three sugar cubes a day, and the bit of jam served some mornings. To keep her going, her friends from different rooms donated their spare sugar rations.

After breakfast, it was time for the "educational program." The program usually consisted of Islamic propaganda or re-runs of prisoners admitting, under pressure, of course, to crimes they had not committed. Prisoners whose prison terms had ended would not be freed without undergoing this ritual of self-defamation. During these programs, everyone was forced to stay in the room, awake and attentive. The only sure way out was to play sick. Most mornings, therefore, many women complained of various aches and pains, only to miraculously recover after the program was over. The woman in charge of the room's "pharmacy" would distribute medications, giving the tactically sick an aspirin or two and a dirty look. Another way out of the "educational program" was to go to the washroom and stay inside. When too many people used the same excuse, however, the room rep forbade leaving the room altogether. Each day, arguments took place between the room rep and those claiming to be ill. There was no way to resolve the conflict and

---

32 *Taftoon* is a kind of traditional Iranian bread made in a special oven called *tanoor*. The *taftoon* bread used in Evin was machine-made and not popular with the prisoners.

both sides knew it. It was impossible to force women to listen to badly made propaganda. The only inmates allowed to go to the yard during the "educational program" were mothers with children – so that the kids would not disturb the "educational" sessions with crying or noise.

We shared the yard with the upper ward. Each day, one ward had the yard in the morning for about an hour and a half, and the other ward had it in the afternoon. During this time, we also had to wash our dirty clothes so that we could hang them on the lines outside to dry. We didn't wait until yard break to wash underwear, however – we hung them from our personal hooks in our rooms, inside a plastic bag to keep the water from dripping on the heads of those sitting beneath.

Every morning the bread ration arrived in heavy plastic bags. When empty, these bags were distributed among the prisoners in each room, according to need. For example, when I was first transferred to the public ward, I was allotted plastic bags to make a small sac to hang from my hook on the wall. This sac held my daily personal hygiene objects – toothbrush, soap and hand cream (used also for the face and body). Since our personal belonging usually resembled one another's, we embroidered our names on the plastic sacs. Since we were all political prisoners and not criminals, no one ever touched anyone else's belongings, except by mistake. If excess bags were available, they were used to make all sorts of imaginative stuff, from baskets to suitcases.

Nothing was thrown away in the ward; everything was put to some good use. Old socks were carefully unraveled and the thread was used to make wallets, headbands, and embroideries. The guards forbade this, but the prisoners always found a way to engage in such activities. Sometimes, the prison store offered pressed dates on its list of items for purchase. We ate the dates and made worry beads and bracelets out of their stones, which helped calm our nerves and give us something to do during the never-ending "educational" sessions.

Many of our creations were taken away during raids launched every once in a while by the guards. They had one goal when it came to dealing with prisoners, and that was to make us as miserable and obedient as possible. Anything that made us happy or kept us busy and creative became an object of punishment. All the guards wanted us to do was brood. They preferred those who sat in corners, quietly crying or looking depressed. Prisoners who seemed to have a plan for their lives in captivity were harassed and frequently transferred from one ward to

Bracelet made from date pits.

another. The *tavvab*s found a way to keep busy, too. They would take copies of the *Qur'an* or other "safe" books and sit in the hall area outside the ward. This tactic brought them peace and quiet for a period of time. We, on the other hand, were driven crazy by the incessant noise generated by so many inmates in such a small space. This problem finally led prisoners to come up with a rule of our own. We decided to have two hours of silence every afternoon to allow everyone to do whatever they enjoyed, from taking a nap to reading yesterday's paper to mending clothes. Whispering was allowed only if necessary. This rule helped keep many prisoners from going mad.

The women had another unwritten rule unknown to the guards. Whenever there was need, we shared everything – but not with the *tavvab*s, who reported even sharing to the authorities. Some women's families lived in other cities, which meant that their visits were irregular. As such, these women sometimes ran out of money and couldn't buy necessary items from the prison store lists that were circulated every so often. The inmates naturally came together in small groups. Everything was shared with the members of the group. No one was left without support of some kind. When someone was transferred to another ward, the members of her group would stuff her bag with whatever they had, knowing it would take her some time to become a member of another group in a different ward. This practice was frowned upon by the prison authorities, who considered these support groups organizations, or "communes," inside prison.

Another unwritten rule was that breastfeeding mothers, pregnant women and small children always got the most nutritious part of every meal. The prison officials didn't provide these mothers with enough

"My Home" carved out of stone. Actual size is 1³/₈ inches wide
by 1⁵/₈ inches high.

Antelope pendant hand-carved in stone.: Actual size is 1 3/8 inches wide by 1 1/8 inches high.

baby formula or food so infants needed to be started on regular food as soon as possible. Sick people, who had special regimens and could not eat certain meals, gradually became malnourished and weak, living off of bread and feta cheese. Inmates always tried to help each other whenever they could, but in cases like this, there was nothing to be done.

On special occasions, like a cellmate's or child's birthday, we made a "cake." We had no access to cooking facilities or kitchen utensils. All we had were plates and spoons, and some raw ingredients which, outside of prison, we would never use in a cake. We had to plan ahead for the feast. For several days, we put aside our rations of sugar, feta cheese, dates or dried figs, and butter. We soaked the feta cheese in water to take out the salt, and placed the dried figs in water to soften. On the day of the celebration, we combined dried bread with the above ingredients and

Ballerina carved from a stone. Actual size is 1 1/4 inches wide
by 2 inches high.

Dove carved out of a piece of tile. Actual size is 1 1/2 inches wide
by 1 7/8 inches high.

added water to the mixture. Then it was time for strong hands to knead
the dough as hard as they could, to turn it into a pliable mixture that
could be shaped and designed like a cake. Then, when no snitch was in
sight, we celebrated and ate the cake as quickly as possible. Experience
had taught us that lingering over the cake could put its enjoyment in
jeopardy. One day, when a group of prisoners had taken their cake out
to the yard to celebrate under the blue sky, one of the snitches informed
the female warden. She descended upon the happy bunch like a vulture,
impounded their cake, and threw it in the trash can.

One autumn morning, which, at first, had the appearance of any
other morning, we ate our breakfast, washed up, and waited for the
dreaded "education" program. All of a sudden, the loudspeaker began
to crackle, as it did whenever the guards were preparing to make an announcement. Then a long list of names from the lower and upper wards
was broadcast. When the guards read prisoners' names for interrogation
or other purposes, everyone listened to find out if their names were
being called. By the combination of names announced, we could guess
where the prisoners were being taken.

On this day, after the first two or three names were read, a morbid
silence took over the ward. The women whose names were being called
were all *sar-e moze'-i* who had been tried but not yet sentenced. As the

This is a notebook made from a tissue box.

reading continued, our suspicion – that these women were all being taken for execution – strenghtened.[33] The list was long – perhaps as many as fifteen from the lower ward, alone. They had been asked to take their belongings with them. There was a respected elderly lady in Room Five, known as Mother Shamsy, who had a daughter in the upper ward. Her daughter's name was on the list. From our room, there was one name: Sheyda.

As soon as the guard finished reading the names, silence turned into commotion. Women moved back and forth between rooms, saying goodbye to friends. Those whose names had been called were busy collecting their belongings, giving away keepsakes and trying to keep their composure. The old lady and her entourage had gone to the bottom of the stairs leading to the upper floor, hoping to catch a glimpse of her daughter upstairs. Mother Shamsy's face was flushed with emotion and her lips were moving constantly, perhaps in prayer. All over the ward, emotions were running rampant. Many were trying hard to keep tears from running down their faces. Others were trying to give support to those getting ready to leave. Still others looked dumbfounded and emotionally exhausted; they gazed around in silence.

Sheyda looked slightly pale, but was smiling nevertheless. She was tall and slender, with blue eyes and chestnut hair. Polite and sweet, she had a heart of gold. She was the centre of attention, which made her self-conscious and bewildered. Everyone was trying to say something to her, but she didn't seem to hear anything.

In the meantime, the female guards kept asking the women to hurry

33 When a prisoner's sentence was death penalty, the authorities did not inform her until the day of the execution.

to the guards' room upstairs. Slowly, the caravan began to proceed down the length of the ward. Many of us were following the women. As they passed each room, more inmates spilled out to hug them and wish them courage. Others gazed at the departing women, trying to imprint their faces upon their memories.

The guards did not allow Mother Shamsy to say goodbye to her daughter. After the women left the ward, she finally loosened her firm grip on the wooden guardrail at the stairs. She went straight to her room without speaking to anyone or showing any emotion. Then, being a very religious woman, she stood in prayer and cried silently under her prayer veil.

We had no appetite for lunch or small talk. We all stared into the void, trying to find some meaning to life in prison. Everyone kept to themselves for the rest of the day, trying to keep busy with trivial work.

That afternoon in the yard, women discussed nothing but the events of the day. Rumours spread from one room to the next. No one rumour was very accurate or more credible than another. We had no new information, only speculation. We tried to hang onto a possibility less tragic than the execution of so many young women in a single day.

In the days that followed, we all resigned ourselves to the reality that the departed women had been executed and were no longer with us. Life returned to the old, unpleasant routine. What we didn't know was that we would soon miss even this unpleasant routine.

A few days later, the damned loudspeaker started buzzing again. We all hated that noise; it was always the harbinger of bad news. The guard began by saying, "The following people should get ready to leave the ward with all their belongings." Then she read a long list of women who had been getting on the nerves of the guards and ward reps. Almost one third of the population of the ward was on the list. This time we knew it was not execution because the women who were called had already been sentenced. Chaos reigned over the ward for about an hour. A large number of women had to collect their belongings and say goodbye to friends. Someone from each group divided up the common goods that had been bought from the prison store. Clearly, the prison authorities had a plan, but it was unknown to us.

Those whose names had been called soon left the ward. The rest of us followed them to the iron bars separating the ward from the stairwell that led to the warden's room. We had all lost a close friend in this transfer, and knew deep down that more bad news was on the way. Just as we were wondering what to do with all of the extra space in our rooms, we heard noises coming from the warden's room. Soon, a large number of women streamed down the stairs and into the ward. Some of the inmates recognized a few of them, and the news was quickly passed from room to room until it reached ours at the end of the corridor: the newcomers were mostly *tavvab*s from Ward One. They had been brought into our ward to weaken the spirits of those inmates who were fighting the rules every inch of the way. We assumed that the women who were sent away had gone to Ward One to be under the supervision of the *tavvab*s left behind. The strategy was to mix the population of the wards and force the "bad apples" into submission.

We quickly realized the type of person that the majority of the newcomers were. They resembled ordinary criminals more than political prisoners. They tried to bully the original inmates of the ward by threatening them with bad reports. They didn't respect the rules we had set for the rooms and deliberately mocked our values. They observed a subtle hierarchy among themselves and were planning to impose it on the rest of us, as well. Even the old *tavvab*s of our ward were surprised to see what was going on, and tried to keep a distance between themselves and this new breed of *tavvab*s. I tried to figure out whom they reminded me of, and the best I could come up with was the "soldiers" in George Orwell's *1984*. They were an unruly bunch, pretending to have repented their past, and ready to do anything to be trusted by the guards and prison establishment. In short, their metamorphoses from human beings to beasts was complete.

As soon as the shock of their arrival wore off, we decided to let them know what kind of a ward we were willing to settle for. We made it understood that if they wanted to live according to the law of the jungle, we were not prepared to be their monkeys. When several of them were isolated and treated like outcasts, they realized that they had gone too far. Clearly, our humanitarian ideas and approaches were far more acceptable to the majority of the population of the ward, than those of the lost souls who had sold their spirits to the henchmen of Evin. When the leaders of the group felt that their methods of intimidation and bullying were not going to be effective, they complained to the warden and requested to be transferred back to their old ward. The warden agreed.

Unlike their sudden and triumphant arrival, their departure was gradual and low-key.

The transfer, however, did yield some very good news. By speaking to the newcomers, we learned that the fifteen women who had been taken away from our ward were, in fact, alive and well, living in Ward One. The whole act of removing the women in such a dramatic manner was an attempt to shock us out of our wits and into submission.

The Children of Evin

Majid often began the day by climbing over my head and making joyful sounds as he crawled out of his mother's bed early in the morning. He was a chubby little boy, born in Evin prison to a working class mother by the name of Maheen. She was imprisoned for organizing workers, and for her ideological convictions. While Maheen was pregnant with Majid, she also had her second child, a two-year-old girl, with her in the public ward. Her greatest concern was that before the baby was born, she'd have to send her daughter to stay with her old mother who was already caring for Maheen's seven-year-old son. The little girl was too young to be separated from her mother, but Maheen couldn't care for two children in prison. In her ninth month of pregnancy, she took her little girl to a family visiting session and sent her out of prison in her mother's custody.

Maheen and I had developed a certain bond. We were both mothers with young children, and we were roughly the same age. When she came back from that visit with her family, she came straight toward me; we hugged and silently cried.

I knew exactly how she felt in separating from her daughter. I had gone through the same ordeal a couple of months earlier. My daughter, Layla, had been with me the night that my husband and I were taken to Evin Prison. Layla was almost three years old. Even though my parents were there at the time of our arrest, Layla would not let go of me and I hadn't had the heart to leave her behind. Despite the fact that we'd arrived at Evin late at night and the principal interrogator was already gone for the day, we were taken for a preliminary interrogation. They made us wear dirty black blindfolds, shiny and smelly from overuse. Layla kept asking me to remove the blindfold. I tried to tell her that this was a game in which her father and I were playing Zorro, a character in a television series she watched once in awhile at home. The interrogator kept asking questions to which we provided no answers. He grew very angry and slapped my husband across the face. My daughter ran over to me screaming, "He is a bad man, a bad man! I don't like him! Let's go home!" I picked her up in my arms and yelled at the interrogator, asking that he show some degree of restraint in front of a little child.

 After more questioning, Layla and I were separated from my husband and taken to the solitary cell that housed our four other cellmates. As soon as we entered the tiny cell, my daughter felt uneasy. She started to cry and scream, asking me to take her home. I could do little to comfort her and she kept crying. I needed to keep my composure and my mind on the situation we were in, but Layla's sobs prevented me from concentrating. A petite young girl in the cell, our fourteen-year-old cellmate, finally came to my rescue. She began talking and singing nursery songs to Layla, which kept her quiet for a while. With their precious sugar cube ration, our cellmates made Layla a glass of *sharbat*, in an effort to keep her happy.

Including Layla, there were six of us in that tiny cell, making it difficult to sleep. My daughter got the best spot in the cell, the space next to the wall. Although it was winter, the cell was extremely hot and stuffy. There was no air, and breathing was very difficult. All night long, Layla kept waking up and showing signs of illness. She was warm to the touch and kept moaning in her sleep. In the morning, I told the guard about Layla's condition and she promised to ask "Doctor" Salman to stop by later. Instead, the guard came back with a bottle of adult cough syrup and a few aspirins, and when I asked about the doctor she said, "This is a prison, not a private hospital!" My daughter kept asking to go play outside the cell. I asked the guard to take the child outside for a short while. She agreed and Layla stepped out. A few minutes later, Layla was brought back, having asked for her mother. All day long, Layla asked to go out, but she always returned soon after. She wanted me with her and didn't understand why I couldn't accompany her outside.

The young girl and the other three women who shared the cell with me looked after my daughter whenever I was called for interrogation. Sometimes Layla cried and asked for me, and the guard brought her to the interrogation room – the last place I wanted her to be. These interrogation rooms were very frightening places. I didn't want Layla to witness people being beaten up and shoved around. Once, I heard my husband calling our daughter by her name. I realized that he was in the midst of interrogation as well, and Layla was roaming around in the corridor. Having noticed her father, Layla ran towards him. When my daughter returned to me in my interrogation room, I asked her, "Did you see daddy?" She replied, "Daddy is playing Zorro, too."

I knew I had to send Layla out of the prison. One day, I wrote a short letter to my interrogator requesting to send Layla home. After our arrest, my parents had been coming to the prison door everyday, asking for the child. The combination of my requests and my parents' perseverance were effective in getting the attention of the prison officials.

One morning, just after breakfast, a female guard knocked on the door of the cell and called my name for interrogation. As usual, she asked me to put on my blindfold and to wait in the long corridor of Ward 209.

After a few minutes, the interrogator came and said, "Get your child ready to send her home, your parents are here."

I knew this might be my only opportunity to do the right thing for Layla. But the thought of being separated from her at such a tender age – without knowing when I would see her again – was unbearable. Tears started rolling down my cheeks, blackened by the dirt from my blindfold.

A prisoner standing next to me had witnessed the scene, and whispered in a low voice, "Don't give them the pleasure of seeing you cry. That is exactly what they want."

I dried my face with the back of my hand and waited for the guard to take me back to my cell, where I could say goodbye to my child. To my surprise, Layla didn't cry when she heard she was going to grandma's. She hated the tiny cell so much that she even looked somewhat relieved at the thought of going home. We kissed and hugged each other and I tried hard to keep my composure.

After Layla left the cell, I let the tears stream down my face. My cellmates were extremely touched by the scene and tried their best to divert my attention. From that moment on, there wasn't a day that passed that I didn't think about my daughter and what she might be doing at home without her father and myself.

The first time I had a chance to visit with my parents, Layla came along too. When I saw them from the other side of the glass, I was so happy that I began to cry. Layla was in her grandfather's arms, kicking and crying with exhaustion and boredom. For a ten-minute visit, the families had to spend long hours waiting in the cold of the winter or the summer's scorching heat.

My father told Layla, "Look! Mommy is here."

Layla stopped crying and turned around. She couldn't recognize me for my black *chador* and drawn face. She kept staring at me with no sign of recognition.

Children of seven years of age and younger were allowed to cross over to the prisoner's side, and visit with their parents in person. When Layla came around, I hugged her, kissed her, and held her close to me for a few minutes. It was as if I wanted to remember her scent. I touched her everywhere, making sure she was healthy. Hearing my voice, she slowly started remembering me. But she kept looking around for *pasdar*s, and refrained from talking. She was clearly frightened.

After a few visits to Evin, however, Layla became more comfortable and felt more at ease. "Why are you in a hospital?" she asked during one visit; we'd been apart approximately one year. Apparently that was what she had been told at home.

"Don't worry honey, I'm not sick. This is a prison," I replied.

"Have you done something wrong?"

"No, dear. Your father and I are political prisoners and there is nothing you should be ashamed of."

I learned later that I was among the lucky mothers in prison. At least I had people who could take good care of my child in my absence. Others, who weren't so fortunate, were forced to keep their children in prison for extended periods of time.

Parviz was a cute four-year-old boy who had been in prison as long as he could remember. He had no recollection of life outside Evin. Once, when his mother had a chance to visit with her husband, he was taken along to see his father. Living in the women's ward, Parviz had never seen a man. He began crying as soon as his father tried to embrace him and refused to make eye contact. Parviz was afraid of his own father.

Every time the technicians, who were always men, entered the public ward to fix something, we were told to wear our *chador*s, as required by the Islamic *Shari'a*.[34] One day, when the technicians were coming into the ward, Parviz ran to his mother and asked for a scarf to cover his hair. He couldn't understand why everybody else had to cover up but him. His mother's explanation – that he didn't need to wear a *chador* because

---

34 The *Shari'a* is the Islamic law which regulates all aspects of life.

he was a boy – didn't make much sense to him and he kept insisting until he was given a scarf.

Assal was another one of Evin's unfortunate children. Assal's father had been executed soon after his arrest and her mother, Mina, would have had the same fate except that soon after being arrested, she realized she was pregnant. She was told that her execution would be delayed until after the child was born and had stopped nursing. When Mina came to our ward, she was still pregnant. She was very bitter and sad, and often kept to herself. She loved her husband very much and would have preferred to die along with him, were it not for the child in her womb. She refused to pray as dictated by prison regulations. This made her a focus for the *tavvab*s, who used every occasion to put pressure on Mina and report her every move to the prison officials.

One morning when we woke up, we learned that Mina had been taken to the prison clinic in the middle of the night and had given birth to a girl. Assal had hazel eyes, blonde hair, and skin as soft as rose petals. She was the most beautiful child I had ever seen. From the moment she arrived in her mother's arms, she became the darling of the ward. Everyone wanted to play with her, and everyone volunteered to take care of her, but Mina was very fussy about who came near her daughter, and was especially careful to keep *tavvab*s away from her. As an experienced mother, however, I had the privilege of helping Mina whenever she needed assistance.

The interrogators took advantage of Mina's love for her newborn baby and put pressure on Mina to change her attitude, become more cooperative, and even collaborate. They called her for long periods of interrogation and threatened to send her baby daughter away. But Mina wouldn't budge. She knew she had limited time to enjoy her daughter, and, as such, she was very reluctant to delegate caretaking responsibility to other prisoners. There were tasks, however, that we could perform for Mina – we washed diapers and other items of clothing, and bathed and cared for Assal when Mina was called for interrogation.

Just before Assal's first birthday, the guards notified Mina that upon her family's next visit she would have to give Assal up and send her out of prison. Mina returned to the ward, pale and distraught. In public, she wouldn't say what was wrong, but later I learned what she had been told by the interrogator. She coped with her sorrow by making keepsakes to send away with her daughter. She made these mementos out of whatever she could find in the ward – date pits, pieces of bone fished out of the *abgousht*,[35] little stones from the yard, and the like.

A few prisoners, who knew how to sew, made beautiful little dresses for Assal by tearing up and re-using the fabric of old dresses and sheets with pretty patterns. A lot of time was spent embroidering and adding delicate additions to these dresses. Everyone knew it was only a matter of days before Assal left the ward. Mina looked dazed and withdrawn. When the *tavvab*s were not around to rejoice in her pain, Mina cried silently. She had relinquished not only the hope of ever raising her child, but her desire to live, as well.

The day finally arrived for Mina to prepare Assal to leave the prison ward. It was a delicate situation. Everyone was happy for the little girl who was finally going to have a chance to live in normal surroundings. But Assal's early departure signalled the possible execution of her mother, who no longer had an "excuse" to escape her death sentence. Mina carefully collected her daughter's belongings, stashing the keepsakes among the clothing, and prepared Assal for a last trip to the visiting hall. When the guard called Mina's name over the loudspeaker, all of the prisoners came out of their rooms and lined up to say goodbye to the little girl they had cherished for eleven months. Some followed her to the ward door to catch a last glimpse of their favourite baby. Most were trying to hold back their tears for Mina's sake. A few wept openly and hid themselves from Mina, who was visibly shaken.

When Mina returned from the visit with her parents, she looked resigned and drained, as if every last bit of energy in her frail body had left with the last kiss she gave her little girl. From then on, she was fair game for the interrogators, who longed to get their hands on Mina without her baby.

Prisoners did their best to be considerate and respect Mina's privacy. Privacy is of the utmost value to anyone living twenty-four hours a day with three hundred people. The only private space where we could hide from the stares of the *tavvab*s, and the inquisitive looks of other prisoners, was the toilet. Out in the open, it was often difficult to hide emotions and keep moods secret. Other mothers inside the ward tried in vain to console Mina and take her mind off her baby. That evening,

---

35 *Abgousht* is a thick soup resembling Hungarian goulash.

she didn't eat and hardly talked to anyone. We all hoped time would heal her wounds.

There was another tiny girl in the ward who was also born in Evin. Her name was Swan and her situation very similar to Assal's. Her father had been given a death sentence. Her mother, pregnant at the time of arrest, had been spared execution until the baby was born and nursed for as long as the officials deemed necessary. Two months after Assal was born, Maryam gave birth to Swan. The baby was very intelligent and precocious. One day, Maryam was permitted to visit with her husband and take the baby along. Upon her return to the ward, Maryam was beaming with happiness at having been able to show her husband their daughter. She didn't question the intentions behind such a seemingly charitable act. At the next scheduled visit with her parents, however, Maryam was informed of her husband's execution. The execution had occurred on the same day that Maryam had met with him. She told only a few friends about this and tried to keep her composure. Still, Maryam knew she would probably meet a fate similar to that of her husband.

One day, when Swan was about five months old, the guards called Maryam for interrogation, which lasted a full day. We took turns caring for Swan until Maryam came back. Maryam was in a horrible shape; her complexion was yellowish, she had dark circles around her eyes, and she was limping and holding her slippers in her hands. She came straight to me and reached for her baby, who was sitting on my lap. She said nothing, fearing that the snitches sitting in the room would report her. Later, Maryam told me that she had been flogged on the soles of her feet and told to stop breastfeeding the baby. If she didn't cooperate, she would be executed like her husband. After the beating she took that day, Maryam's breasts hardly provided enough milk to satisfy the baby. She had to supplement Swan's nourishment with whatever baby formula she could borrow from other mothers, because as far as the authorities were concerned, Maryam was still breastfeeding and as such, would not receive a ration of baby formula.

Swan, like Assal, was a darling of the room. She was the sweetest and most clever child I had ever seen. She was very generous with her smiles, and would begin dancing as soon as we hummed a tune, even before she could walk. She was the object of the prisoners' attention, especially those mothers who were reminded of their own children left at home. When she was almost a year old, Swan, like Assal, was separated from her mother and sent home to her grandparents. The guards were paving the way for the savage interrogations and intimidation of Maryam that would begin after her baby's departure.

There was one more child in the ward, a five-year-old girl. Because she was older, Pari suffered more than the other children. She could not be sent away; there was no one outside who could take care of her. She was old enough to understand the abnormality of her situation. There was nothing to keep her busy, and she wasn't learning anything in the arid atmosphere of the ward. All day long, she had nothing to do but accompany her mother everywhere and stare at the walls. Some prisoners tried to teach Pari how to draw. Once, when a woman drew her a flower, she asked what a flower was. There was no vegetation in the prison yard for her to see. Pari started acting strangely. She'd move aimlessly from room to room, making funny gestures and sounds. She was obviously bored to death.

The prison authorities did not concern themselves with children's well-being. As far as they were concerned, all of us, including our children, belonged in the darkest corner of hell.

The life of children in prison was cruel and inhumane. But their presence was a blessing to the inmates. They brought a sense of normality to the hollow life of prison. They represented life, growth and innocence. Their presence refreshed the rigid, brutal atmosphere of the ward, and made it more tolerable.

I can't bring this story to an end without mentioning all the dedicated relatives who went to so much trouble to raise these small children while their parents were being tortured and mistreated in the hellholes of Iran's medieval regime. That so many of those children turned out to be healthy, normal young men and women is a credit to those who cared for them.

A Trial in Ramadan

It was a hot summer night during the month of *Ramadan*.[36] In Evin, everyone was fasting. No one had the option of not complying with the religious rules except for non-Muslims and women who were menstruating or ill. Those who refused to pray and fast were flogged seventeen times at every one of the three calls per day to prayer. How did the guards know who prayed and who didn't? The *tavvab*s supplied this information. The *tavvab*s also made sure that no one was spared the torture of having to wash faces, arms and feet with cold water, even during the frigid temperatures of the winter months, before standing to pray. They reported the slightest defiant gesture or comment to the female guards and the interrogators. The *tavvab*s also made sure prisoners observed the irrational rules imposed, such as complete silence during the "educational periods" which were, in fact, brainwashing sessions.

During *Ramadan*, food was served twice a day, once at dusk to break the fast, and once at dawn to begin the day of fasting. For the dawn meal, we were awakened around three in the morning to eat and pray before sunrise. At such an early hour, no one had any appetite for the greasy prison food that was usually cold by the time it was brought from the kitchen. The worst part was that the loud sound of religious chanting over the speakers awoke us. That was enough to kill anyone's appetite for even the most scrumptious food in the world. Prisoners preferred to be left alone to sleep, and skip the meal altogether. However, we were forced to get up and pray, or pretend we were praying, to satisfy the snitches. Even if we were exempt from praying (during menstruation or illness), we had to rise from our sleep, gather the bedding from the floor, and stack it up against the walls to make room for the large plastic cloth upon which we set the dishes and the food.

The ward consisted of two levels, both below ground. The prisoners from the two levels did not see each other because our short daily outdoor breaks were at different times of the day. However, the same guards were responsible for watching over both levels, and the same loudspeaker was used to call prisoners for interrogation and other mat-

---

36 *Ramadan* is the Islamic month of fasting according to the lunar calendar.

ters. Although the prisoners from the upper and lower levels did not have any contact with one another, we sometimes peeked through the painted windowpane to catch a glimpse of a comrade whose name we had heard on the loudspeaker. We also gathered information during visits with our family members. Families spoke to each other and relayed the information to their incarcerated children and siblings.

It was through this channel that we learned there was a woman in the upper ward, a member of a leftist organization, who refused to pray. The guards decided to teach her a lesson during the holy month of *Ramadan* and make an example of her for the benefit of the other prisoners. That warm morning, the food was served and sleepy prisoners began eating in silence. Suddenly, we heard noises from the upper level. Then a chorus of voices began counting in unison, "One, two, three, four, five…" We realized the guards were flogging the woman who had refused to pray. The *tavvab*s were counting the lashes. She was shouting something, but we couldn't make out what she was saying. The ward fell silent. Prisoners stopped eating. We couldn't react for fear of reprisals by the guards or the interrogators; it was evident no one had any appetite left for food. Some had tears in their eyes, and others were bursting with anger and disgust. Some prisoners even risked being punished by commenting on the savagery being committed by the guards. After seventeen lashes were counted, there was a long period of silence. Our food lay cold and half-eaten. Then the guards started broadcasting the chants that preceded the morning prayers during *Ramadan*. The radio announced that ten minutes remained until fasting began. We had to finish eating and get in line to brush our teeth.

After the wash-up and prayer, the prisoners went back to bed to brood over the incident in the privacy of darkness. It was an unnerving early morning, very demanding on everyone's emotions. For some time after the lights were turned off, I could hear the women tossing and turning, unable to put the nightmare behind them.

I am usually a terrible sleeper even in the best of circumstances. That particular night, I had even more reason to suffer. I thought of all the *Ramadan*s I might have to spend in this dungeon, and the total obscurity of what lay ahead of me. I had been left in the lower ward of Evin to rot. No one called me for interrogation anymore. I knew they were testing my patience. They figured I would come around one day and confess to all my "crimes" against the "revolutionary" regime. After a while, I must have dozed off, because I woke to the sound of some-one calling my name and shaking me. It was a cellmate who told me my name was being called on the loudspeaker. I had been in a deep sleep when she called me, and had a hard time focusing on our conversation. I kept asking, "What time is it?" When she told me it was half past four in the morning, I was anxious to know why they were calling me at this early hour. One woman suggested that during *Ramadan*, it is customary for the interrogators to work after their morning meal until noon, and then go home to sleep the rest of the day until sunset, when they could eat again.

I got up and washed my face with the cold water, which helped me to wake up and be alert. Other women, who had also awakened and wanted to be supportive of me, were helping me get ready to go. One handed me my slippers, another, my blindfold, and still another, my veil – the customary attire in prison.

Because all the women were covered from head to toe, the guards could tell the prisoners from the female guards in two ways: we wore slippers and they wore shoes; we wore blindfolds and they didn't.

I went up the stairs to the guards' room. They usually told us where we were being taken. Fatemeh, a young female guard, a theology stu-dent, was on duty that night. She was always eager to convince everyone that she was very pious and quite knowledgeable about Islamic Law. She wore white gloves to keep men from seeing her hands, even though according to the Islamic rules of *hijab*,[37] women are not under compul-sion to cover their hands, the round of their faces, or their feet. She was also quite cruel to prisoners and treated them like criminals. As soon as she saw me, she said, "Administrative Quarters," which meant one of two things. Either I was going to be executed, or I was finally going to be tried. Since I had not yet been to a court (no matter how bogus the courts were), my guess was the second. For the first time since I was ar-rested seven months ago, I was going to find out with what I had been charged.

A few women from other wards had also been called. The male guard, who had come to take us to our destination, told us to follow him in single file, each of us holding onto the veil of the person in front. We were all blindfolded and couldn't see where we were going. The first

---

37 *Hijab* is the Islamic cover required for women.

woman in line held one end of a pencil, and the male guard led her by holding onto the other end in order to avoid bodily contact. To our dismay, it was still dark outside and we could hardly see anything. Even though we always left the ward blindfolded, we usually managed to peek out from under the dark fabric at the beautiful old trees in the garden surrounding the prison. This was made possible by subtly pulling at a few threads from the blindfold. We only left the ward when we were summoned, or to see immediate family members on visiting days, or to take part in compulsory gatherings at the *Hosseyniyeh*.[38]

In the administrative building, we were taken to a corridor where various courtrooms were located. I sat on the floor in front of the door of the courtroom, waiting to be summoned inside. After a long wait, perhaps an hour and a half, a guard told me to enter the room. I had heard that the clergymen who act as judges ask prisoners to take off the blindfold upon arriving in the room. I waited for this request and, when he said nothing, I asked if I could remove my blindfold. To my surprise, he said, "In my court, I don't allow this, but if you have an objection, you can go back to the ward, write a letter to your interrogator and ask him to arrange a trial with a different judge." Such a process would have taken at least another six months and perhaps result in some form of retaliation. I wasn't going to jeopardize my chances of knowing the charges brought against me by postponing my trial. I consented to staying blindfolded for the procedure. The judge began the relatively short process that would decide my fate.

After asking my name, he asked about my religious affiliation. He wanted details about what denomination of the religion I belonged to, and whether or not I was a practicing Muslim. Then he began inquiries into my political affiliations, my beliefs, the reasons behind those beliefs, and why I did not choose to be a practicing Muslim even though I was an "educated woman." He was convinced that anyone with some education and half their senses would choose Islam over other religions and philosophies. But by far, my greatest sin was to have defended women's rights in public and in writing, both before and after the Revolution. Everything he charged me with had to do with my political beliefs, and nothing else. It was a twentieth century Inquisition. Though I managed to control myself and reply as moderately as possible, I found out later

38 The *Hosseynieh* is a huge hall in a building on a hill in the Evin Prison compound.

that my non-confrontational replies were enough to land me many years in prison.

My trial lasted less than fifteen minutes, an average length trial in Evin. In those fifteen minutes, judges who had already decided that we were guilty as charged made life and death decisions. Often, the inter-rogator's report to the judge included suggested sentencing; everything that followed was nothing but window dressing. The accused didn't know with what he or she was being charged before walking into the room. We didn't know the dates of our trials so we were unable to prepare, and we had no lawyers to defend us. The young teenagers, who made up a sizeable portion of the prison population, often didn't understand much of the vocabulary used by the clergymen who acted as judges.

After leaving the courtroom, I realized how difficult it was, for those inexperienced youth brought to trial, to defend themselves before judges who deeply believed that anyone who didn't share their religious beliefs – often a particular interpretation of that religion – was wicked and guilty. This was why so many of these youth were sentenced to death or long prison terms for "having participated in anti-government demonstrations, armed with salt."[39] Some high school students had been tried for that exact "crime" in Evin at the onset of the crackdown on dissidents.

As I was being brought back to the ward, I realized I didn't have the faintest idea what my sentence might be. I could expect anything from freedom to execution, for there were no known criteria on which judg-ment was based. The Iranian penal code had been rewritten after the Revolution. The new one was mainly based on the laws of the *Shari' a*. Even educated adults knew very little about the consequences of their actions according to the new penal code. Acts which were totally legal before the Revolution had become offences punishable by law. I had no idea about the consequences of the charges that the judge had brought against me. Immersed in my thoughts, I was returned to the ward along with the other women who had undergone the same ordeal.

A month later, as I was pacing back and forth in the yard, a cellmate shouted from inside the ward. I was being called on the loudspeaker. I got ready and climbed the stairs to the guards' room. She told me I was being summoned to the sentencing office. Once inside the minibus for

---

39 "Armed with salt": some demonstrators carried salt in their pockets with which they would protect themselves by throwing it in the eyes of their attackers.

the ride to the administration building, I felt a sense of relief. One way or another, I would soon learn my fate. During the short ride, I thought of everything from death to freedom.

Once I arrived, the guard pushed me into a small room with a desk in the middle. The desk was piled with papers. I was handed a piece of paper and asked to sign it. I pushed my blindfold slightly toward my forehead to read what had been handed to me, and replied that I needed to read the document in order to know what I was signing. I was so anxious, I could hardly see the words hastily jotted down on the paper. I asked the man standing behind the desk what it was that I needed to sign. He chuckled and said, "It's your sentence!"

I managed to see a number in the midst of all the gibberish written on the paper – the number nine. The first thing that came to my mind was how old my child would be by the time I got home to her.[40] On the one hand, I was relieved. I could now count myself amongst the living, although I had done nothing to deserve a death sentence. But, nine years in the Islamic regime's prisons were not to be taken lightly. I heard the man shouting, "Hurry up, I haven't got all day!" When I objected to the harsh sentence, he told me I could decline to sign and request another trial. Then he added, "Maybe next time you'll get lucky and be sentenced to death," and chuckled sheepishly. I realized I couldn't expect justice from close-minded theocrats who had the power to do as they pleased. I signed my name at the bottom of the sheet of paper and left the room.

Some of my cellmates came to meet me as soon as I entered the ward, questions written all over their faces. They had guessed where I had been and couldn't wait to find out how I had fared. When they heard my story, one of the women said, "Don't worry, these sentences don't mean anything!" It was only in 1988 that I realized the veracity of her words, when thousands of prisoners, with sentences ranging from one year to life, were executed in a single month.[41]

---

40 In 1981 and part of 1982, sentences were calculated from the time of arrest. But in 1983, when I went to court, sentences were calculated from the date of the trial. Since most of us were tried 6-12 months after our arrests; this meant longer sentences.

41 In the summer of 1988, thousands of Islamic Republic's political prisoners who had been sentenced were executed for being "infidels" and "incorrigibles."

A Fishing Expedition

The absence of privacy is a major annoyance that prisoners experience in any detention centre. One never feels alone, not even in the most seemingly private spaces. There is always some way to trouble and torment an inmate. At Evin, one such practice was the prison search. The search was repeated every now and then at irregular intervals, and at the most unexpected times. Prisoners knew they could not hide anything from the authorities for long. Nevertheless, we kept improvising ways of hiding small objects, like handmade tools, a piece of poetry, or even an artifact we had created without the guards' permission. The prison authorities wanted to ensure the inmates didn't possess anything meaningful that would keep us alive and happy. They believed we all needed to come to terms with our past, repent our "sins," and form new beliefs and attitudes toward the system. Any "distracting" activity was deemed not conducive to positive change.

Prohibited activities included reading (except for religious books and the *Qur'an*), sewing and embroidering, stone and bone carving, painting and drawing, and writing. Possession of pen and pencil was forbidden. On Fridays, we were allowed a limited number of needles and scissors per room for mending our clothes, but only by prior reservation and with the provision of a legitimate reason for their use. We could also use the scissors for giving haircuts, but only with prior permission from the head guard, Mrs. Bakhtiari. For a period of time, permission was not granted to young girls because Mrs. Bakhtiari believed girls in short hair looked like boys, and would be too sexually tempting to other girls! Later in the day, the needles were counted and collected along with the scissors.

At times, while thick fabrics were being sewn, needles would break into two pieces, and one of the pieces could not be found and returned. In such cases, the guards would punish the whole room by depriving us of these tools for one week. Each room, which held an average of seventy to ninety inmates, received one pair of scissors and four or five needles. We shared the scissors and needles according to our needs. If someone required the tools for longer than ten minutes, another person

This embroidery is made with coloured threads that were obtained by unravelling towels. It was a New Year's gift to Sousan from a friend.

This piece was crocheted with a safety pin bent into a crochet hook, and sewing thread.

would extend their time slot to that individual and instead use the tool the following week. Once, an inmate who was mentally ill asked for the scissors to cut her own hair. The guards had not given her permission for a haircut. But, on a Friday, when it was our room's turn to use the sewing tools, she asked a cellmate if she could briefly use the scissors for something urgent. Then, she cut a chunk of her hair so short that the guards were forced to let her cut the rest of her hair, too. The *tavvab*s had relayed the information to the guards, who promptly came to the ward, collected all of the scissors, and punished our room.

Embroidery work given to Sousan by Ashraf. Embroidered in white on the right are lines by a popular Iranian poet:
In the green flourishing heart
of each leaf,
life is blooming

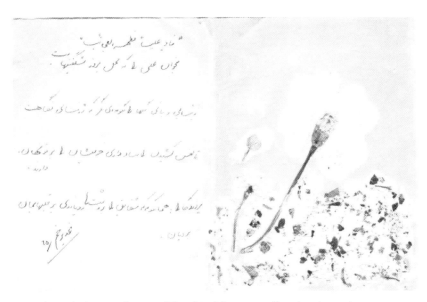

A card given to Sousan. The dried flower is affixed with toothpaste.

Sometimes, women pretended to have lost a needle, and hid it to do embroidery or other "illegal" activities later, when the ward was less crowded, or in the toilets. A needle was considered quite a treasure. The guards raided our ward every so often, carrying away whatever we had painstakingly collected. This included pencils, which were granted to prisoners a few times a year to write letters to our families. The letters were prearranged forms with only seven lines provided for the prisoner and a space for reply on the same page. This way, family members always sent the letters back, and authorities were able to deprive inmates of the opportunity to later prove that we had served a sentence at Evin as political prisoners.

It was late in the afternoon on an autumn day and the ward was getting ready for evening prayers and dinner. That day, I was in a particularly bad mood. I paced the narrow corridors of the ward like a lion in a cage. Since they had transferred me from the solitary cell to the public ward, I had not been called for interrogation. This was before my "trial" and I had no idea what they were going to charge me with. I was absorbed in my thoughts when suddenly, I heard thumping from the stairs leading to the guards' room. Before I could turn the corner of the corridor to see what was happening, male guards in uniform and boots descended upon us like falcons swooping down on thin prey. Women from the first corridor, closest to the door, started screaming and running inside their rooms. It seemed like we were being raided. Normally, the female guards did the task themselves, or told us to cover up if men were entering the ward. This time there had been no notice. Perhaps, in order to keep this raid a total surprise, the female guards had not been notified. Some women were bathing, and the guards opened the bathroom door and closed it when they realized there were nude women inside.

Then, a female voice was heard belatedly over the loudspeaker, ordering us to cover up and get out of the ward and into the courtyard. We had very little time. Some women grabbed the first thing that they could get their hands on and covered their heads. Many couldn't find their slippers and ran outside in bare feet. We were pushed and shoved by the guards and told to stand in the middle of the yard facing the wall. Though we could not speak openly, we whispered to each other about possible scenarios. Some women thought it was a raid, while others speculated on darker plans, including mass execution. I was among the barefooted, and my feet were freezing. We stood facing the wall, while inside, the guards threw our belongings onto the ground and made all sorts of scary noises. We could hear them sweeping the wide air conditioner pipes sticking out of the windows and talking to each other in loud, angry tones. It was getting dark but we were still standing in our bare feet, staring at the brick wall. This might have lasted around two hours, but given the circumstances, it seemed like we were there forever.

Finally, we were told to go back inside in an orderly manner. From the sounds of disbelief coming from the rooms, I could tell a horrible experience awaited us. When I reached our room, I saw a pile of clothing on the middle of the floor. All of our bags had been thrown to the ground and opened. We had no idea how to distinguish our underwear from someone else's. Most were purchased from the prison shop and looked alike. We picked out what we could and threw away the rest, even though we were all in need of more clothing. For a long time after, we were still exchanging items that had been taken by mistake.

Some prisoners had to disinfect their toothbrushes, which had been found on the floor, trampled by the guards. To lose an item of necessity, like a toothbrush, was a disaster. We never knew when the guards

The back of a card given to Sousan for New Year's.

would circulate another shopping list. At times, we were left without the most urgent items: sanitary napkins, facial tissues, toothpaste, and soap. We borrowed from one another until the next shopping list. Every time there was a raid, we lost precious, hard to replace belongings.

It took us a long time to tidy up the cell and have dinner. Afterwards, we were all so exhausted that we prepared our beds on the floor and fell asleep. That night I thought to myself, It could have been worse! In prison, don't take anything for granted. Just live your life, one day at a time.

A few weeks later, we found out what had taken place that crazy evening in Evin's Ward 246. A prisoner, who was a member of the *Mojahedin-e Khalq* Organization,[42] had, for a long time, pretended to be a *tavvab*. She had apparently organized a group of inmates and was engaged in various types of activities, using her favourable status as a *tavvab*. To make sure she could not destroy any evidence that she or members of her group might have possessed, the guards had made the surprise call and in the process, scared the prisoners out of their wits. The woman was sent to solitary confinement and later executed.

Life went on inside Ward 246. More needles and pens got lost. We were raided many times over. Every time we heard of a raid in another ward, we started cleaning up our rooms. Papers, and anything we had made, were flushed down the toilets.

In fact, a few days after one raid, our toilets backed up. The smell of sewage filled the ward. We sent the *tavvab* ward representative to the guards' room to request that someone fix the toilets. She came back and relayed the message from the guards: "You can tell them to clean it up themselves, it's their own doing and they must take care of it on their own." This claim was far from the truth. Even though we put small objects in the toilets, the real culprit was the prison's archaic sewage system, which was badly in need of repair. Even when we took showers, we were ankle-deep in filthy sewage water which would not drain.

We spent the whole day cleaning the corridors and the toilets, picking out the larger pieces and putting them in a bucket. At the end of the day, those who had done the bulk of the dirty work took a shower with cold water. But throughout the day, even when our hands were soiled

---

42 The *Mojahedin-e Khalq* Organization was formed in the 1960s to fight the government of the Shah Mohammad Reza Pahlavi. It continued its anti-government activities in the Islamic Republic.

with the filth coming out of the toilets, women kept their sense of humour, laughingly calling the exercise a "fishing expedition," referring to the solid crap fished out of the sewage that covered the floors.

The Event

It was a hot summer day in 1984. We had just finished breakfast and were cleaning up, as usual. In a few minutes, the "educational program," consisting of videos of lectures by *mullahs*[43] and other ideologues of the Islamic regime, would begin. During these sessions, which lasted two to three hours every morning, we were not allowed to talk, sleep, read or engage in other activities. We sat on the floor around the room, and pretended to listen while our imaginations took us to more interesting places. A few women, pretending to be sick, put bandanas around their heads to fake headaches, or shawls around their waists for kidney pain, and lay down to sleep.

The only time everyone watched with some interest was during Arabic language classes, or during the lectures of a young *mullah* by the name of Moussavi who tried to refute Marxist philosophy for the benefit of leftist prisoners. His logic was so full of holes that at times it was like listening to a comedy show. Whenever he had trouble refuting a Marxist tenet, he would get very angry and say things like, "I can carry a cow on my shoulders up the mountain slope. Can any of you Marxist intellectuals do this?"

Once, he even attempted to hold a debate with the "leaders" of various banned leftist organizations who had been imprisoned because of their ideological inclinations. Obviously, whatever the leaders might have said during the debate could have severe consequences for them. Thus, they declined Moussavi's offer. This led him to boast that no one had the guts to debate him because they knew they could not win! Moussavi's arguments were so amusing to us that we couldn't help but laugh. Of course, the names of those who laughed openly were reported to the female guards by the snitches planted in various cells. We knew there were consequences, and sometimes we paid dearly for the fun.

Prison conditions were very bad. We always wondered why no international organizations were lodging protests against the Islamic Republic of Iran for its mistreatment of political prisoners. Since the only news we received were the broadcasts of the official media, we didn't

---

43 A *mullah* is a member of the Islamic clergy.

know that during the summer of 1984, the U.N. Envoy for Human Rights demanded to visit Iranian prisons and check firsthand on the rumours of prisoner abuse. When Mr. Galindopol arrived in Tehran for the purpose of speaking with political prisoners, the prison officials rounded up the *tavvab*s to meet with the U.N. Envoy at the *Hosseynieh*. The *tavvab*s claimed everything was fine and that they were treated very humanely. But some of them later let the cat out of the bag by boasting about the meeting to some of their friends. Rumours began to fly about the presence of the U.N. Envoy in Tehran, but there was no additional information among the prisoners.

On this particular day, the loudspeaker started crackling like it always did when the guards wanted to make an announcement. The authorities communicated with prisoners primarily through the loudspeaker. They seldom came down to the floor of the ward, except at night to check that everyone was asleep. Finally, the guard began to speak: "Attention sisters.[44] Take the following items with you and be ready to leave the ward in ten minutes: a plate, a spoon, and a cup. No one is allowed to stay behind."

For a few minutes, everyone just looked at each other, perplexed. Why were we all leaving the ward at the same time? If we were changing wards, why weren't we taking our belongings? There was a lot of specu-lation, some of which was as drastic as a possible *coup d'état* by foreign powers. The strangest thing about this situation was that this was the birthday of Imam Reza,[45] a national holiday. We knew the interrogators didn't work on holidays. So, where were we going?

We got ready as best we could, grabbing the supplies that we were ordered to take. Some women could not find spoons or cups because when damaged, cups and spoons (which were made of nickel and easily breakable) were often not replaced. Furthermore, when new prisoners were added to a room, the prison administration did not provide us with additional cups or cutlery, so we had to make do with what we had.

Finally, we were told to line up so that we could be taken to our destination by the male guards. Because we were all so anxious to find out what was happening, everyone was trying to get out of the ward as

---

44 This is the way guards and interrogators liked to address each other and prison-ers. Mr. or Mrs. was considered the pre-revolutionary form of address.

45 Imam Reza is the eighth Shiite Imam. He died in 818 A.D. His birthday is a national holiday.

quickly as possible. Any event that shattered the boredom of prison life was highly appreciated. We found it strange that no one was to be left behind. Normally, we could get out of attending some of the ceremonies held at the *Hosseynieh* by claiming to have a bad back or some other medical excuse. This time, however, no excuse was accepted.

We lined up and climbed the stairs to the supervising guard's room. From there, we were loaded, in groups, onto minibuses. We watched in amazement as our minibuses turned in a direction we had never taken before – toward the hilly section of the huge prison compound, far from the wards. This was where executions were thought to take place. In fact, if someone went to court and did not receive a sentence within a month or two, we jokingly referred to that person as *tapeh-i*,[46] or destined for the hills. Of course, anyone taken in this direction had never come back to tell us what happened there, so we were sure this was our last day in prison.[47] Fortunately, we stopped among the trees, just short of the hills. We sighed with relief. We were ordered out of the minibuses and told to stay put as another group of women was leaving the area.

We were delighted. There was no execution. We were among the shady old trees of the Evin garden and we were going to spend some time here in the open, breathing fresh air instead of the stale and polluted air of the ward. In total amazement, we started walking around the area to which they had us confined, touching tree trunks and leaves. We could hear sparrows gathering noisily in the branches of the old trees. From the courtyard of our ward, we were only able to see the top of a barren hill: sometimes a couple of stray dogs ran down its slope or a huge old crow sat on the barbed wire. That was the extent of our exposure to nature. Walking through bushes and old trees was a luxury that, in prison, we could not even dream of.

After half an hour, one of the female guards told us to climb the stairs leading to a higher terrace. Because the prison had been built on a hill, the garden was made of terraced areas joined by flights of cobblestone stairs. We found ourselves beside a large pool with several wooden poles floating inside. The water was greenish-brown from dirt and algae. This was the pool used by male guards for military training. Beside the

---

46 *Tapeh* means "hill," and *tapeh-i* means destined for the hill.
47 During the Shah's regime, some prisoners were taken to the hills of Evin and ordered to run. They were shot in the back and killed. It was claimed they were attempting to run away.

pool were very tall poles with protrusions attached to them for climbing exercises. A few yards away stood a large grey metal door, through which cars could enter and exit.

After a few minutes, we had finished exploring the area and found out everything there was to know about it. The female guards told us we could swim in the pool if we wanted. When no one volunteered to swim, fully clothed, in the filthy water, one of the guards said, in a sarcastic tone, "What's the matter? Isn't our pool good enough for you ladies?" No one answered. One of the guards tried to be "friendly" and jokingly pushed a *tavvab* into the pool. This was a perfect excuse for the rest of us to play "friendly" with the guards. Under the pretence of having a good time, the women went wild with a game of pushing and shoving. Some guards could not swim and had to be rescued from the pool. It wasn't long before the guards reigned in the rowdiness, and told us to dry off and get ready for lunch. They realized that jokes could get out of hand and result in something for which they were unprepared.

Women with wet clothes sat in the sun to dry off. We had all uncovered our heads and were basking happily in the summer warmth. When we were inside the ward, we could take off our scarves, but as soon as we stepped outside into the yard, we had to keep our heads covered – even if there were no men around to see us. We used to joke that we were covering ourselves for the male crows flying in the sky above. So uncovering our heads, even for a few minutes in the sun, was a great opportunity we did not want to miss.

Suddenly, the big door opened and a pickup truck rolled in. The female guards screamed, and yelled at the male driver for not notifying them of his impending arrival. The man bringing our lunch was no other than the new warden of Evin. He was quick to look away and make himself invisible inside the truck. The guards made sure everyone was covered, and then let the men unload large pots and a number of huge watermelons from the pickup truck. Once the men left the area, we uncovered the big pots, and the smell of *aash-e reshteh*[48] filled the air. We hadn't seen this much food in years, and couldn't believe there were no strings attached to this generous meal.

The only other time we had experienced such generosity was on the eve of the Fourth Anniversary of the Revolution, when I was living in

48 *Aash-e reshteh* is a thick soup made with vegetables, noodles and legumes.

the solitary confinement cell. To our surprise, we were each given rice and a big piece of chicken for dinner. A few hours later, after lights had gone out, everyone came down with food poisoning. We took turns using the only toilet inside the cell. In the adjacent cells, toilets flushed all night long. Later, through the tiny opening in the ceiling window, we heard the guards on the roof talking about the rotten chickens they had fed us in celebration of the important day. So we had good reason to be suspicious of today's large amount of food, especially the watermelons.

By the time we finished eating the watermelons, we were feeling bloated and needed to relieve ourselves. The authorities had not foreseen the need for a toilet and told us to wait until we returned to the ward. Some girls relieved themselves outside, while others coped painfully with the situation by sitting still.

A couple of young prisoners – a chubby girl with short black hair and a petite pale teenager – started climbing the poles used by male guards for military exercise. This was a shock to the female guards. In their view, women were incapable of such physically demanding acts fit only for strong men like the male guards. They started shouting at the girls to come down immediately, not only because it was dangerous, but because from the tops of the poles, the girls were able to get a full view of the prison. The female guards would definitely be reprimanded for this breach of security. The guards continued shouting. The girls, trying to stay up as long as they could, pretended they couldn't get back down the poles. There was no way to resolve the situation. Male guards could not be called in to catch the girls because it would be indecent to touch them. The female guards could not do it because they were incapable of climbing the poles in their *chador*s. When the shouting didn't work, the female guards began begging that the girls come down. The commanding tone disappeared. The guards looked truly pitiful.

When the girls were finally ready to come down, they made their descent with triumphant smiles across their faces. They had spent the day doing something new; they had overcome the boredom of the ward. They showed that they were better and braver than the guards who played god inside the ward. The prisoners who braved the poles had very sore palms and inner thighs, but they would not have traded that experience for anything.

In the afternoon, it was time to return to the ward. We were being imprisoned once again. The day in the garden had taken its toll on everyone. We were all so tired that upon our return to the cells we fell silent. In the quiet, we thought of our days of freedom, when we could travel and hike, and go wherever our hearts desired. That night, the day's activities helped everyone fall asleep early.

The next day was a Friday. As usual, we turned on the television to hear the sermons that preceded the Friday prayer.[49] We listened to the sermons regularly because they often discussed current politics, and as such, served as our window into the domestic and foreign policies of the Islamic regime. That day, to our great amazement, Asadolah Laje-vardi, then the Prosecutor General of Tehran, was one of the pre-ser-mon speakers. In his speech, he boasted about reforms that had taken place in Iranian prisons, and noted that prisoners were now regularly taken on picnics! He then blamed the Great Satan – the United States of America – for inciting the United Nations Human Rights Commission to accuse Iran of mistreating its political prisoners. He even dared Mr. Galindopol visit Evin Prison to ask the prisoners about the conditions in which they were living.

Suddenly, the reasoning behind our "picnic" became crystal clear: it was to demonstrate to the U.N. Human Rights Commission that we were "safe and sound," and going on picnics while incarcerated! Needless to say, this was the only "picnic" that ever occurred at Evin.

---

49 The Friday prayer was usually preceded by two sermons: one was of a political nature and dealt with the issues of the day, while the other dealt with religious subjects.

The Quarantine

In the summer of 1983, there was a rumour floating around Evin concerning those women who, some time ago, had been transferred to Qezel Hessar Prison. According to this rumour, some of these women had vanished from its public wards and no one knew where they were. It was during visits with family members that we heard the rumours. They said some families had attempted to visit their children at Qezel but were turned away with the explanation, "Your kids don't have visiting rights until further notice." At first, these families thought their children had been executed. But in the case of execution, the standard procedure was to return the prisoner's personal belongings and will to the parents.

It seemed that in the course of a week, scores of women from various wards of Qezel had been rounded up and taken away, and no one had heard of them since. Usually, when prisoners were transferred from one prison to another, it would take, at most, a month to find out where they'd landed. The vanishing of the recent transferees had become an enigma. We expressed our concern to our families, but they had no news with which to relieve us of our anxiety.

One day in the yard, I noticed an unusual commotion among the prisoners. Women kept exchanging walking partners and I could see clear signs of excitement on their faces. A friend from another room must have seen the curious look on my face, for she approached me and quietly asked, "Have you heard the news?"

"No, but I can tell something's going on. What is it?"

"We know where the transferred women are. They're in quarantine."

"Are they sick?"

She laughed. "No, don't be silly. They've been quarantined from the rest of the prisoners for political reasons."

I was dying to know the details. "Do we know where they are and what's happened to them?"

"Somewhere in Qezel, but not in the regular wards or punitive cells. All we know is that they must be living in horrendous conditions because they still don't have visiting rights."

Because we were only allowed ten minutes to visit with our families, it was extremely difficult to take care of all of our personal concerns, and find out about other prisoners. I knew we would have to wait and put bits and pieces together in order to come up with a complete picture of what had happened to the vanished women.

A few months later, I was transferred to Qezel. Approximately twenty of us were loaded into a bus with curtained windows, and the driver started toward the city of Karaj. Qezel was located near Karaj, about forty-five kilometres west of the capital city of Tehran. We were told to stay quiet and refrain from talking. Grim-looking armed guards pointed their machine guns at us.

Once we were on the Tehran-Karaj highway, we were allowed to open the curtains and look outside. For the first time in three years, I saw normal people going about their business. I envied every free man and woman that I saw on the road, rich or poor, young or old. At Evin, I envied the stray dogs and crows that looked for food on the hill just past our prison yard. There on the bus, I couldn't believe that while we were in prison, people were living their lives as if nothing had happened. Then I smiled – and quickly covered my mouth with my black veil – at the thought of what would happen if someone suddenly stopped the bus and freed us all.

Immersed in my thoughts, I suddenly noticed the beautiful mountains I had once climbed with my husband. The green pastures and orchards along the way looked so calm and inviting. I wanted to jump out and run until I dropped, but I knew that given the condition I was in, I wouldn't get very far.

I was so busy admiring the scenery that I didn't realize we were nearing our new living quarters. I saw the watchtowers first, and then the tall brick walls topped with barbed wire. The prison was very large and, surrounded by acres of pastures, tucked far away from public eye. Here, not a soul would hear our cries, or the sounds of bullets piercing prisoners' bodies.

We went through a huge iron gate. The bus stopped in front of a large, box-like building that, constructed during Reza Shah's rule,[50] boasted the architectural style of the period. We were told to put on our

---

50 Reza Shah Pahlavi ruled from 1925-1941. He was the father of Mohammad Reza Shah Pahlavi whose rule came to an end in 1979.

blindfolds, enter the building, stand against the wall and wait to be taken to our designated wards. In Qezel, Wards Three, Four, Seven and Eight were set-aside for women, and Wards One, Two, Five and Six for men. Wards Three and Four were ordinary wards while Seven and Eight were punitive wards and had their own peculiar rules and regulations. We were assigned to Wards Three and Four.

Inside, two female *tavvab*s serving as caretakers of the ward met us in the area known as *zir-e hasht*.[51] For the first time since entering Evin two years ago, I saw a small mirror on one of the walls of the room. While prisoners were being counted and registered, I cheerfully approached the mirror and took a look. Then I backed away in fright and amazement. The face I saw in the mirror looked nothing like the one I used to see every morning before going to work. In Evin, we used the water cooler for a mirror and it spared us the agony of seeing so clearly the metamorphoses of our physical appearances. I could see the toll that the Evin years had taken on me.

In order to assign us to cells, the women in charge talked with each of us and asked about our backgrounds. Prisoners inside the ward were waiting impatiently, clutching the iron bars and sticking their noses through the openings between the bars, to see if they could find an old cellmate or a lost friend. We felt the same way and waited anxiously for the chance to get inside and see if we could find any familiar faces. As soon as we learned our cell numbers, we hurried in to get a bite to eat and rest. Because we had missed the distribution of food in both prisons, we had not had any food or drink all day. We were also exhausted from the long trip.

As soon as I stepped inside the ward, I recognized Maheen walking the long hallway. When she saw me, she ran toward me and we hugged for a long time. It was good to see a familiar face. Maheen could let me in on the secrets of the ward and help me put the inmates in perspective. She quickly told me about some of the people in my cell and noted that our room was among the better cells of the ward, with only a couple of *tavvab*s in it. I asked about her son Majid,

---

51 The *zir-e hasht* refers to both the area between the prisoners' quarters and the corridor of the unit where the female *tavvab*s resided, and to the area outside the ward, where *pasdar*s and other prison officials congregated while on prison duty. It was also where prisoners who broke prison rules were beaten and tortured.

who was born in Evin. She said she had recently sent him home to her mother.

Once inside the cell, the room rep approached me with a smile. She didn't have the look of a *tavvab*. She introduced herself and some of the women present. Six three-level bunk beds rested against three of the cell walls. The fourth wall consisted of iron bars, separating the cell from the long corridor into which all cells opened. On both sides of the corridor there were sixteen cells: half of the cells were smaller, bearing only three bunk beds apiece, and the other half were larger and held six bunk beds.

In every cell, there were more inmates than there were beds. We took turns sleeping on the floor. As soon as the tea was brought in, those sleeping on the floor had to get up to make room for the plastic cloth that had to be spread on the floor in order to serve breakfast. Since I was a newcomer from Evin, where everyone always slept on the floor, I was assigned a bed right away. I guess they wanted me to experience how it felt to sleep on a bed after such a long time. The girl who gave up her bed for me was tall, slightly chubby, and very young. Marjan had a strong sense of humour and laughed easily. She later told me stories about the first month of her arrest in 1981, when the Islamic Republic was still disorganized and didn't have the proper means of maintaining so many political prisoners. There was a shortage of food and inadequate hygiene facilities, and the prisoners hadn't yet realized the seriousness of their situations.

At first, glance the ward seemed more spacious than that of Evin. That one wall of the cells had bars contributed to this impression. Unlike Evin, where we spent a lot of time inside our cells, here we spent more time in the corridor. In fact, there was very little room inside the cells for sitting down and talking. Most of us stayed on the highest levels of the bunk beds because on the first and second levels, we had to slouch or lay down in order to fit between the boards.

After dinner, we all walked back and forth in the long corridor to digest our food. At ten o'clock, the lights inside the cells went out and no one was allowed to talk. The only lights that stayed on after-hours were in the washroom area and the corridor, the latter being very dim and unhealthy for reading. Despite these unfavourable circumstances, some of us who had trouble falling asleep at such an early hour would keep on reading.[52]

Life in Qezel had not always been this "good." The infamous warden of the prison, Hawji Davood Rahmani,[53] had recently been dismissed for certain "excesses" against the prisoners. Reading after lights-out and certain other behaviours became possible only after his dismissal. Some of my old friends, who had been transferred to Qezel earlier, told me horrible stories from those days. I felt very lucky to have been spared their painful experiences.

As I began to make new friends, I noticed certain women looked different. They walked alone, spoke little and preferred to stay relatively isolated from their cellmates. I was curious to find out why, so I asked one of the old-timers of Qezel. She said it was a long story and that I would find out for myself soon enough. She mentioned, however, something about their having been in quarantine. Suddenly, I recalled the horror stories I had heard in Evin about those women who vanished from the wards of Qezel.

One day, entirely by accident, I made the acquaintance of one of the quarantine women. I was sitting by the flowerbeds with Shohreh, an old friend from Evin days. We were admiring the beautiful pink and purple morning glories that we had planted in the yard, when a woman by the name of Niloufar approached. She was taking her usual slow walk, totally immersed in her thoughts. As she passed by, Shohreh greeted her and introduced us. Niloufar nodded politely, smiled shyly and, to make small talk, asked when I had arrived from Evin. I replied, "With the latest transferees." As she was getting ready to continue her solo walk, Shohreh asked her to sit with us and chat. Niloufar reluctantly sat down and looked away toward the flowers, avoiding my curious stare. After some small talk, Shohreh left to wash her clothes and hang them to dry while the sun was still warm. Niloufar seemed more relaxed, perhaps feeling that as a newcomer, I wouldn't judge her. She asked me to join her in a walk. I gladly accepted. We walked and talked for an hour.

---

52 After the 1984 reforms in Qezel Hessar, prisoners could request reading material from the prison officials. Books and other materials made the rounds and prisoners registered their names on a list for the material they wanted to read.

53 Hawji Davood Rahmani was the notorious warden of Qezel Hessar Prison, known for his extreme cruelty towards prisoners. He was removed from his position in 1984, after a more liberal faction of the government took over the prison system temporarily.

We found that we had a lot in common and were able to keep each other company talking about our past experiences. And so, we became friends.

Though I was dying to ask Niloufar all kinds of questions about her experience in quarantine, to respect her privacy, I refrained, and let her choose the timing herself. Several other women in the ward had also been in the quarantine. During the twenty-nine months I spent in Qezel, I was able to gather a lot of information from the women who had been confined in the place referred to as "hell," "quarantine," "grave," "coffin," "doomsday" and "box."

To understand why the "quarantine" came into being requires a bit of history. Prior to 1984, prisoners who failed to comply with the inhumane rules of Evin were transferred to Qezel to be "broken in." At first, they were sent to Wards Three and Four. If they still showed signs of non-compliance, they were transferred to punitive Wards Seven and Eight, which were smaller, with much harsher living conditions. Life in Wards Seven and Eight was not easy to endure. The cells were two by one and a half metres, with a single bunk bed and over twenty prisoners in each cell. Often, cell doors would be shut to further punish occupants.

This is how M. Raha, the author of *Haghigha-te sadeh (The Simple Truth),* a book about the political prison system of the Islamic Republic of Iran, described her experience in one of these cells:

"[T]hey put over twenty people in one cell. They opened the door only three times a day for washroom breaks. Obviously, this many people didn't fit in a 2 by 1.5 m cell. In each cell there was one bunk bed with three levels. At night, five people slept under the bed, with only their heads showing. On the first and second levels, we put the sick inmates, to give them a bit more comfort. On the third level, four to five people slept along the width of the bed, with their legs dangling in the air. To improve the situation, we tied one end of someone's veil to the bars of the cell and the other side to the window latch to support our legs. There were still people left who had nowhere to sleep. They had to sit all night long in the space between the cell bars and the bunk bed. We took turns sleeping and sitting. One night, when it was my turn to sit, I felt really thirsty. I got up to ask someone in the corridor for a glass of water (not all cell doors were shut. There were degrees of punishment, even in the punitive ward). Two of the women who were sitting on my sides slipped in their sleep and filled my space. They looked sound asleep and I didn't feel like waking them up. I spent the rest of the night with one foot on a bar and the other on the side of the bed."[54]

Prisoners were punished for every small disobedience, from demanding to eat in the corridor instead of the overcrowded cells, to refusing to attend prayer sessions held in the long corridor outside the ward, to asking to be taken to the washroom too often.

Niloufar described the punishments she and her cellmates had endured for demanding to simply eat with the cell doors open. "For the slightest disobedience, Hawji Rahmani came inside the ward and began insulting and beating us. He used a variety of weapons, from whips to a broomstick to wooden fruit boxes to his heavy boots. He seemed to get a kick out of beating us so savagely. If we screamed or objected to the beatings, he beat us harder until we shut up or fainted on the floor. Once he started beating us, he kicked us in the back, on the head or between the legs, without mercy. Often we had bruises everywhere, in which case he would take away our visiting rights so our families wouldn't see the bruises. Another form of punishment was making us stand on our feet facing the wall for over thirty hours at a time. Many among us had lower back and knee problems as a result of this type of punishment and the beatings."

During the same period, the Attorney General, Ayatullah Ardabili, came to inspect the prison to see if the complaints he had heard from families of prisoners were true. He stopped at the door of one of the cells and asked if anyone was ill that hadn't yet been taken to the clinic. What happened if someone spoke about an untreated ailment was well-known. One woman showed a lot of courage by saying, "Someone in another cell is very sick but no one has taken her to see a doctor." Rahmani and Lajevardi, the man in charge of all prisons in the country and the ex-Prosecutor General of Tehran, were both present, and stated that all of these women were liars and should not be believed. Even though

---

54 M. Raha, *Haghigha-te sadeh (The Simple Truth)*, Part 1, p. 133. Independent Iranian's Women's Publication, Hanover, Germany, 1992. The translation is mine.

the Attorney General seemed to note the overcrowded living conditions of the prisoners and some of the bruises on the women, nothing changed after his visit.

As time went by, rules of conduct in the ordinary wards became harsher and harsher, leading to more disobedience and more transfers to Wards Seven and Eight. Prisoners were not allowed to exercise together, share the goods that they bought from the prison store, or even eat together. They couldn't talk or walk together. Isolation was the rule of the game. Learning foreign languages – which we taught each other to pass the time and occupy our minds – was forbidden. Anyone who refused to pray was considered "impure," or untouchable. They weren't allowed to engage in work that involved the use of water around the ward. It was the *tavvab*s who assigned the day's ward work. When prisoners divided the chores among themselves, they did so taking women's conditions into consideration; those prisoners who were physically or mentally incompetent didn't participate in heavy work. The *tavvab*s, however, didn't care about inmates' conditions and assigned heavy work to those women that they didn't like. Rahmani had demanded that the women participating in the day's ward work be referred to as "homemakers" rather than workers. According to Rahmani, the word "worker" had socialist connotations and shouldn't be employed! The TV was turned on and off by the *tavvab*s in charge of the ward, and they used their power at will to infuriate the prisoners.

Rahmani's rules were ridiculous and objectionable to the inmates, which led to more dissatisfaction and disobedience. Thus, an increasing number of women were sent to the punitive wards to experience the savage beatings of Rahmani and his gang of *pasdar*s. The tug of war between the warden and the prisoners could not go on forever. Everyone knew that Rahmani was looking for a resolution to the problem. He had once threatened, "I have a good plan to turn you animals into human beings." It was only a matter of time before something drastic happened in Qezel. What follows is the story I heard from prisoners of how Hawji Rahmani's sick mind finally resolved his "problem."

One evening, the woman in charge of Ward Eight demanded that prisoners go out to the corridor to listen to some *mullah* refute Marxist philosophy. During his speech, some prisoners started shouting their grievances against the prison establishment and the harassment they experienced at the hands of *tavvab*s. Rahmani was present from the beginning. Lajevardi showed up later, when the meeting got rowdy and out of hand. That night, Lajevardi promised the prisoners would receive due punishment for their behaviour.

Another evening, the ward rep asked the prisoners to take the rug from inside the ward and spread it out in the long corridor for prisoners to pray. Some prisoners refused, saying "Whoever wants to go outside and pray must spread the rug." After the prayer was over, Rahmani and his attack squad came into the ward. They took all the leftist prisoners out into the corridor and began beating them savagely. A few prisoners sustained serious injuries. One woman had a torn eardrum, and another had a bloody head.

A few days later, Rahmani came back. He selected twelve people from the cell nearest to the ward door, and took them away. That night, as a consequence of another dispute with the ward rep, Rahmani returned, lined up more prisoners, and sent them to the prison *zir-e hasht*. Everyone was told to cover up and go outside, where the truck used for transporting meat to the prison kitchen was waiting. The women were led onto the truck without being told where they were going. Some women thought they were being taken to Gohardasht Prison.[55] But the truck stopped in front of another building inside the Qezel compound. The women were pushed inside the building and made to stand one metre apart, facing the wall. The *pasdar*s beat anyone who expressed any objection to having been taken to this location. From far away, the muffled voice of a woman could be heard, her words indistinguishable in the distance. The women spent the night sitting on the floor.

The next morning was visiting day. The women were sure they would not be taken for their scheduled visits looking the way they did. That afternoon, the *pasdar*s took the women inside another room that was too small for forty people. In the corner, a few military blankets were piled up on the floor. The women immediately spread the blankets on the floor and tried to rest. They were all exhausted and hungry. Suddenly, a guard kicked the door open with his foot, and slid a tray of food inside. It was, at best, enough to feed five people.

During the first few days, the women had nothing, not even sanitary napkins. The room was so small that they were unable to sleep properly. After continual protests, the women were grudgingly brought the

---

55 Gohardasht was another prison near Qezel Hessar that had very small punitive cells which prisoners called *sagduni,* literally meaning "dog's den."

minimum products necessary for keeping clean. Every once in a while, Rahmani came back with an excuse to beat them up. A few days later, the women were moved to another room, which had a shower and a toilet, though no hot water. This room was also too small for so many people.

Here, the women's connection to the outside world was totally severed. No TV, no newspapers, no one to talk to except for the *tavvab* supervisor and Rahmani, who only showed up to beat people. They tried to exercise, but there was so little room that it was impossible to move. They finally decided to stand, one behind the other, and walk around the room in a line, then reverse the direction to avoid nausea. They also decided to try to learn a foreign language. One of the women was familiar with French, but it was difficult to study a language without pen and paper.

One Friday evening, after a month in the new place, the women were told to collect their belongings and get ready to move. Once again, they did not know where they were going. The women had given up on speculating. They collected the blankets and their meager personal possessions, and waited. They were led through several corridors and finally arrived in a larger area. They were told to sit on the floor facing the wall and refrain from speaking to one another. After a while, the women started whispering to each other and when nothing happened, they cautiously looked around and realized they were alone. They also noticed that the cellmates who had been previously taken were there. They saw how filthy the room was, and realized that this must be what prisoners called "The Stable." It was even dirtier than a stable. Inside the big room was a bathroom and a toilet in which large worms lazily crawled. The women had no option but to try to clean up their new quarters as best they could.

It was late October and the room was damp and cold, but the women were still in their summer clothes. They had been promised their warm clothes from Ward Eight, but these items were never delivered. Once more, a guard slid a pot of food inside. The food looked like leftovers from other wards. They were told not to wash the pot because "dogs are impure"[56] and should not touch the pot with wet hands. A few days later Rahmani returned, selected some prisoners, beat them, and

---

56 Leftist prisoners were considered "impure" because they didn't pray.

took them away. These women had no idea where they were being taken, but they were sure it was an even bigger hell than the one in which they had just been. They were blindfolded and taken to another room where they were told to sit on the floor, one metre apart. They were told not to speak or remove their blindfolds. At night, there was still no change in their situation. They slept in their veils with their blindfolds on. A female *tavvab* was constantly watching them. Every morning at six o'clock the *tavvab* ordered the prisoners to wake up and immediately sit up straight. At ten o'clock at night she told them to sleep. If they did not obey the orders quickly, Rahmani would come with his whip and teach them a lesson.

One morning, Rahmani came in, and in a sarcastic tone, said that the women would soon have their own beds. He also threatened, "You'll remain here until you turn into human beings." Then the guards entered and ordered everyone to line up against the wall. The women could hear nails being driven into wood, but couldn't see anything. After the guards were finished, they shoved and kicked each one of the women inside a separate box. As the women sat facing the wall, they felt two short wooden walls on either side of them, like sitting in a coffin. The backs of these boxes were open so that the *tavvab* could keep watch on every move made. The women could not lean against anything to rest. They sat straight up all day long, without seeing or hearing anything. They were to raise their hands if they needed to speak to the woman standing watch. She took them to the washroom three times a day, and told them they had one minute each to do what they had to do. If they took longer, Rahmani would return and beat them again. Sitting all day long made them badly constipated, and their bottoms unbearably sore.

Massoumeh was another woman who had lived in the quarantine. She told me how she coped with the conditions inside the box: "The horrendous circumstances were driving many of the women crazy. After a couple of months some of them raised their hands and told the *tavvab* they were ready to comply with Rahmani's conditions. They were forced to repent in front of other prisoners. They would recount their sins, which often included immoral acts and personal incentives for whatever they had done. These acts of self-degradation were called 'interviews' and were broadcast for the benefit of the women who were stubbornly still sitting in the boxes. The women often cried very hard when confessing in front of other prisoners. This was Rahmani's way of breaking and manipulating them. He didn't stop at forcing the women to do the 'interview.' He also asked them to provide him with all the information they had on other prisoners who were once their closest friends."

Massoumeh continued: "I was becoming increasingly anxious. Whenever I fell asleep, I dreamt that my parents, who had to come in from another city to visit me, had fallen into a ravine and died. Then I would wake up screaming. All day long, there was nothing to do but listen to the 'interviews' and religious chanting broadcast over the loud-speaker. I was dying for some sleep, but I was so scared of my night-mares that I resisted falling asleep. A young girl in the box beside me, who had kept some of the dough from her ration of bread and covertly played with it under her veil, was 'discovered' and severely punished. Any stimulation for the mind was forbidden. The fabric of my veil was patterned with tiny flowers. I had counted the flowers many times and they had become my friends. I had even begun talking to them without using my voice. One night, I couldn't resist anymore, and I fell asleep. I had the same dream. My parents were coming to Karaj to visit me and on the way, they drove into a deep ravine and their car caught fire. All I recall is that I screamed very loudly. I don't remember anything else. When I opened my eyes, I was lying on a bed in the prison clinic. When I asked the nurse why I was there, she told me that I'd had a nervous breakdown. Later on, I learned that I had been unconscious for forty-eight hours."

When these women returned to the regular wards, they were sepa-rated from the rest of the prisoners to prevent them from recounting their ordeal and getting the support of other cellmates. They existed among other women, but were isolated from them. As time passed, more women returned from the quarantine under easier conditions. But some courageous women stayed there until the end, when the warden was finally removed from his position and the quarantine closed. Its closure was the result of a temporary victory won by the moderate fac-tion of the government, led by Ayatollah Montazeri. This period of the "liberalization" of the prisons only lasted a couple of years, but during this time, prisoners' records were re-evaluated and many were released under easier circumstances.[57]

The quarantined women came out of the boxes seriously harmed. They had endured not only physical torture and harsh circumstances, but psychological damage, too. They were deprived of visual and auditory stimulation. They couldn't talk to anyone except for the woman standing watch. In their isolation, they were deprived of the only thing that kept all prisoners alive: the support of other prisoners. They had no way of knowing what was happening to their comrades in other boxes. They heard nothing but religious chanting and confessions. They had no idea what those comrades who had left the quarantine had revealed to Rahmani. In short, their world was a big blank page.

Several victims of Rahmani's barbaric tortures could not shed the effects of the experience and later attempted suicide. Some survived, but others were not so lucky. Many more suffered numerous physical and mental disorders. No one came out of "quarantine" intact.

---

57 Under the old system, even if a prisoner's sentence ended, he or she could not leave the prison system without taking part in an "interview" in front of other prisoners. Prisoners were required to admit to crimes and "sins" even if they had not committed them. Because they refused to participate in this spectacle, many prisoners remained in prison well beyond their sentences.

Friday Afternoon at the Movies

In Qezel, Fridays[58] had a special routine. It began with breakfast at the usual time, then washing and cleaning up. Then, as soon as the door to the yard opened, we ran outside to cleanse our lungs of the stale air circulating inside the ward. This was especially true in the summer, when the outside air was fresh and warm and the sun shone almost every day of the week.

Qezel was conveniently tucked away outside the city of Karaj. The prison sat amid grazing pastures. There were no human beings within several kilometres in any direction. Being in the middle of so much grass and hay caused hardship for inmates who suffered from seasonal allergies. During spring, we woke up to the sound of violent sneezing from the adjacent cells. The shortage of tissues was felt more severely by those prisoners with allergies, who made small handkerchiefs from old clothing and washed them regularly.

The prisoners had obtained permission from the prison authorities to plant flowers and herbs in the prison yard. We paid a guard to buy us the necessary seeds and planted a variety of herbs, vegetables and flowers. In the summer, when the herbs matured, each cell's inmates took turns waking up early in the morning to cut the herbs for the day's lunch, before they wilted from too much sun. At noon, every cell received their share of herbs, which supplemented the bland prison food with something fresh and nutritious.

Usually, prisoners spent a good part of the morning walking alone or in pairs. Sometimes they talked; sometimes they just walked side by side in complete silence. It was as if we needed each other's support to carry the burden of thoughts too difficult to discuss. During these walks, most prisoners spent some time beside the flowerbeds, admiring the unbelievable shades of the stonecrops and the stunning beauty of the morning glories and hollyhocks.

In the background, we could hear the clicking of the ball hitting the table, as women played table-tennis in pairs. The new prison administration, which replaced the barbaric gang previously running Qezel, were

---

58 Friday is a day of rest in Islamic countries, and a holiday.

trying to prove that they were different from their predecessors. They had allowed us to collect money from the inmates and purchase a table and a few pairs of rackets. Prisoners took turns playing by registering their names on a list that was kept by a volunteer who had agreed to the responsibility. Everyone had the right to play, whether or not they had contributed to the fund. And it didn't matter if you were an expert or just a beginner. Anyone wishing to play could do so when it was her turn. But, with a single table, your turn did not come very often. If you missed your turn for whatever reason, the next person on the list would play instead.

By noon, we were all tired and ready to have lunch. For a short period of time, on Fridays, we had *chelo kabob*[59] for lunch. This was a real treat, especially for those of us who had come from Evin, where food was very scarce and of bad quality. Some cells chose to spread out a couple of blankets in the yard near the flowerbeds, and eat lunch outside. Others preferred to eat inside and forego the extra work required to carry the blankets and dishes outside and then back inside when lunch was finished. The decision about whether to go out or not was usually left to those in charge of the day's cleaning responsibilities in the cells.

After lunch, the dishes were washed and the area was cleaned. Around two o'clock, it was time for the radio news. At the end of the news, speeches from the high-ranking officials of the Islamic Republic at Friday prayer in Tehran were broadcast over the ward's loudspeakers. These were very important to hear because they told us what was going on inside the seemingly monolithic government of the Islamic Republic. This was how we became aware of the rift among the different factions of the government. Among other things, the rift concerned the treatment of political prisoners, during 1983-4. One Friday, an official would be demanding to cleanse the prison system of the "germs of corruption and infidelity." The next week, another would be asking for the elimination of "corrupt elements" and "blood-sucking leeches" from the system of government. Listening to the news was our way of finding out who was winning the fight between the two factions.

After the news, it was time for relaxation. Some prisoners stayed outside to take advantage of the peacefulness of the yard. Others sat in

---

59 *Chelo kabob* is a dish favoured by Iranians but seldom served in prison. It is comprised of skewers of barbecued beef or lamb, on rice. The *chelo kabob* served in Qezel was made of ground meat.

front of the TV in the corridor, next to the set of iron bars that separated the prisoners from the quarters of the *tavvab*s who ran the ward. On Friday afternoons, the first scheduled TV programs were usually suitable for school children and small kids. These were followed by a movie for the general public. Most who opted for the TV program also stayed for the movie. The program usually consisted of badly made propaganda films that dealt with the Iran-Iraq war, which was still raging in the southern and western fronts.

Once in a while, however, there was something worth watching. On this particular Friday, the movie was advertised ahead of time. It was about prisoners of war during World War II. The film was *Escape to Victory*, with Sylvester Stallone, Michael Caine, and the famous Brazilian football player, Pelé, a favourite with Iranians. Naturally, many people were sitting in front of the TV set, waiting for the film to begin.

I was usually among those opting for more fresh air and silence. I tended to stay out in the yard as long as possible. As I was walking, engrossed in my thoughts, I heard clapping and cheering from inside the ward. Curious to find out what was causing the stir among the prisoners, I rushed inside. To my amazement, I saw everyone's eyes enthusiastically glued to the TV screen. Everyone looked cheerful and absorbed in the story. I thought it must be a fun movie to watch, so I sat down.

In the scene that had caused such excitement, the Allied prisoners of war were playing a soccer match against a team of German soldiers. The POWs had a plan to escape the camp at the end of the soccer game. As the game progressed, our cheering for the POWs became louder and louder, and our whistling was deafening. For a while, we forgot where we were and what was expected of women in the prisons of the Islamic Republic. All we were thinking was that some lucky prisoners were going to escape and the bad guys were losing the game. The soccer match, with Pelé on the prisoners' team, added to the excitement.

Suddenly, the prison guards appeared at the door of the ward, questioning the *tavvab*s' ability to control the "unruly bunch." One of the *tavvab*s, who had gone to answer to the guard at the door, returned and threatened us over the loudspeaker, saying that if we didn't behave, the movie would be discontinued and the TV set would be turned off: "The brothers are complaining that your cheering can be heard all the way down to the end of the unit corridor.[60] They say you are acting very un-ladylike and that they have never heard such noises coming from women before. They want you to shut up or face the consequences."

With this ultimatum, the women calmed down a bit. But many complained loudly to guards who were still at the ward door. One prisoner said, "Can't we even watch a movie without a chaperon?" Another added, "Yeah, haven't you heard? Women have to be quiet as mice!" Others kept adding more derogatory comments until the mood began to calm down. Gradually, the voices subsided and the movie resumed. The lively mood that had reigned over the ward for a short while was gone. Many left the corridor for the yard, where they could complain amongst themselves and walk off their anger.

From that day on, women didn't show as much interest in films shown by the prison system. They had come to the conclusion that even good films, when screened in prison, could have a bad aftertaste.

---

60 Qezel Prison consisted of three units, each possessing eight wards. We were in Unit One.

Freedom at Last

One day, as I was walking in the yard, I heard noises coming from inside the ward. I could tell something unusual was happening. I rushed inside and asked a cellmate what was going on.

"They're reading names of prisoners who are going to be released soon."

I jokingly asked if she had heard my name on the list.

"I don't know," she replied. "I came in late, but don't you have nine years to serve?"

I smiled and said, "I'm glad you're not on the review board!"

I stood there listening with envy to the names being read. I knew I still had several more years to serve. But the new judicial system had promised to look into our sentences and reduce those considered unjustly long. Many of the judgments delivered during the 1981-83 period[61] were haphazard and excessive. Therefore, many of us could qualify for the file review.

The women who had been called were cheering in disbelief. Many of us stood in line to congratulate and wish them well. They came from various political backgrounds. Among them was my French language teacher, whose classes had been responsible for shattering the boredom of prison life for many women, after Hawji Rahmani's dismissal.

The women finally left the ward and the excitement subsided. We felt drained of energy. Another opportunity had come and gone, and no one knew when another one would come knocking. After dinner, I went in the corridor looking for one of my French language "classmates." There she was, smiling broadly. She was one of the quarantine women, who had endured the boxes until the very end.

"I knew you'd come!" she said. Who's going to correct us now when we make a mistake?"

"Let's practice and see if we still remember what we've learned," I suggested, and on we went, walking down the corridor, speaking in French.

---

61 Summer of 1981 was the beginning of mass unrest, and the Islamic regime's suppression of dissidents.

I spent another winter at Qezel and forgot all about the promise of prisoner file review. I was convinced I would remain in prison until I had finished serving my full sentence.

Towards the end of winter, a cleric affiliated with the judiciary, who was in charge of file reviews, came to Qezel. He sat in the room referred to as either the Library or the *Mosque* – depending on who was speaking. We had noticed his entrance and anticipated some good news.

One of the *tavvab*s in charge of the ward entered the *Mosque* and came out with a sheet of paper in her hand. By now, half the population of the ward had gathered in the front section of the corridor, near the microphone. The *tavvab* said, "Those sisters whose names I read should go to the *Mosque* immediately."

All eyes were glued to the bars dividing the corridor from *zir-e hasht*. I stood in front of our cell and grabbed the cold iron bars.

The woman started reading from the list, and with every new name announced, sounds of excitement were heard.

"…Niloufar Mandani, Maryam Barzegar, Nazila Bakhshi, Mahboo-beh Kamali…Azadeh Agah."

Suddenly, the woman standing next to me hugged me and said, "It's your name they are calling! Hurry up and go!"

I didn't trust my ears. I needed assurance. Was I really being called into the Library?

A close friend ran toward me. "Hey, didn't you hear? They called your name!"

I was starting to believe that something was about to happen. I got ready and went into the room where the *mullah* was waiting.

After what seemed to be a long introduction, he said, "Several files have been reviewed and you have been found eligible for pardon." He made sure we understood how lucky we were to have been selected for "pardon" and how disappointed he would be if we didn't abide by the rules.

What he called a pardon was, in fact, a kind of parole. If, during this period, we reverted back to our previous "subversive" activities, we would have to serve the remaining years of our sentences. He then laid out the conditions of our release: we would have to report weekly to the nearest neighborhood *comité*;[62] we needed the *comité*'s permission to

---

62 Revolutionary Guard stations in every neighborhood.

travel within Iran; we wouldn't be able to apply for passports until our suspended sentences were over; before leaving the prison, we would have to sign a form promising not to engage in any anti-government activities. In fact, we were leaving Qezel Hessar for a larger prison.

We had one week to decide whether or not we would consent to the conditions. It was now up to us to decide our fate. We returned to the warm embrace of our jubilant cellmates, who were waiting for us impatiently near the bars separating the ward from *zir-e hasht*.

The following week, a heated discussion raged among the prisoners. Should we sign the form? In principle, we should have been freed unconditionally. But there was no guarantee we would fare better if we refrained from signing the forms and stayed in prison. Those who were in favour of signing the form argued that no one knows what faction might replace the group currently running the prisons, and that this might be our only chance to get out. Even if we were to serve our full sentences, the officials wouldn't let us out of the prison without some sort of non-involvement guarantee. Thus, staying in prison was not a wise and viable alternative. Those opposed believed if we signed the forms and accepted the "pardon," we were in fact, admitting to wrongdoing. We didn't believe we had committed any crimes. It was difficult to convince the followers of either group to change their minds. There was some truth to both arguments. Finally, some women decided they didn't want the pardon, for they had done nothing illegal. The majority of us decided to sign the form and get out while the opportunity was present.

Still, something in the back of my mind made me feel uneasy. I needed to weigh the positive and negative outcomes of my decision. What if this was a gimmick to keep us engaged in wishful thinking? What would happen to all of the women left behind – those who didn't get reviewed, those who wouldn't sign the form? Though I was delighted to go home to my daughter, I felt sad leaving my comrades and cellmates behind. They had become my new family. I felt safe among them. The world outside was full of uncertainty, hardships and responsibility.

During my next visit with my family, they told me they'd been contacted by the prosecutor's office about arranging for the conditions of my release. The office had requested for a government employee as guarantor, and a piece of property as collateral for my release. Things were beginning to roll. My family reassured me of my pending freedom.

Spring was coming and the air was filled with the smells of nature. Ever since I had been notified of my possible release, I was spending more time in the yard, walking and planning for life outside the cage. Nothing topped walking when I needed to relax and think. As I walked, I tried to remember every detail of the prison compound. There was still no sign of freedom for my husband, so I would have to raise my daughter single-handedly. I knew many problems awaited me outside of prison. I would have to find a job to support my family. I wasn't sure I could go back to my old employer. I now had a record and many doors would be shut in my face. But I had skills and I could manage to earn a living.

I gave away most of my belongings to my friends, as keepsakes. There were items that I couldn't take out with me, and some that I would probably never use outside of prison. Days went by and still no news. I was beginning to doubt the possibility of being released. On visiting days, I kept asking my family if they had any idea why we hadn't been called to the Freedom Room. They kept repeating, "Soon." The other women were in the same boat. We often speculated about the reason; none of us were ever correct.

One day in late spring, after breakfast and just as I was getting ready to go outside for my morning walk, the microphone started to buzz. Everyone began talking at once. The *tavvab* responsible for the ward asked the women to be quiet so she could continue talking. Then she read our names from a list and asked us to be ready with all of our belongings as quickly as possible. Everyone knew the list by heart; we could tell where we were going.

Women rushed to say goodbye to their friends and cellmates. They surrounded me and began pulling me in all directions. My friends and I were crying and hugging for the last time. I didn't realize how attached I was to them until that moment. The *tavvab* kept shouting, "Hurry up, don't you want to get out of here?" After many warnings, we were finally ready and, accompanied by the women of the ward, walked toward *zir-e hasht*. As I was leaving the ward, I looked back for the last time to capture the faces and events of that moment in my mind.

We were told to line up and follow a *pasdar* toward the prison *zir-e hasht*. From there, we were taken to a bus and were counted as we climbed inside. The bus doors closed and we started our journey toward Tehran. This time, the road was much more beautiful, with blossoming trees and yellow-green mountain slopes. As I admired the scenery, I thought of my husband, who was a great nature lover, just like me. I felt sad. But I knew he was happy that at least one of us was going to be with our daughter when she went to school for the first time.

We stopped in front of Evin and were told to put on our blindfolds. Then the bus entered the Evin compound and stopped in front of the administration building. We were told to get off the bus and stand to be counted once more. We were all wearing black *chador*s and black blindfolds. Anyone looking at us could not differentiate us from one another. The *pasdar* who was given the job of counting us had a difficult task indeed. At one point, he came up with the number fifty, and at another, only forty-nine! He must have counted us ten times. Our muted laughter under our veils, and our constant shifting about added to his confusion. He finally swore out loud and yelled at us to follow him into the ward. We still had to get processed before being released, and that was why we had been brought to Evin.

After a couple of days, they began calling women to the administration building to sign release papers. I was among the last group to be released. On a beautiful spring day, a minibus took us to the parking lot of an amusement park called Luna Park, where our families were waiting to receive us. From the window of the minibus, I could see my daughter, Layla, jumping up and down with joy. My family had a hard time controlling her as she ran towards our still moving vehicle. I was delirious with joy. I got into my sister's car with Layla and my nieces, and we drove off to my parents' house.

Layla didn't want to leave my side. She followed me as though she was my shadow. Everyone wanted to know what I needed or desired. My sister-in-law had brought me a cake from my favourite pastry shop. Relatives poured in to see me that night and the days that followed. I tried to spend as much time with Layla as possible. But life was hectic and I was in great demand. I didn't have proper clothing. Most of our belongings had been spread among family members' homes. I looked really awkward in the outdated, made-for-prison clothes. I felt dependent on my family members for everything. I was afraid to go out alone. When I had to go out, I kept looking back to see if someone was following me.

I sometimes forgot to take care of my daughter's needs. I had temporarily lost my sense of responsibility as a mother. In the beginning, I followed prison routine by force of habit. I woke up early in the morning and wondered where I was. When I realized I was home, I would smile and close my eyes with satisfaction. I didn't realize it was now possible to have snacks or fruit between meals. I waited until others offered me something to eat. In the evenings, I paced my parents' courtyard for a long time. This was my way of letting off steam and calming down.

I had to report to the *comité* once a week. At the door, they gave me a filthy blindfold to wear and sent me upstairs to a scantily furnished apartment. Someone showed me to a metal folding chair behind an old metal desk. I sat there waiting and thinking about the best way to cope with this degrading life of "freedom." Certainly I didn't feel free.

A man stepped into the room, and an hour of interrogation followed. I was reminded of the early months of my time in Evin. At each visit, I was to report all of my activities to him. If I saw a fellow ex-prisoner, I had to report the meeting and the subject of our conversation. I was told it was my "duty" to inform the *comité* of any "suspicious" person or activity. In fact, they planned to use us as free informants. This procedure would go on until the *comité* decided I was no longer a threat to society. Needless to say, no one reported their visits with ex-prisoners and everyone took trips inside the country between visits to the *comité*, and didn't report it!

I could now visit my husband in prison on visiting days. The ten-minute visit usually required a full day. Families of prisoners often gave each other rides to and from prison. Layla had started school, but I would let her miss classes every other week so that she could come along to see her father. I decided to tell Layla's teacher about Layla's situation; she promised not to report Layla's absence to the school administration on those particular days. I found most people sympathetic to the plight of political prisoners. People were often helpful when we were in a jam and needed assistance.

Slowly, I began adjusting to my new life. I started looking for work and soon found a job in a private institution. Though we lived with my parents, I tried to make Layla feel as if she were independent, and in her own home. We had private outings for just the two of us. Layla had been the centre of attention in the absence of my husband and I, and now she needed a routine. I tried to normalize our situation as much as possible. Now, all we were hoping for was that my husband come home and complete our family.

On a hot summer afternoon about a year and a half later, our wishes finally came true. This time we were experienced, and arranged for the conditions of his release ahead of time. Once more, our family was complete.

Life is not empty
There is kindness, apple, and faith
Yes
One must live as long as there are poppies

Something is lurking in my heart like a bush of light,
Like slumber before daybreak
And so restless am I that I wish
To run to the end of the plain, climb to the peak of the mountain
There is a voice in the distance that is calling me.

Sohrab Sepehri *

*   An excerpt of a poem called *Dar Golestaneh* by Sohrab Sepehri, a contemporary Iranian poet. In Sohrab Sepehri, *Hasht Ketab*, Tahoori Publishers, Tehran, 1984, pp. 348-51.

The Five Seasons

SHADI PARSI

The Day of My Arrest

THE LARGE GLASS DOORS of the *comité* were dark and grey, and when they were closed behind me soon after my arrest, everything in my life became blurry, as dark and grey as those doors. That morning, I had been distributing leaflets for the political party I supported. Everything was fine until I slipped a leaflet in the mail drop of one particular house. A furious, bearded man opened the door, ran out, and jumped at me, swearing and shouting. It was around noon on a weekday and there was hardly anyone on the streets. As I ran, the man chasing behind me, I saw a single shop, a craft store, among the many houses. I tried to enter, but it was closed: it was lunchtime, noon prayer time. I often ask myself, "What if the shop had been open?" There is no way for me to know the answer to that question; I can only make guesses about the possible scenarios. Deep down, I believe it wouldn't have changed the course of events. Wouldn't the angry man have easily found me inside the shop? There was only one shop on the main street, one place I could have hidden in – unless one of the neighbourhood people had let me in their house. Even if that had happened, the man could have gone to the nearby *comité* and asked for an area house search.

So there I was in the middle of the street, surrounded by *pasdar*s and a small crowd of passers-by. There were three *pasdar*s, two males and one female, asking to see the contents of my bag. I refused to comply. The angry man was showing everyone the pamphlet I had delivered. With outrage, he yelled out its slogans: "Down with the Islamic Republic of Iran…" The pamphlets were not in my bag; they were neatly tucked and secured in my pantyhose at the waist of my skirt. In a brief hand search, the leaflets would have been hard to feel and spot, but even so, I refused to show the *pasdar*s my bag, insisting that my basic rights would be violated if I obeyed them. People just watched. I could see traces of sympathy in their eyes at the unfairness of it all, and felt their urge to interfere and protest, coupled with the human tendency to remain silent to protect their own lives and families. Stronger than all of these paradoxical feelings was the fear I saw in their eyes. They stood there and watched as the *pasdar*s took me to the *comité*.

I was arrested in November 1981, when I was eighteen years old. If I had been distributing political leaflets five months beforehand, it wouldn't have been a big deal. Five months before, we could have book and newspaper stalls anywhere in the city. It was a period of relative open political activity that had resulted from the people's revolution in 1979, and the government could not suppress such a widespread movement easily. Everyday, we would set up our booths or stalls at certain spots in major squares and intersections. I had just finished high school, and the universities were closed due to the so-called Cultural Revolution. The Islamic regime wanted to purge universities from all symptoms and traces of "imperialism" and "Shah's Decadent Regime." This meant firing many professors, arresting students, and changing the content of textbooks. There were no university studies, and no jobs for the youth of my generation. Our days were free; we had a lot of time on our hands to devote to political activities. In a way, it felt like work: selecting a certain location everyday, setting up our stall, displaying the books and newsletters, putting up the banners, and getting ready for the anticipated heated arguments. A few minutes after we set up our stall, fans of other political parties would join us and set up their materials.

Those days were filled with demonstrations, marches, book fairs, political discussions, and people gathering around us to discuss political issues and current news. Recently, our days often ended with an attack; an individual or a group of thugs calling themselves *Hezbollahi*[63] would appear from nowhere, and tear our banners, shout slogans, swear at us, accuse us of being traitors, and, sometimes, beat us and take away our books and newspapers. We had accepted it as part of our day, and were gradually developing ways to cope with it as best we could.

What drew a line between that era and the day of my arrest were the events of June 20, 1981. The *Mojahedin-e Khalq* Organization arranged and held a number of simultaneous mass demonstrations. This wave of protests drew a violent reaction from the Islamic regime. To nip the protests in the bud, the Islamic Revolutionary Guards – *pasdar*s – poured onto the streets and arrested anyone they deemed suspicious. Mass arrests, and executions of those already in prison started. After June 20, 1981, one could easily end up in prison: by looking "suspicious" to the *pasdar*s, possessing a left-wing book or newsletter, being an unveiled woman, or dressing in a certain way. The government announced that after June 20, any gathering, publication, activity, or demonstration by any opposition group was banned and considered against the law. Therefore, anyone involved in such matters would be arrested. Remembering all of this on the day of my arrest, I tried to face the fact that it was no longer five months ago, and that despite the June 20th announcement, I had chosen to distribute leaflets for the left-wing organization I supported; I therefore had to face the consequences.

Back to the large glass doors – the moment they closed behind me, I was cut off from the familiar world in which I had lived all my life. It occurred to me that I used to know what to do in almost all typical situations of my eighteen-year-old life. Not anymore! At that moment, it was as if I was watching a movie, and had some sort of vague affinity with the main character. It wasn't me going through the motions; it was the main character of this movie. I made an effort to guess and determine the best course of action for her, but couldn't. It was interesting that I

---

63 A *Hezbollahi* is a member of the *Hezbollah* (Party of God), loyal followers of Ayatollah Khomeini. *Hezbollahi* were armed, self-styled, unofficial defenders of the revolution. They could be mobilized by the government at any time.

wasn't feeling sad or even scared. I should have, naturally, having been arrested by a regime that was famous – or infamous – for its ruthlessness towards political prisoners and opposition groups. I just didn't have the capacity to feel fear or miss my family and friends. My urge was to think and act rather than to feel. Feelings could wait.

The *pasdar* in charge of the office made me stand at the far end of a big hall after his routine interrogation. How did I get the leaflets? Who gave them to me? Who were the others involved? Names and addresses? Long ago, I had lined up my story; I'd spent many sleepless nights thinking about possible scenarios and the best ways to cope with them, what stories had the least possible plot holes. I just picked one of the best and narrated it with as much confidence as I could muster. To them, I had to appear to be a simple eighteen-year-old going through the passionate years of her teenage life, excited about politics and political activities, as was the trend, as was cool! I provided minimal information about addresses and contacts. I tried to play a simple teenager who wanted to distribute leaflets to fit in with her peers, not someone deeply involved with ideologies and real politics. It was too early to judge its effectiveness, but for the first interrogation, it worked.

That night, in my solitary cell, I stayed up for a very long time. I had been strip-searched thoroughly and blindfolded. I still felt the rude violation of their hands on my skin; I hated the feeling and longed to be able to wash it off. In the coldness of my cell, I started to think, for the first time, about my family and comrades. My mind began to penetrate through the prison walls to the outside world. I was back in my familiar life, and my mother came to soothe me with her doting hands. She was the first to come into my thoughts, and she stayed longer than everyone and everything else. My sister, father, and comrades were next. So far, I had managed not to give out any names. But a nagging, disturbing thought was eating me from inside: would I be able to stay decent and human? What was my tolerance level? How far could I bear physical and emotional torture? I had done okay for one day, but there was an endless array of days and nights stretched out in front of me. I was solely on my own to make numerous important decisions about myself and others.

The thought of rape crept into my mind and soon filled my whole being with paralyzing fear. I was alone in a cell, in the middle of nowhere. Anything could happen, and the only thing I had control over was how I perceived and reacted to the events. My mind was too numb to think about the details, but one thing became very clear amidst the chaos: I had a deep, clear, beautiful need to stay human, to be true to the essence of my being. I had to do all I could so I wouldn't hate myself for the rest of my life. If I didn't, I would be unable to rely on and live with myself. In a very basic, naive way, my decision was made: "I'm going to stay true to *me,* and keep that truth alive, at all costs, even if sick and bruised and beaten. So long as I wasn't dead, there would be hope to survive." It was only after this thought that I could sleep for a few hours that night.

The Fake Execution

Three days after my arrest, in a different cell with two other prisoners, I was lying on the ground. The door of our cell was knocked at, hard. Dinner had come. I didn't even bother to sit up. Dinner was some flat bread, butter and watery carrot jam. My cellmate covered my body with a blanket. It is not appropriate for a Moslem man to see a woman lying down since the sight might arouse him. Although I knew this, I neither moved nor cared.

That morning, I had been called for interrogation six times. Each session lasted about twenty minutes, at which point I was returned to my cell, and then called again in less than half an hour. They were asking for information about the organization I supported, the person who had given me the leaflets, and anything else that could lead to more arrests. I kept giving them the same information: that I was not an official member of the opposition, that I just distributed their leaflets out of the respect and love that I had for the one person I knew and saw regularly, that I did not know anyone else, that I didn't have the address of my one connection; I just met him regularly at a specified place and time once a week. At the end of the sixth interrogation, the interrogator put yet another sheet of paper in front of me. At first, I thought it was one more page of questions that needed answers. What I saw from under the blindfold was a blank sheet of paper, with only one word written, in red, at the top of the page: WILL. He was asking me to write my will.

"You are lying and obviously not cooperating. I'm not going to waste my time further with you. Write your will, and you'll be executed tomorrow."

I was shocked and out of ideas in terms of how to react. A sudden rush of images from my past marched into my mind, like a movie flashback, and then died away, replaced by the piece of paper in front of me. I said, "I don't know anything other than what I've already told you. What do you expect me to do? Lie? Give you the address of an innocent person just to prevent my death?" At some point in the midst of these interrogations, a sharp burning pain had developed in my stomach. Now, it was excruciating, slicing my insides with a sharp knife.

The *pasdar* took a few steps towards me, hit me in the head with something hard, and said, "Nice try, but you all say the same thing." Then, mockingly, he added, "I don't know! How can you distribute a leaflet with a death sentence to an entire government and not know anyone else in that organization? How am I supposed to believe that? We're running out of time. Write the will."

The burning sensation in my stomach boiled up and came to my throat. The room started to spin around. I threw the paper on the floor, said, "I'm not writing this. You're asking me for information I don't have," and got up. Another blow to my head threw me to the wall, and I was taken to my cell. I had been lying down since then, with my cellmates sitting at my side, talking to me, when the dinner came.

As the guard delivered the food trays, he signalled to me with his head and said to one of my cellmates, "Tell her to get up and eat. It's her last meal."

"Don't you think she has had enough?" she said with disgust.

The guard grinned, showing off his ugly, bad teeth, and left.

My other cellmate soon fell asleep. She was so tired and depressed that she slept most of the time. Sara, the one who had spoken to the guard, stayed awake beside me, keeping quiet to let me fall asleep. I felt like I had a very high fever. Things seemed unreal and too far away, as if they were not happening to me. Memories crowded my mind. I was neither awake nor asleep, and it was in this state that I told her my address and asked her to tell my family how much I was thinking about them on my last night alive, in case she got out of prison one day.

Her eyes filled with tears. She came closer to me and whispered, "Would you give them the information they want if you had it?"

Without hesitation I whispered back, "No, I wouldn't."

She nodded; that was the answer she was expecting.

"Tell me about your family," Sara said, and I started to talk to her, trying to make my last impression on earth as meaningful as I could to the last person in the world that I trusted in that moment. Somewhere in the middle of my talk, we heard the morning *azan* and knew it was shortly before sunrise. The *azan* brought with it childhood memories: my safe home, my parents fasting for the month of *Ramadan*, listening to the *azan* early morning in my bed, knowing that it was coming from the alarm radio to wake my father and pulling the blanket back over my head because I still had one more hour to sleep before I had to get up for school.

We heard heavy footsteps in the hallway. They stopped at our cell door. The key turned noisily in the lock, and the door opened. It confirmed my theory that executions usually took place early in the morning. I knew immediately what the guards had come for. Someone called out my name, and the giant octopus of fear wrapped me in its multiple arms.

With my eyes closed, I walked outside, and climbed what seemed to be a rocky hill. My knees were not mine. They were automatic devices dragging me along; they seemed to know where they were going. A *pasdar* had asked me to follow him to the place of execution, but I was far away, floating in a crystal ball above all that was happening, watching from a distance. Even death could not touch me here; I was watching myself walk to death. This "me" was invincible, and would never die; it was devoid of any emotion: fear, sorrow, love, hatred. It had turned into a big nothing, with no worries. I was incredibly relaxed. For the first time in days, I felt liberated. It didn't matter what they did to me; I was free from all the bonds within which they could possibly enslave my life.

The cool early morning breeze blew on my face. To my surprise, I did not enjoy it; I just felt it. I was beyond nature, going through the last season of my life, the last day, the last hour, the last few minutes. For a split second, I thought, "Why doesn't my ideology, my belief, save me? Why doesn't it try to define life and death in these last minutes?" This thought passed. I was ready, absolutely ready, to go. It is strangely easy to die when you don't feel or think anything, when you don't even feel that your body is yours. It was so easy, so dignified. I was ready.

He stopped; I stopped.

His harsh voice cut through my comforting vacuum. "You seem so honest and young. They don't believe this, but I do. Talk to me; tell me everything, there's still a chance to save your life. You're so young, why die so early?"

I was not quite sure what this meant, so I didn't respond. I preferred to keep walking and lingering through the beautiful nothingness in my mind.

He pulled me back. "I'm going to ask them for a second chance for you. I'm sure you will come around. Let's go back."

I tried to say something, but the depth to which I had sunken was so far below that I couldn't surface.

"I will talk to them, tell them to take you to another place and give you some time to think. I'm sure you will change. When you do, remember that I saved your life."

All of a sudden, I felt dizzy. It was as if something had collapsed inside of me, and I wanted to sit down. The soundless beauty that had gradually built up within me ruthlessly shattered. I was out of the crystal ball and back in my body again, face to face with the ugliness. I felt so vulnerable, like anything could hurt me. After cutting loose all my ties to life, coming back was very hard. I couldn't bring myself to want to see another minute, another season, another year. This execution had been a bluff, and I hadn't realized. I had gone along with it, had let them walk me through all the phases of the experience. What a fool I was, and how I hated them.

"Aren't you happy for a second chance?" he asked.

My lips could not part to say anything.

"Let's go. The car is waiting to take you to another place."

I got in a big van with dark windows. From under my blindfold, I saw other prisoners in the car. I closed my eyes to rest – I was exhausted from the roller coaster I had just been through – and waited for the next blow that life had in store for me.

Evin Prison

The unusually cool breeze, ice-cold water, endless interrogations, torture, and numerous executions: this is how I remember Evin Prison, in this very sequence, with the elements of nature first, since my mind wants to postpone the darkness of the rest as much as possible. When I think about Evin, the first thing I remember is the incredibly refreshing cool breeze that brushed my face when I was first taken there. We were blindfolded, but the moment we stepped out of the big van, I knew we were no longer in Tehran, that this must be Evin. Tehran hardly ever had such cool breezes. The breeze became the signature of Evin. On that day, and later on, during the long, hot summer days that I lived with more than one hundred other prisoners in a small room for the five years that Evin was my home, whenever I sought a small escape from the bestiality that surrounded me, I thought of the breeze.

Then the freezing water: I had never before experienced tap water so cold that it burned my hands. We often had to wash our hands and faces in a rush, just to get rid of the pain. It was only in summer that the coldness became something to look forward to. I often had to wash my whole body with that water since there were long periods of no hot bathing water in prison. Even though it was ice-cold, it was still water, with the potential to cleanse us both externally and internally. To take away a bit of the coldness, we used to fill pails and small clothes tubs with the water, and put them in the yard under the sun for hours. After the water had absorbed the hottest rays of the sun, we took the pails and tubs inside, and used the water to wash ourselves.

Life in Evin was life in limbo. In Tehran, prisoners were usually arrested and first taken to various small *comités* or other buildings that *pasdar*s had turned into little jails all over the city. Though prisoners were sometimes kept in these buildings for several days, eventually, they would be taken to Evin. Evin, a political prison built during Shah's regime, didn't have as many cells and prison buildings as the Islamic government now needed. They had to build and expand to accommodate the increasing number of prisoners. In a short time, they added several new buildings in the area. The youth of Tehran were being followed, chased, and arrested with unbelievable speed, and in less than a year, it was rare to meet a family that did not have a relative in prison.

Prisoners were kept at Evin as long as they were under interrogation, or awaiting trial, if there was going to be one. This could take a long time. Even after getting a sentence, many prisoners were still kept at Evin; others were transferred to other prisons to serve their terms. Staying in Evin meant living a life of absolute uncertainty. Everyday, names were called for interrogation. Each morning, before or at breakfast – which wasn't much: a little tea saturated with and stinking of camphor, a tiny piece of bread and a tinier piece of cheese – we perked up our ears to find out who was being called for interrogation and torture. It didn't end there. All day long, names were announced. It was only at night, when names weren't called, that our minds were put at relative ease. On those occasions that a new piece of information had been revealed and needed immediate attention and questioning, names were called late at night. Even our bath time started late at night – they didn't want to call somebody's name while that prisoner was in the shower.

Those who were sick and those who had been tortured were given priority in the showers, since they couldn't take a shower with five other people, hands and elbows hitting their bruised bodies every few seconds. Also, according to Islam, women who have just finished their menstrual period have to take a shower to be cleansed before they are able to start praying again, so the religious prisoners put their names on a priority list. Only after these people could other prisoners take turns to bathe. When it was our turn to take a bath, our bath monitor would wake us from sleep. This was a very paradoxical feeling: it was difficult and unpleasant to have to get up in the middle of the night, when sleep was the best escape out of the dark world of prison, and go straight under the usually lukewarm water; at the same time, it felt great to get clean, even though we were given an unreasonably short time to do so, and there were so many people around in the process. Anyone who passed on their turn would miss their chance for an unknown period of time. Sometimes the water would stop running in the middle of our shower – technical problems or intentional pressure reduction, who could be sure which? – and we had to rinse ourselves with the freezing cold tap water, if it was still running. Sometimes, there was so little water coming out of the taps that it didn't reach the shower and five or six people had to share the lower tap while the bath monitor shouted our names and announced the end of our time.

Life in Evin was absolute uncertainty: living under constant threat of being called for interrogation, endless nights spent lying awake think-ing about what to say if certain questions were asked. Waking up in the middle of the night, sweating and panicking, and believing that the nightmare was real, thinking to oneself: "I have given the interrogators information about my friends; I haven't been able to tolerate the tor-ture; my friends have been arrested because of my incompetence; I'm responsible for their suffering" – and taking a long time to realize that it was just a bad dream, not yet true. Nights of holding hands with the person lying down beside you, and whispering in the dark about our-selves, trying to rekindle our faith and devotion to our beliefs, confiding in each other, crying, and consoling each other. Days during which we witnessed many become *tavvab*s.

Because it was a house of torture, Evin became the birthplace of *tavvab*s. These were prisoners who claimed they had seen the light and found their true calling in Islam and the Islamic regime; they had to denounce their political party and all previous affiliations. In order to prove themselves to prison authorities, *tavvab*s were expected to do certain things. These expectations grew at a constantly increasing pace and scope. At the beginning, giving out names and addresses of friends would have been enough. When more and more *tavvab*s started to do this, however, even more was expected of them. Some began to assist in the interrogation and torturing of other prisoners. These *tavvab*s worked in the interrogation hallways, distributing food, checking on prisoners to make sure we didn't talk or exchange information, and taking us to the washroom or for interrogation.

Some helped interrogators draw the organizational charts of vari-ous opposition parties. The charts started with minimal names and lev-els of responsibility, and expanded each day as the number of *tavvab*s increased. This task was initiated by *tavvab*s, but later on, all prisoners whose names came up somewhere on the chart were called for inter-rogation and clarification. These prisoners could not easily deny their place in the organizational chart. All the important details had been re-vealed by others. If it weren't for the collaboration of *tavvab*s, the gov-ernment could not have arrested such a huge number of people in such a short period of time. Everyday, new team houses were attacked and there were more arrests, thanks to the information the *tavvab*s provided. The prisons were being flooded with the youth of Iran.

*Tavvab*s made calls to friends on the outside, who did not know that the tavvabs were in prison. The *tavvab*s would set up appointments with these unsuspecting friends, and then watch as their friends were arrested.

One day, about two years after my arrest, a *tavvab* told me and a friend of mine the story of one of these arranged arrests. She had planned to meet a friend in a familiar restaurant where they used to frequently hold their meetings. She explained how her friend had tried to escape from the back door of the restaurant when she noticed the suspicious situation. According to their usual arrangement, if such a thing happened, they were to use the restaurant's back door. This *tavvab*, however, had told the *pasdar*s about the back door arrangement, so the *pasdar*s were waiting for her friend outside. She gave us these details with such enjoyment; it was as if she was reliving the "fun" she had had then. As she got to this last piece of her story, I felt all my insides rise to my throat. It was not just her story that caused my feeling of sickness, it was the way she was narrating it, the way she laughed and joked as she described the shocked expression on her friend's face when she opened the restaurant's back door. This friend was later brutally tortured and, because she didn't collaborate with the guards, executed. When the *tavvab* told me this, I charged to the washroom to throw up all the ugliness that I had just heard. I could not understand how she could live with herself, so untouched and carefree.

Another case that I will never forget was a *tavvab* that was asked to reveal the hiding place of her brother. She was tortured for several hours, and by the end of it, she was ready to tell them everything. The problem was that she didn't really know where her brother was. She solved the problem by telling the *pasdar*s that her mother would certainly know his whereabouts. They arrested and tortured the mother. She denied having any information about her son, but because her daughter kept insisting that she was lying, the mother continued to be beaten and tortured by the guards. The pain of torture had become so unbearable to the *tavvab* that she was willing to do anything to save herself from further flogging.

The *tavvab*s were sent to the cells and prison units to watch the prisoners closely and report back to the guards. They eavesdropped, lip-read, and formulated theories about the relationships between prisoners. They interpreted the simplest daily activities as forms of protest: reading the paper, laughing out loud, exercising, humming, sewing, or eating together. Worst of all, some *tavvab*s in Evin participated in the executions. To put the final seal of approval on their repentance, these *tavvab*s were asked to perform the last shot to the head after mass executions. I met a handful of such *tavvab*s who were proud of having had such an "honour."

Because the *tavvab*s were present in the wards all the time and there was no escape from them, they were worse than the guards. It was painful because they demonstrated to us how low each of us could potentially sink; they showed us the dark side of our own selves: the tendency to preserve our physical and emotional well-being at any cost. They reminded us that staying devoted and committed was not that easy, and that we would have to watch every small and big decision that we made: whether or not to buy fruit from the prison store, talk to someone who had just been tortured, or celebrate our New Year – *Nowrouz*. Life in Evin was a minute-by-minute trial, in which our various limits were consistently being tested: limits for bearing physical and emotional pain, loneliness, boredom, missing family and friends, hunger, lack of hygiene – the list goes on and on.

Life in Evin wasn't all ugliness, mind you. It also included friendships so beautiful and pure that they were enough to keep you going amidst the utmost inhumanity. Sacrificing a piece of bread, giving up sleeping space to a sick friend and sitting up all night to watch over her, sharing clothes, washing the clothes of a cellmate with tortured feet who couldn't walk, massaging someone's bruised feet, listening to a mother incessantly talk about the child from whom she'd been separated, carving a stone for a friend's birthday – there were times when we could easily forget where we were, when we could actually laugh and tell jokes, sing, or make up plays and then act them out. We could imagine families for ourselves, have mothers and sisters who were not our own, fall in love and create bonds so tight that years and bars and death could not cut or damage them. Among the lessons I learned during my five years in Evin, this was the only one that was beautiful. In prison, I made the best friends of my life, and not only that, met the best people I could ever imagine. I also met the worst people of my life in Evin, but no one said it was going to be all roses. If true friendship is what I got out of those five years, I believe it's a good price for my youth, my health, and for growing old too soon.

And the regime knew this very well. It was enough for the guards to hear about a close friendship; they would immediately take one of the friends away, either to another room or another prison. When the *tavvab*s would spread rumours about close friends having a homosexual relationship, the women in question were whipped in public a number of times. Homosexuality is an unforgivable sin in Islam. The prison authorities did everything in their power to cut the only tie that motivated us and kept us alive and strong.

I have said a lot about Evin, but there is still more. Evin was the house of torture. During the first days of arrest, prisoners were tortured, usually without exception. Of course, this was not called torture by the prison officials or *tavvab*s; it was called *ta'zir*. *Ta'zir* was flogging of the feet with very thick cables. First, the prisoner was tied to a bed. If it was a woman, she was covered with a blanket before being tied her up so that her body parts would not be revealed when she struggled hard under torture. This could arouse the male *pasdar*s who were beating her. How they could find a bruised, swollen, sweating body in inhumane pain sexually arousing is beyond my understanding. A dirty piece of cloth was shoved inside the prisoner's mouth to muffle cries of pain. Then, the prisoner was flogged on the soles of her feet, until she either passed out or was ready to confess. Sometimes, the torturers had an order from the interrogator for a certain amount of flogging, and stopped when they met the target.

After the flogging, the *pasdar*s made the prisoner walk on her painful feet. This was one of the worst kinds of pain, but it helped reduce the swelling, so the feet could be flogged again. We saw all sorts of feet after such torture, from mildly swollen to badly bruised to torn apart, a red blob of flesh and blood. In some cases, the prisoners had to undergo surgery to take skin from other parts of their body – such as the thighs – with which to patch the foot. Some prisoners lost a number of their toes as a result of the floggings.

Other kinds of torture included hanging prisoners from the ceiling for long hours, whipping the palms of prisoners' hands, and *qapaan*,[64] wherein a prisoner's hands were tied behind the back for hours. Prisoners who had experienced *qapaan* said that trying to bring their arms back to a normal position was excruciatingly painful. Beating, kicking and slapping were also quite ordinary occurrences that could be expected at any time.

Torture was not only physical. We could be interrogated in the same room where another prisoner was being flogged, or we could be kept in solitary confinement with no basic facilities. The prison authorities would arrange fake executions for us, or tell us lies about our families or friends both inside and outside prison: "Your brother died in a street shooting," or, "Your friend collaborated and confessed everything."

Executions were Evin's specialty. The main method of execution was via firing squad; less frequently, prisoners were hung. The names of prisoners from different units would be called in the early afternoon. When such groups of prisoners were about to leave, a deadly silence initially prevailed. Then, prisoners from other rooms would begin flooding the rooms of the summoned. These were incredible moments; we knew these people were going to die that very night, and yet they smiled and asked us not to cry. Some asked us to sing, some told us to be brave, and some just said goodbye in the most casual way and left. One element, however, was always the same: the summoned never panicked, seemed afraid, or regretted the way things had turned out for them. We would sing and slowly walk these people out of the unit, all of us crying but them.

I have many examples – and am sure each survivor of the Islamic Republic of Iran's prisons does – of unique individuals who went to their death with incredible strength. There was a mother who had been tortured extensively upon her arrest. Her son had been executed, and her daughter, also in prison, was a *tavvab*. Because of the extreme torture she had suffered in prison, she had to take numerous medications. The torture and the medications had seriously affected her hearing and her sight, so she wore very thick eyeglasses, without which she could only see vague colours and silhouettes. She had white hair, too white

---

64 *Qapaan* was a form of torture in the prisons. The hands are tied at the back in an awkward manner for long periods of time. It is very painful to bring the hands back to a normal position, and there is usually numbness which may or may not disappear.

for her age – she was only forty-five – which made her look even more motherly and kind. She couldn't see or hear us, but we communicated by writing on the palm of each other's hands. She was very good at this, but I wasn't. Over time, I gained more speed and skill in understanding her and writing to her. Because she had become deaf, she wasn't aware of how loud she could be when she spoke. Her voice would suddenly rise and everybody could hear what she was saying. This could be troublesome at times, if she was saying something about the *tavvab*s, her opinions, or her life story. That was why we tried to use the palm writing method most of the time. Eventually, the *tavvab*s began to react to this and said that the mother was influencing younger prisoners with her opinions, so this coping technique had to go underground as well.

The mother and I got closer to each other. I began to help her organize her things, wash her clothes, and wash herself. Because her entire body was scarred and bruised, she would get a cabin all to herself at bath time. I was with her, of course, since I was helping her. That was the only place where she and I were together unsupervised. I washed her quickly so that we could spend some time writing on the palms of each other's hands without fear of the *tavvab*s. This woman was undoubtedly one of the most amazing women of strength that I have ever met. She had not been sentenced, which was not a good sign in the Islamic regime's prisons. Prisoners with no sentence would either be released sometime in the future, or be executed. *Madar* Mehri[65] was one of the latter. She was aware of her fate, yet still radiated strength, faith and love.

The day she was taken for execution, I was looking for the spring of a friend's watch in the yard. They called her name to go to the prison clinic, but she somehow knew her time was up. Whenever prisoners were about to be executed, it came in the form of a call to the clinic, or a trip to the office with all of one's belongings. *Madar* Mehri's beautiful green eyes sparkled behind her thick glasses. She pressed my hand hard, smiled her gorgeous smile and said, "It's finally time. I'm going to finish what I started and thank God it's with dignity."

They took her and that night, we heard the shots as usual, and

---

65 As a sign of respect, mothers who were in prison were often called "Mother of" followed by the name of their son or daughter (e.g. *Madar-e* Ali, Mother of Ali). Sometimes "Mother" was followed by the woman's name (e.g. *Madar* Mehri).

counted them in deadly silence. First, there were a series of bullets, and then one by one, the last shots were made. It was these final shots in the head that we counted; they told us approximately how many executions had taken place that night.

Years later, when I was released from prison, I went to the *Behesht-e-Zahra* cemetery in Tehran, to the section for the executed prisoners. I wasn't looking for anyone in particular. I was just walking and reading the names on the tombstones, if there were any. *Pasdar*s did not leave us alone at the cemetery either; they marched back and forth to check on anyone who stood at a grave for one minute too long, and interrogated them: "Who is this person to you? Are you related? Say your prayers and leave." Suddenly, there she was, my *Madar* Mehri. She didn't even have a tombstone, just a mound of soil with a sign propped up on a stick that had her name, and date of birth and death on it. I forgot where I was; I started to yell and shout out her name, and my tears were endless.

Evin was a strange world, a world of people who put *Madar* Mehris in prison, and tortured and executed them. But, if it weren't for people like *Madar* Mehri, I would have lost my faith in humanity and myself much sooner, in the early years of my youth, before it had even fully blossomed.

My Trial

It had been more than a year since I was in the public ward. Day in, day out, the routine was more or less the same. One of the most depressing things in prison was not knowing how long our imprisonment would be. Moreover, we didn't even know when we would stand trial. There was no standard procedure or rule for that. We could not aim for anything or set any goals for our lives in any real sense, and this, in itself, emptied our lives of the meaning we needed in order to carry on. The future did not mean the same thing to us as it did the people outside prison. I had ceased to be able to visualize any future for myself beyond the bars. With the passage of time, normal life outside became more and more ghostly and unreal. Even in dreams, I always saw myself in prison.

The passage of time in prison is a strange and paradoxical thing. On one hand, it is so slow that you feel every second as it is passing by. Only a few people had watches and the rooms did not have clocks. Time seemed to pass in slow motion. Sometimes, I used to recreate the ticktock of a clock in my head and follow its rhythm for several minutes. This would give me a hypnotic feeling and take me away from the life around me. It would also create a sense of normality; to experience the passage of time is to believe you are alive and that life is going on. However, feeling time pass reminded me that *this* was now my life, and deep inside, I wanted it to pass more quickly. I was willing to give away days and years of my life as fast as possible, just to be happy that another day was over. One morning, we were still in bed – although you could hardly call the rough blankets beneath us beds – but hadn't got up yet. As we were silently looking at the ceiling and wondering what time it was, one of the prisoners with a sense of humour said, "My God! I used up all my energy yesterday to make my day end, and look: it's morning again." Yes, time really went by very slowly.

Because all of our days were relatively the same, it was hard to distinguish between the days of the week and the weeks of the month. Newspapers, TV, and nature told us what day and month it was, but the variety necessary to set them apart was missing. So, when we looked back at a month ago, it felt just like yesterday. This monotony blunted the feeling of time, and as a result, sometimes caused the illusion that time was passing more quickly.

It was on one of these monotonous days, when I had stopped waiting for trial or anything else that would create change, and was entrenched in prison routine, that my name was called for interrogation. I wore my black *chador* and used a scarf as a blindfold. I went out with a group of prisoners whose names had also been called. In the larger hallway upstairs, we had to wait again, and they separated us according to where we were headed. It was then that I realized I was going to have my trial.

I was not exactly happy, but I felt satisfied because a trial would give me some certainty, some control over my life. At least I would know how long I could expect to stay in prison if things ran their normal course and if an emergency did not arise. One always needed to leave some room for emergency in prison. Even if we had a sentence, something could happen in the society at large that would affect our fates in prison. A sentence could change at any time. Still, having a sentence was better than not having one, I decided.

After waiting for what seemed to be hours, I was taken into a room that was supposed to serve as the court. I was asked to remove my blindfold, which I did immediately. It took my eyes a while to get used to the light and actually see anything. What I saw was a room with only one desk and two chairs. The flag of the Islamic regime was up on the wall, and beneath it, sat a *mullah* dressed in black, from top to bottom. Everything about him was pitch black, from his turban and robe to his eyes, eyebrows, and beard. He was frowning and looking at me angrily. When our eyes met, he didn't lose one second, and said, "Sit down, you traitor!"

I took a few steps to the desk, and sat down, not knowing what to expect. I had not really expected an actual courtroom with a special stand in which to sit, or a lawyer to defend me. I was aware that the international rules and standards wouldn't mean anything in Evin, that the courtroom dramas I'd seen in movies and read of in books would not approximate my own experience. Despite all of this, I expected, in the very least, more than one person to judge me. Even a group of *pasdars* would have been better than having just one person there with me. A group would have represented different points of view and different personalities, which may have created an air of fairness – though deep inside, I knew that would have been a show, as well.

The *mullah* proceeded to read my charges. He started with "In the Name of God, the Compassionate, the Merciful," but there was no mercy in what he read, or in the way he read it. I could not believe my ears. It was as if he was talking about someone else since lots of the items did not even apply to me. Among the items on the long list was that I had been teaching karate in Tehran schools. All my life, I had been made fun of by my brother, cousins and friends, for not being fit and for getting low marks in physical education. I didn't know the basics of exercise, let alone karate. Another item on the list was that I had participated in all the demonstrations and events of the organization I supported, and that I was a main distributor of political pamphlets and newsletters in my region. There was no mentioning of how they had come to these conclusions, or any evidence except for the leaflets with which they had caught me.

I didn't interrupt him, maybe because of the courtroom movies I mentioned earlier. I thought that somewhere at the end, there would be time for me to defend myself and at least address the items that did not apply, so I waited patiently and listened.

When he came to the day of my arrest, he started to read out loud one of the leaflets I had been distributing. At first, he read each statement with a clown-like singsong tone. Then, when he came to the more direct slogans at the end of the leaflet, he lost the sarcastic tone, and got angrier and angrier. It was ironic to hear those slogans coming out of his mouth, slogans which I believed in so fervently. His face was blood red as he almost yelled, "Down with the bloodthirsty Islamic regime." He stopped and, in a voice muffled with anger, said, "A bunch of stupid well-to-do kids knowing nothing and trying to fight Islam and God… This is a regime supported by God. Who are you to wish for it to go down?" Without giving me a second to respond, he went on: "Will you do a TV interview and say that you repent from all these crimes?"

"My Dad would kill me if I appeared and spoke on TV," I replied. "I can't do that."

He got redder. "Where was your Dad when you distributed these leaflets in the streets? Why didn't he kill you then?"

"He didn't know."

مترجم رسمی زبان انگلیسی دادگستری جمهوری اسلامی ایران

تهران :

OFFICIAL TRANSLATION

EMBLEM
ISLAMIC REPUBLIC OF IRAN
JUSTICE ADMINISTRATION
TEHRAN PROVINCE JUSTICE ADMINISTRATION
  Penal Record Section

SEALED PHOTO OF HOLDER

Date:
Ref.:
Representative Book No.:

Certificate

According to records kept with Tehran Province Justice Administration

    Ms.

D/o   , holder of ID card No.   , issued from Tehran, born

in 1963, has penal conviction records of five years prisonment that

is ended and no civil disability (deprivation from Civil Rights)

pronounced in the writ.

Signed and Sealed:
Head of Admin. Dept.

TRUE TRANSLATION CERTIFIED

TM

The authenticity of the seal
Signature of the official translator
marked(x) is certified without any
consideration to the content

Translation of security clearance certificate needed to prove
persecution to Canadian immigration authorities..

The *mullah* continued. "What about the prison's closed circuit TV? Will you interview for that?"

I was trapped. "It would be the same. If he hears about it, I am history."

He grinned. "You are history anyways…What about an interview in front of other prisoners in the *Hosseynieh*?"

Again, I shook my head and replied that I didn't have the required public speaking ability.

He flushed with a fresh surge of anger and got up as if he couldn't contain his anger anymore. He tapped his paper with a pen and shouted, "Then just come and sign here! I'm not going to waste my time to ask if you will at least write that you are regretful, because I know what sort of creature I'm dealing with."

With shaking knees, I went forward, took the pen and signed under all those items that were not true. The situation was so absurd that I could only react to it in an equally absurd way. Would it make a difference if I had argued with him, asked for evidence, or requested time to defend myself? Did he even consider me a human being with all those rights, or just a "creature," as he'd put it earlier?

After I signed, he shouted at me coarsely, "Get lost! Get out of my sight before I beat the hell out of you!"

That was my trial, summed up in a few minutes. I left the room. As I was sitting in the hallway, waiting to be taken back to my ward, I thought about my trial. They had made up their mind about all of us, and the trials were mere formalities. I had heard about other prisoners' trials; they were more or less the same. The way we responded to the last question – whether we agreed to appear on TV to show our repentance and denounce our political beliefs – affected the result of the trial. And from the anger-swollen veins on the *mullah*'s neck, I knew that he wasn't happy with my response. I tried to return to the ward routine and forget about the trial and its result.

A week later, I was called for interrogation again. Most prisoners, especially those who already had their sentence, unanimously agreed that I was going to learn my sentence. This time, I didn't meet the *mullah* in black. They just called me to a room, and without asking me to take off my blindfold, gave me a small folded piece of paper that looked more like a drycleaner's receipt than a document that held my fate. I unfolded the paper and read my sentence: imprisonment for five years without any possibility of parole. Initially, I felt relieved, happy to at least have some certainty about the future. But by then, I had been in prison for a little over a year, and my sentence seemed like an eternity. How could I bear four more years of imprisonment? It was just the beginning. I realized that before my trial, as hopeless and indifferent as I seemed to be, I must have been nurturing some kind of hope, some unrealistic belief that I would, by some miracle, get out of prison. Now, I had a paper in hand that was formally telling me I was to stay there for at least four more years. My sentence gave me a sense of certainty and a kind of stability, but it also cut loose the narrow string of hope I didn't realize I'd been harbouring. My next challenge was how to break the news to my family, especially my mother. My mother had taken refuge in a dream of naive hopefulness: that I would be released if I were tried, that if they really looked at the evidence and what I had done, they would let me go and everything would be all right. Had it not been for this hope, she wouldn't have been able to get through her days and nights. I had a week of sleepless nights to reflect upon how to tell her about my sentence, that it was not a misunderstanding that had been cleared up, that she had to accept our current situation as an established one for at least four more years.

Egg Salad: Religious Minorities in Prison

Eighteen years later, in Canada, in the kitchen of our small apartment, I am making egg salad. A very simple and innocent task; one would normally perform it automatically, without any hesitation or mental challenge. The image of the eggs mixing with other ingredients, however, takes me back to the time I spent at Evin as a political prisoner of the Islamic Republic of Iran.

On Friday nights at Evin, our food was very predictable: hard-boiled eggs and potatoes, sometimes with a little butter. This plain food was very popular because many prisoners used it as an opportunity to feast with friends. They peeled the potatoes and eggs and mashed them with the tiny piece of butter, using the bottom of a plastic tumbler. Once the mixture was ready, four or five prisoners shared the food on one plate. In Iran, Fridays are the weekend. Even in prison where there was no work or school or leisure, Fridays were different from other days. To begin with, the interrogation building was closed for the day. All morning, the Friday Prayer ceremony that was held regularly in the University of Tehran was broadcast over the loudspeakers, and the prisoners had to observe silence and listen to the speeches and prayers. Every Friday, the atmosphere was gloomy and boring. The prison kitchen was also closed on this day, so the easiest food to prepare was eggs and potatoes. Prisoners celebrated the end of a depressing, monotonous day with the tidings of eggs, potatoes, and a food-sharing ceremony.

There was a time when none of my close friends were in the same cell as me. Then, the unit we were in was L-shaped, with cells – usually called rooms – along the hallways. The doors of the rooms were open, so we would take our share of eggs and potatoes out to the end of the hallway, mix it in one plate, and eat it together, laughing and joking the whole time. We called this our "Friday night party." There were five of us between seventeen and nineteen years of age. One of us was an Armenian Christian.[66] This made no difference to us. None of us was religious. We were all arrested for supporting communist

---

66 Armenian Christians have been a continuous presence in Persia-Iran since at least the 13th century.

opposition groups. Aida was just one of us. She was very humorous and made us laugh.

We enjoyed our Friday night parties for a few months, until one day, an announcement was made through the loudspeakers. The religious minorities – Christians and Jews mostly – were pronounced *najes*,[67] which means unclean in Islam. It is true that their religion is mentioned in the *Qur'an* and their prophets are respected by Moslems. But it is also an Islamic notion that if they touch anything with wet hands, that object becomes unclean, or *najes*, and should not be touched by a Moslem unless it is thoroughly rinsed with water.

At the beginning, like several other new rules in prison, we did not take it seriously. Aida still walked and talked with us, and we ate from the same plate. One day, Aida's room representative – a *tavvab* – told her that she should eat from a separate plate at all times, wash her plate and spoon separately, and keep them in a sealed plastic bag so as not to mix with dishes that belonged to Moslem prisoners.

Making egg salad at home in Canada eighteen years later, the sight of the mixture reminds me of Aida's face, shadowed as it was by utter bitterness.

She dragged herself up from the floor and went to the bathroom alone to wash her dishes. When she returned, she dried them slowly with a cloth, and then put them in a plastic bag which she tied tightly and placed at the far end of the shelf, far away from all the other plates and spoons.

Dirty dishes were washed by the day's workers after each meal. Prisoners had developed a schedule to take turns with chores – sweeping the floor, washing the dishes. So, each day, a certain group was responsible for these tasks. Aida, however, was only allowed to do "dry work," which meant sweeping and dusting. She wasn't allowed to participate in dishwashing, since her wet hands would make the dishes *najes*. From that day on, she was sentenced to a solitary life among so many people. She became a black sheep: always noticed, always seen, but never recognized.

We still continued to eat with Aida on Friday nights. These were the only nights that you could see light in Aida's eyes and a smile on her face. For a few minutes, she forgot all the ugliness that was surround-

---

67 *Najes* means religiously impure.

ing her, and took refuge in our world. But this did not last long. Soon we received warnings from the *tavvab*s and the prison office that if we continued to eat with Aida from the same plate, it meant that we were non-believers and would be considered *najes* just like other non-believers and non-Moslems. We still brought our food share to the hallway and mixed it all together on one plate, but we'd divide it and give Aida her share on a separate plate. Even though we were still eating together, the wholeness was ruined, the circle was broken. We felt that we had betrayed her, and she felt that she was putting us in danger. None of us could laugh and joke anymore, and the magic simply ceased to be there. Gradually, the Friday night dinners lost their appeal for our group. Aida lost her appetite, not only for eggs and potatoes, but for everything. She ate less and less. She was alone most of the time. She would lie down and hide her face under the blanket.

About two months later, Aida was taken to solitary confinement. In a way, it was very ironic, since she had already been forced to live in solitary confinement among four hundred prisoners for months. I wondered if it might be easier for her in solitary confinement – at least she would be the only black sheep, and her colour wouldn't matter.

Back in Canada, at home in the kitchen, I pour the egg salad into a container, and think of how deeply the prison memories are imprinted upon my whole existence. Nothing, no matter how ordinary, is simply what it seems. Everything can also be something else: egg salad can be just egg salad, but can also be a symbol of harmony and sharing and togetherness against all the odds. It can trigger the distressed face of Aida, a friend in prison, when she was treated like a leper.

The Executions

It was late in the afternoon. In our room, in one of the public wards of Evin, we had just finished our lunch and were spending our afternoon rather quietly. Some were talking, some were napping, and others were just thinking their own thoughts. In a corner, a few prisoners who had just been flogged on the soles of their feet had stretched out their legs and friends were massaging their bruised feet. The smell of the ointment they were using – *Dopal* – filled the room. It was pungent and strong.

The relative calmness of the afternoon was disturbed by the muffled crackling of the loudspeakers. Someone had picked up the microphone in the guards' office. An announcement was on the way. We perked up our ears in anticipation. What was up? Was someone going to be called for interrogation, clinic, or trial? The announcement was made: a series of prisoners' names were called, and they were told to leave the ward with all their belongings. Three of these prisoners were in our room.

A deadly silence took over the ward. A sequence of names called in this manner could mean one of the three things: a transfer to another prison, solitary confinement, or execution. The names that were called that day, without any doubt, were meant for the last. They were all prisoners who had had their trials, but no sentences had been given. Now, we all knew what their sentences were.

Everyone stopped what they were doing: those sleeping sat up, massagers stopped massaging, and walkers froze in the middle of their route. It was as if a spell had been cast upon everyone.

The first reaction came seconds later from Zari, one of the summoned prisoners who lived in our room. She got up, smiled, and looked at the picture of her little daughter that we had taped to the TV with a piece of dried date. In the middle of the room, she stood, arms crossed, and looked at us mischievously. "Give me a proper goodbye, all of you. I want to hug every single one of you."

The prisoners got up one by one, and encircled the three friends who had been called. A *tavvab* from outside the circle said, "Don't block the way. Let them take their stuff with them. The announcement said come with all your belongings." At least forty pairs of eyes turned furiously towards her. When prisoners were being taken for execution, the *tavvab*s wanted everything to be as eventless as possible. The *tavvab*s kept repeating that the prisoners weren't being taken for execution. They didn't want things to get out of hand, which could easily happen since these moments were loaded with the strongest of emotions: love and fury.

Who were the three prisoners in our room that were called that evening? Zari was the mother of an adorable one-year-old daughter. Since the day Zari came to our room, she planted love for this little girl in all of our hearts. Her daughter's picture was soon taped on the TV. Zari constantly talked about her daughter's words, habits, and physical features. Whenever Zari opened her mouth to say something, we joked with her and said, "What story are you going to tell us about your daughter this time?" She never talked about her husband, and we all understood why. He was not yet arrested and as such, needed to remain a mystery to us and to the prison officials. Zari had been arrested recently, and was not allowed to have visits with her family. The only connection she had to her daughter was the two pictures she'd had with her at the time of her arrest.

Amazingly, I saw a picture of Zari and her daughter many years later. I was watching a documentary about the execution of prisoners in Iranian prisons and the lives of those surviving family members who now lived outside Iran. One of the people interviewed was the daughter of an executed woman. A picture of Zari and her small daughter, the picture that was taped to the TV in our room, appeared on the screen. I couldn't believe my eyes. The small daughter in the picture was now an eighteen-year-old I had known for at least four years, without realizing she was Zari's daughter. She was the daughter of a good friend of mine, who, now remarried, had never met anyone who had seen Zari in prison. I was able to tell him about Zari's final days and moments!

Zari was very funny. She told us stories about the first week of her arrest, when she was being kept in another prison called *Comité 3000*, which was in fact the head office of all the *comité*s in Tehran. During that time, she had been in a cell with the mother of a famous Kurdish political leader. The Islamic regime hadn't been able to arrest the leader himself, but had managed to bring his old mother to prison. One of Zari's stories that I remember the most is about this mother. Zari told us how the woman did not know one word of Farsi and spoke Kurdish all the time. Although Zari didn't understand Kurdish, they had become friends and began to find a way to communicate. The mother was apparently arrested wearing her traditional Kurdish attire. The Kurdish pants are very large and loose. Since other prisoners in their cell did not have enough clothes, she tore up her pants and made three skirts for the three women in her cell. Zari showed us her skirt and, giggling, she said, "Imagine how big the pants were!" A few days before her execution, she divided whatever few belongings that she had among us, and that blue skirt became mine.

Jila was the second of the three summoned. She was seventeen, a beautiful, simple girl from the north of Iran. She had been arrested in Rasht, a large city in the north, where she'd been kept in a prison for a few months, and then tried. According to her, there were not many other prisoners there with her. Most of the time, she had been with one or two other prisoners in the cells. In her trial, she had defended her political party and beliefs wholeheartedly and without hesitation. She was sentenced to death. After her trial, they brought her to our public ward in Evin. There, she learned that other prisoners did not defend their beliefs in trials openly. They tried out other strategies because they knew that the Islamic regime could put an end to their lives as easily as killing a fly. Gradually, Jila talked to other prisoners in our room and realized alternative ways she could have behaved in court, but it was too late.

From Jila, we had learned a song in Gilaki.[68] You could see the blue of the sea in Jila's eyes. She was from a small city called Masouleh,[69] and the song she taught us was about this city. It told the story of a flood in the city and how it affected people's lives when it destroyed their houses. It ended with the hope that the Masouleh children would grow up and make a change in their primitive life conditions. She had taught us the words and their meaning, and it had become one of the songs we sang in our room.

The third woman was Shohreh, the only religious prisoner in our room at that time. Everyone else, except the *tavvab*s, was non-religious

---

68 Gilaki is spoken by Iranians living in the northern Iranian province of Gilan, on the Caspian Sea.
69 Masouleh is a picturesque village near the cities of Rasht and Fuman in northern Iran.

and arrested in connection to various communist parties. Shoreh had been brought to our room a short time before, with bandaged feet that were injured severely because of flogging. We massaged her feet often, and that had enabled her to take short walks in the room and even out in the hallway.

Shohreh didn't seem to feel lonely among us. She had a free spirit that did not bind her to one ideology or religion. In less than a month, we had come to accept and welcome her as one of our own. She was very secretive about her life, both inside and outside prison. I have learned that about most of the people who were eventually executed, especially those executed soon after their arrest. They didn't talk much, and if they did, it wasn't about themselves or their life outside. In some cases, it was because others involved in the same political activities had not yet been arrested, so keeping quiet protected them. Other times it was because others had been arrested along with them but were in other wards or prisons, and the guards did not know much about their connections and degrees of involvement in political activities. In prison, there were always secrets to keep, not only from the prison authorities and inter-rogators, but from other prisoners as well. You might have been able to trust other prisoners according to who they were at the moment, but you never knew what would happen in the long run.

We had come to know and love Zari, Jila, and Shohreh by the time their names were called that gloomy fall afternoon. It was a moment we had all been thinking of, but for which we'd never really prepared. It was a mystery to me: the way they felt when they knew what was going to happen, the thoughts that went on in their heads, and whether they were scared or not. These were not things you could ask a prisoner awaiting execution. From what I observed that day, there was no panic, no last minute pleas for life, and above all, no regrets. There sure was a lot in life they were going to miss, so many things they still had to see and taste and do. But the three of them were the first ones to stand up bravely that day, the first ones to shake our shocked selves back to conscious-ness and into the reality in front of us. They were the stronger ones, and yet, we were the ones who would keep on living.

It was very hard to come up with an appropriate way to react in such a situation. Cry? Put on a brave face? Act as if nothing was happening? Get carried away with the moment and express the full scope of emotions that were raging inside us? Or to think way beyond the present, and the consequences such a full expression of feelings would bring us?

Zari's invitation to give her a hug was a call for our numbed bodies to move. We took turns hugging the three of them and saying goodbye. In their ears, we whispered how strong they were and how much we admired their courage, while we wiped our tears and smiled. If they were agitated or scared, I didn't see any trace of it in their faces or behaviour. They were their usual selves, only stronger and more assertive, as if by stepping on the floors of the ward that day, they were making eternal footprints. We had no sense of time of day or year, no concept of where we were, no real understanding of our limitations. We had only a few minutes to draw every single positive characteristic out of the departing friends so that we could recall them in the tough days ahead, and take their stories with us everywhere we went.

I feared my turn to say goodbye; I didn't want the line to end. When it did, I wasn't prepared. Speechless and tearful, I hugged Zari first.

She touched my chin gently and said, "Cheer up, my young poet, you've got a lot to write about!"

My crying got worse, and I just let go of her. Now my shoulders were shaking, but I had no time to spare. I hugged Jila, not having the heart to look into her clear blue eyes, and then moved to Shohreh's arms. I wanted the moment to go on forever; I simultaneously wanted it to end immediately. My heart was exploding with emotions I had never known before.

Once everyone in the room had said goodbye, Jila said, "Now it's time for our room's National Anthem – sing it for us."

That request was the final blow. Over the past few months, we had started to sing, either one by one or as a group. Singing had become a favourite pastime, filling our long nights with excitement and inspiration. Obviously, we could not sing any songs that were overtly political or connected to certain groups or ideologies. But there were certain songs that we had chosen to sing. These were usually classic songs that talked about nature and love and people – those that talked about spring coming and buds sprouting and flowers blooming, about an end to winter, about better times, reaching for the stars, or dreams. Something in those songs had to possess the essence of purity and honesty for us to choose to sing them in prison; those were the qualities that we most needed to feel. It was no surprise, then, that some of these songs turned out to be children's songs: pure, simple and innocent. One of these songs, funny and light, had, over time, become known as our room's "National Anthem." It didn't have any serious uplifting message; it told the story of a naughty child, a greedy child who wanted everything she saw, asked for too much food, had no table manners, slurped her soup, wiped her dirty hands on her dress, and wet her bed. While we sang, we made funny faces and laughed out loud. It was comic relief for us, something that made laughing possible when there was not much to laugh about. We sang it to lift our spirits when all else failed, when there was nothing rational or serious or sensible that could make us feel better. In exactly such a moment, Jila had asked us to sing it.

But how could we? How could we sing such a light, meaningless tune at the time of death and loss? What kind of a request was that? We all shook our heads no, but Jila was disappointed: "But this is my real request. Isn't that important? I do want to hear it one last time." In the moment, we realized they were still alive, and we would not mourn their deaths before they actually happened. We could not stop what lay ahead of them, and in the very least, owed them a last token of life and laughter. Somehow the song began, and we all joined in with full force. Tears occasionally interrupted the clarity of words, but we were singing nevertheless. Once we started, it all made so much sense. What else could explain the rationale behind what was happening? What serious conversation could have made it easier to bear? It was a response to an abnormal situation. Years later, in Dr. Victor Frankl's book, *Man's Search for Meaning*, I read that an abnormal reaction to an abnormal situation is considered quite normal, psychologically.

When we finished singing the song, we moved on to *Masouleh* – Jila's song – and then another. We had come out of our room and were moving along the hallway. Other rooms were having their own farewells and stepping out, and in a short time, all the prisoners in the rooms were together, strong, marching towards the main exit of the ward, seeing off the departing friends. It looked and felt so much like a demonstration: everyone marching along with a common purpose and a feeling that united them. The atmosphere was emotionally charged, ready to erupt in fire. Other rooms joined in our singing.

When we reached the main exit, we stopped. Those who were leaving turned back towards us and took a long, meaningful glance at our crowd. For a split second, we stopped singing and breathing. Then suddenly, someone in the crowd started to sing the *Internationale*. This was a different song; it wasn't one to sing aloud in prison. It was the song that communists and socialists around the world sang for the unity of the proletariat of the world, in the hopes of a final battle that would end in international peace and the liberation of mankind. Singing such a song would definitely have serious and grave consequences.

We didn't know who started it. It began as a feeble, unnoticeable voice, and then got stronger and stronger. We all forgot where we were. and, heedless of the consequences, felt solidarity wrap itself around us, a warm blanket. It was a short-lived victory, a bold declaration of our beliefs in the most unusual of circumstances. It was also a most powerful act to be part of, an act that defied death and suffering.

The guards had obviously heard us. We heard several footsteps running towards the ward, and furious swearing. The main door was immediately opened and the first row of prisoners was pulled out of the ward violently. "Stop singing. Shut up! What do you think you are doing? This is prison; we'll make you understand that." And they pulled the summoned prisoners out.

As calm as a gentle breeze, each of the prisoners looked back once more at us, and we could see the sparkle in the eyes that told us the *Internationale* had done its job for them, and that was all that mattered. We didn't know that the next day, large groups of inmates would be called for interrogation and severe flogging because of singing the *Internationale*. A moment like this never happened again, but as long as I live, I will remember the power and strength in the prison hallways when we were singing that song to our friends for the last time.

That night, as we were lying down on our black, coarse army blankets, staring at the ceiling, waiting in vain for sleep to come, we heard the executions. First it was a series of shots that tore into the silence of the night. We all sat up instantly. We knew it was our friends' end. Then, one by one, single shots were heard, those final shots in the head to make sure they were all dead: Zari, Jila, Shohreh, all gone in a matter of a few seconds. As the final shots were fired, prisoners counted: one, two, three, four… That night, there were fifteen executions. One of the prisoners, Zari's closest friend, began to bang her head on the wall, not in a hysterical, out-of-control way, but in the manner of a mourning ritual. I found myself banging my head with the same rhythm, along with her. Somehow it made their lives echo through the night and in my head; I felt I had something to do, that I wasn't helpless. As more and more cellmates joined in, I closed my eyes and continued to bang my head on the wall, fifteen times.

My Family and the Dark Years

My mother's eyes had finally closed after a strong shot of tranquilizer. For a whole week, she had been sitting on the chair by the phone. Since the day of my arrest, she had refused to go to bed, and had sat on that chair all the time, in hopes of hearing from, or of, me. She had no response for those who told her she was accomplishing nothing sitting there and refusing to go to bed; she just felt she had to stay there, awake and alert, to be there to take any possible calls with news about me.

It had been a few months since I had left home and by the time I got arrested, I was staying with my relatives. It all happened after an anonymous, mysterious phone call which I answered myself. We never knew who made that call. The caller's voice was husky, and obviously disguised. It reminded me of the scary voices I had heard in thriller movies. I couldn't tell the caller's gender or age. The message was short and clear: our home was under surveillance and was not considered a safe place for me anymore, and that I should leave. Following that phone call, my family became obsessed with my staying at home. My mom began to burn every book that might arouse suspicion, and every pamphlet or newsletter that could be linked to a political party. She started to notice and trace every unidentified noise, and jumped up with every ring of the doorbell. Eventually, she could not bear to live under the constant threat and fear of my arrest. She could not sleep well at night and got severe migraine headaches during the day. For a while, I stopped my political activities, which included distributing newsletters and leaflets and attending small group meetings to discuss our party's political points of view. My friends and teammates thought it wise for me to take it easy until the upset of the phone call wore away and things got back to normal.

On the day of my arrest, I was at my aunt's house. That my mother had not been able to see me one last time that day bothered her immensely. After my arrest, she started to blame herself, thinking if she hadn't insisted on me leaving the house, I might still be safe at home. She saw my arrest as inevitable in a sense because she could not stop me from being involved in anti-government activities. However, she regretted the days she had not spent with me, the days she had sent me away in an unsuccessful effort to protect me.

When my aunt told her that I hadn't returned to home in the evening, everyone started to search frantically for me, at friends' places, in hospital emergency rooms. There was no trace of me anywhere. Somehow they knew what had happened, but they needed confirmation and more details. Some of my friends called to inform my family that I had been distributing leaflets that day, that I had probably been arrested, that no one knew where I was. After all the phone numbers in my phone book had been tried and every possible route checked out, my mom sat in the same chair, day and night, keeping vigil beside the phone.

When the phone rang suddenly late in the evening of the eighth day, my mother, under the spell of a tranquilizer and only a few hours of sleep, fell off the chair. Despite the drowsiness that invited her body to relax and go back to sleep, she groped for the phone, her body still partly on the floor. Her voice was full of expectation. "Hello?"

Someone confirmed our family name and phone number with her, and asked if she knew me.

Her limbs went numb. She shouted, "Yes, she's my child. What happened? Where is she?"

The message was short, but its resonance went on forever in my mom's head. She felt the whole world collapse on her, as the voice said, "Come and take her body. She was executed tonight," and hung up. The phone fell out of my mom's hand, and she passed out.

Our house was full. Almost all of the family was there, trying to make phone calls, say a comforting word. Some were out on a mission to find a way to verify the call's authenticity. One of the ways to do this was to check the morgues for my body. My parents were in no state to investigate anything; all they could think was that their youngest child had been taken away from them in a matter of a few days. My mom went over the details of the call again and again, and each time, it seemed less and less real; it made no sense. Why would the caller ask them to go and get their child's body without telling them where to go? Why would the caller remain anonymous? Everyday, the names of the executed prisoners came out in the national newspapers. Killing the "anarchists" and "terrorists," as they called political prisoners, was the Islamic regime's joy and pride.

The secrecy present in the phone call had aroused some doubt among my family members and with it, a faint flicker of hope. Maybe I had not been executed after all; maybe the call was fake. But what kind of a person would do such a thing? What purpose could be served in telling parents that their child was dead? Later on, we heard that such calls were being made to the families of other prisoners as well. We never found out who made these calls or why. Was it part of the psychological torture, extended even as far as prisoners' families? I sometimes wonder what would have happened if someone in my family had had a heart attack when they heard this news.

My family gathered and began to brainstorm. They wanted to find someone who knew people in the system, who could verify the news of my execution. Everyone put together their networks of people and from that pool, they found a guard that had once received a favour from someone in the family. He was contacted immediately. He called his connections and could come up only with the fact that my name had not been on Evin's list of the executed prisoners that night. As uncertain as the news was, it was still a glimmer of hope for my family. Now they had to search and find out where I was. My mom was scared to return to the chair by the phone so she started to go through the motions of the day, trying to find other ways to connect to me. Eventually, my family found out, through the same acquaintance-guard, that I was in Evin.

The first days were the most difficult ones. Early on, my sister decided to hide all her feelings in order to help my parents get through the pain. Obviously, she saw that if she gave up, there would be no one to hold things together. Her strength, pure honesty and sincerity, and her uniqueness, had always inspired me. It's from her that I've learned a lot of my lessons: to follow a cause and feel it to the marrow of my bones, and to be ready to pay the price with my soul and body; to cut down the pretences and empty words, and go after what I believed in without fear of consequence. She had a unique sense of humour, too, and knew exactly when and how to use it. Even in the darkest of moments, she could see something to laugh about. Years later, on the day of our first and only face-to-face visit in prison, her sense of humour showed itself in a conversation with a prison bus driver. My family had had a hard day. Initially, they had been told that the visiting time was over and they wouldn't be allowed to see me. Then, after a series of negotiations led by my sister, my family and the rest of the families that had been denied visits were given permission. When they got on the bus that would take them to the visiting area, my sister looked for a seat and found none. She was exhausted, so she sat on the edge of the bump at the right side of the driver. This is a common practice on minibuses in Tehran's public transit system: when there are no seats left, it is okay to sit on the bump.

When the driver opened the door to get on, he saw her and rolled his eyes. "I won't be driving this bus," he said.

All the families protested in frustration, "Why?"

"Well, I don't want to sit beside *her*!" The driver was referring to the fact that a Moslem man cannot sit that close to a woman.

My sister was beyond herself, and said, "Really? I'm surprised. Haven't you received the love letters I sent you? Didn't the letters say that I am *dying* to sit beside you?!"

Giggles filled the bus and the atmosphere shifted. The driver swore under his breath, got on and, without a word, started to drive.

Despite my sister's efforts to hide her stress, my arrest struck her very hard. Each day, she summoned all her courage to inject hope and power in my parents' veins. She pulled my mom out of the list-less cocoon she'd been gradually building around herself, a cocoon that prevented her from seeing and being seen, somewhere she could live with numbed feelings. My sister took my mom out shopping to buy me books, clothes, and all sorts of gifts. It gave them a sense of connected-ness to me; as long as they bought me things, they could still believe that I was alive and expect me to return home to them. During the day, my sister did not cry or break down. But at night, when she stared at the darkened shapes of the room, trying to sleep and forget, the only image she could see was that of someone being ruthlessly beaten and tortured. She'd jump up covered in sweat, unable to go back to sleep, afraid to close her eyes again.

My mom began to knit for me. When I came out of prison, I had a closet full of colourful sweaters that she had knitted for me over the years. In another attempt to reach out to me, she started to write to me in a small journal, day after day. Since the day she gave this journal to me after my release, I have not been able to read it without bursting into tears. I don't have the heart to read the narrative of her tortured soul during those years. Day by day, it is a journey of poetic word: my birth-days, my childhood, remembering the red coat I had when I first started school, the dark anniversary of my arrest, the cycle of nature and seasons without me. It moves from tears and pain and hopelessness, to anger and rebellion, to the rekindling of and its consistent dissipation. Through this notebook, I can feel the sharp pangs of pain that pierced her soul, the roller coaster she rode for five years.

In the first winter, she writes: "Today it's snowing. When I looked out the window, tears rushed to my eyes and poured down my face. I remembered how you loved to walk in the snow, and that you can't do that now. I thought to myself, 'What can I do to make her feel the snow under her feet?' And then, without giving it a second thought, I went out in the snow, and walked for two hours. I must have looked like a mad woman to any observer. All the time, I keep thinking that if I do the things you like to do, it may somehow get to you; you may feel it, too, and even if you don't, it makes this painful feeling of guilt in me subside a bit. Because I feel guilty that you're in and I'm out, that you are so young and innocent and imprisoned, and I'm middle-aged and free, that you can't go wherever you want and I can, that I was the one supposed to protect you and I failed. I wonder, where did you get all this power and courage? Please teach me some of it."

When my family finally found out where I was, it was forty days before I was allowed to have a visit with them, from behind the glass, over a phone. Our visits were usually twice a month, and I could only see my parents; no other family member was allowed. I did not get to see my sister for over four years, until they allowed us to have a face-to-face visit with sisters and brothers present.

My mom and dad behaved quite differently in the visits. My dad kept his sad, desperate look trained upon me at all times, and whenever he got on the phone to talk to me, his voice broke with tears after just a few words and he could not continue. He frequently said that talking to me was very challenging for him and the surge of emotions he felt in the moment did not let him speak. He sometimes told me about his dreams. Whenever I was very sick or in pain, he saw it in his dreams. I remember once, I had an infected tooth that was painfully pulled out. I had gone through a very hard time before and after the procedure. During our first visit after this, my dad got on the phone and told me that he had seen me in his dream, lying down on a surgery bed, that a doctor had pulled out both my eyes and I had shouted out in pain. That was all he could say, before his sadness took over and he had to pass the phone to my mom. He had a strange affiliation with any physical pain that I suffered.

My mom was different. She cried sometimes, but tried to use the few minutes we had together as best she could. She gave me news of family and friends. She told me about those friends who had left the country and were now safe, so I could relax and not worry about the possibility of their arrests. She asked me how I spent my days, my time, the seasons. She wanted to know if I was warm enough, had sufficient clothing and money, if I felt lonely often. She asked me about the things I needed and the things she could do for me. During those five years, some of the things my family did and the effects they had on me are really worth mentioning.

One of the things that filled our monotonous, empty, strict, bitter days was to keep busy with various crafts: embroidery, sewing, making small gifts out of paper, carving stones or date pits. Of course, these activities were totally prohibited by the prison guards. They believed any involvement in such crafts would take our minds away from prayer, reflection, God and the Hereafter, and the instructional religious programs on the closed-circuit TV. Every now and then, the guards stormed the public ward, sent us out into the yard, and rummaged frantically through our belongings, looking for handicrafts. What they took with them was always a piece of carved stone, a drawing, a poem, or an embroidered piece of cloth.

We loved to make these crafts and we needed materials. Our resources, however, were limited; we drew colourful threads from our towels and undid our old socks to use the thread. But we needed more. Once, I had a plan to embroider a piece for a friend's birthday, and I needed bright, colourful embroidery thread to do it. One night, when I was thinking about everything and nothing in particular, just to help me fall asleep, I had an idea. During our next visit, I told my mom that I needed some thread. I had to say it indirectly, in a way that only she understood, and she nodded to let me know she had got the message. At our next visit, she said, "I have sent you some clothes this time. There is a skirt there, too. I wasn't sure if it is the right length, though – I had to estimate. Check it out; you could adjust the hem if they let you use needles." Back in the ward, I went straight to the skirt: a huge braid of silky, colourful embroidery thread ran all the way through the hem of the skirt. All I had to do was to take it out and hide it somewhere safe.

Another time, we were planning to make a blue prayer mat for a friend who loved the colour blue. She had always wondered how good it must feel to pray under the blue of the sky, to feel its vastness above your head and bow down to it. To make the prayer mat, we needed a blue piece of cloth, which was a total luxury in prison. So I went back to my mom, wondering how she would manage it this time. My next bag of clothing included a large, square piece of sky-blue cloth loosely sewn to look like a skirt. In those days, these seemingly small things were great sources of joy and pleasure. Apart from providing me with the means to keep busy in a meaningful way, they were signs that the domain of the enemy was not as invulnerable as it seemed. We could still get some of the things we wanted despite the walls and bars and weapons. The embroidery thread and blue fabric in my hand told me that even though we looked captured and trapped, there were ways to conquer the enemy.

My family made other impressions on my prison life as well. One of these moments relates back to a time when I had been separated from very close friends. These friends had either been transferred to other prisons or released. Whenever two or more prisoners got close to one another, they were separated; this was a very frequent occurrence. Even while we were in the process of making friends, we knew very well that it was not going to last long. Knowing that, however, did not stop us from reaching out to each other. That was about the most vital and powerful tool we had to preserve our strength. We kept making new friends and bonding in ways that people in ordinary circumstances would not truly understand, and the guards kept separating us.

During one of these experiences, my mom asked me, at a visit, why I looked so sad. I told her casually that my only friend had been taken to another prison. She reflected on this for only a few seconds and then nodded. At the end of the visit, just as casually as I had expressed my sorrow to her, she said, "You can write one of your letters to your sister, you know, it would be a nice way to show her you are still close to her," and smiled knowingly. I got it there and then; she was suggesting I write a letter to my friend.

We were allowed to write a short letter to our family – only parents, siblings, spouse and children – once a month. The letter was to be no longer than five lines, so we usually wrote in the smallest handwriting that we could manage. My plan was to write a letter addressed to "my

Letters from prison.

sister." Then, my mom would contact my friend's family and give them the letter. In turn, her parents would copy the contents of my letter on the letter form they were sending their daughter, and during a family visit, let her know that the letter was actually from me. She would be able to write me back a letter addressed to her family. The letter would then travel to my parents, and get copied down on a letter addressed to me. Exchanging letters from prison to prison was an achievement I could not even have dreamed of before.

This kind of communication drew families closer to one another too. On the mornings of each visit, they gathered in the parking lot of Luna Park, an amusement park very close to Evin Prison. The families lined up and waited for their turn. The visits took place in alphabetical order. As each family's turn came, they were told if their prisoner was still alive or had been executed. Each time, families had to go through the same experience, oscillating between life and death, hope and despair. While they waited, they made friends. If they found out that their prisoners were close friends, they felt closer to each other, and began to communicate beyond the usual small talk. They supported each other by offering rides or words of comfort. When some families got the news of a prisoner's execution, the other families were there to support them. During this once-a-month ritual, and all the time in between, our families lived in the space between fear and hope.

During another period of time wherein I had been separated from a close friend, it so happened that my family did not show up to visit me on the scheduled day. Names were called, but mine was not on the list. This had never happened before, and it brought all sorts of upsetting thoughts to my mind. Had anything happened to anyone? Were they all right? That night was restless and long. The next day, at around noon, my name was called for a visit. It was a shocking surprise because that was the visit day for another ward – the ward to which my departed friend had been taken. It was then that I knew what was going on: my parents had deliberately missed the visiting day for our ward, and showed up the next day. Meanwhile, they had made arrangements to attend the visiting day with my friend's family. They told the guards that because they had not been feeling well, they had missed their visit. Would the guards please let them see me with the other ward? The guards had let them in.

In the corridor, I was lined up with the other ward's prisoners, and there, I heard my friend's name called. Quickly, in a moment of risk, fear, and anticipation, I changed my spot in the line and stood behind her. I squeezed her arm and said hello. Because we took off our blindfolds during visits, I got to see her face. I was even able to talk to her in

Letters in purse made in prison.

brief intervals. This particular experience was the best gift that my family could have given me during those hard times.

These were gifts, favours, and extras, but there is one thing my family provided for me that stands above all the rest: the values and beliefs they instilled in me over the years, the pool from which I unconsciously drew to remain a good human being.

From my mother, I received the spark and love of life, the unconditional love that embraces all, the talent to easily make friends and not expect too much from them, the ability to beautify ugliness and thus be able to tolerate it. I decorated my cell with cushions to make it look a bit more like home. From my sister, I learned to fight, to go head-to-head with whatever stands in my way, to not ever give up, to keep my values no matter what, to be true to myself and others. I learned to keep going and learning and achieving, to reach for the stars. From my father, I learned to compromise, to assess situations, be cautious if necessary, to not bang my head against the wall if it is only going to hurt, to withdraw when needed, to not trust everyone, to keep myself from harm whenever possible.

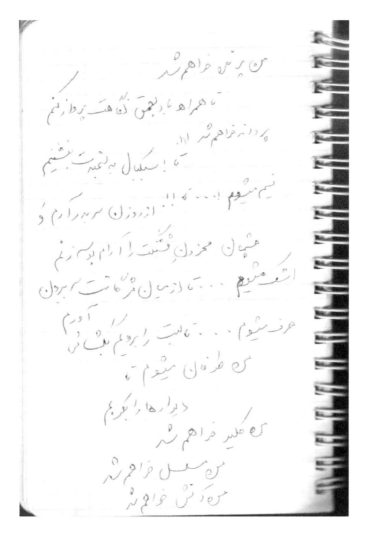

Original of the poem in Shadi's mother's "little notebook."

Sometimes, when I think about what happened to us and our families, I clearly see the depth of the harm it has done. The scale and scope of the arrests in those years was so great that it affected a vast majority of the population. Every family either had someone in prison, or knew someone who did. But truly, who suffered more? We prisoners, or our families? That is a question I have asked myself many times.

During the five years I was in prison, I observed the gradual fracturing of my family. My mom and dad starting to blame each other for the way things had turned out for me. My dad began to look to other sources of consolation for his deep, unbearable pain. My mom developed a serious heart disease that resulted in open-heart surgery. My sister had chronic nervousness and feelings of instability and uncertainty. Trying to go on despite their child's pain, my parents trod a thin line between life and death for years. They tried to hold things together, but with every effort, they lost strength.

When I finally returned to them, I found that some wounds healed, but others haven't. All of the scars are still there. There are certain depths of pain that, once experienced, transform people forever. During those Evin years, my family experienced a range of emotions through which they otherwise wouldn't have gone, extreme emotions that kept them consistently on edge for a very long time. I can still see the harm that this experience has effected upon all of my family members.

Towards the end of my mother's little journal, during her fifth winter away from me, she writes:

I will be a bird
and fly in the direction of your glance.
I will be a breeze,
and kiss your sleepy face.
I will be a tear,
and wash your grief through your eyelashes.
I will be words,
so you open your mouth for me.
I will be a storm,
and break down the walls.
I will be a key, a gun, a flame of fire.

I will open,
I will fire,
I will burn down the walls,
down to the last brick.

Friendships in Prison: Lost and Found

In the hallway, someone called out *"Jadidi!"* The call blew fresh breath into everyone's soul. Ward newcomers were not necessarily newly arrested. They might have been in prison much longer than any of us. But the fact that they were new, that they came from the world beyond the yellow iron bars of our ward, was enough to make them important, the centre of attention. They came with news of other friends, other forms of punishment, different rules and regulations, other prisons. It broke the monotony of our lives.

The appearance of these newcomers coincided with a particularly difficult time in my life. For a while, I had been through a critical time in terms of my beliefs. Deep inside, I had been ruthlessly questioning my philosophical, ideological, and political beliefs. I did not dare talk about it to anyone. If I did, I would have risked being viewed by other prisoners, even my friends, as "unreliable," and maybe at the early stages of becoming a *tavvab*. At least, that was what I thought at the time. All day long, I put my belief system on trial, attacking it with the unsettling questions that troubled me. With disbelief, I saw that it was unable to defend itself. In prison, it was crucial for me to have a strong system of values and beliefs, and feeling its instability was beyond my tolerance. Frequently, I woke in the middle of the night thinking, "What if God does exist? What if I die and realize there is a God? What if I die this very minute?" The idea did not appear improbable or ridiculous to me at all. Death was a highly probable occurrence, and its possibility brought thoughts of "afterlife." At other times, I felt extremely lonely; the presence of even my closest friends did not help mitigate the loneliness. My internal world had become a gigantic, dark hole that was swallowing me. The ground under my feet, once solid, was caving in, bit by bit. It was in this context of inner turmoil that the newcomers came to our ward.

To avoid the unrest that prevailed every time we had new prisoners in the ward, the guards ordered that we stay in our rooms for an hour. Although our doors were open, we weren't allowed to go into the hallways or other rooms until the *jadidis* had settled in their rooms and the commotion had fizzled out. As I was watching the news on TV, I craned my neck to see far down the hallway. All I saw was a rush of unfamiliar faces. They were each given a cell number. None stopped at our cell door. I tried to take in as many faces as I could, hoping to see someone familiar. Several newcomers had been sent to our adjacent cell, Cell Six, where two of my closest friends resided. I decided to pay them a visit and take a glance at their cell's *jadidis*.

The newcomers in Cell Six were clearly supporters of the *Mojahedin* Organization, and I didn't know any of them. One by one, I surveyed their faces. I looked a bit longer at a girl with olive skin and very straight black hair, so straight it showed the unevenness of an amateur cut. Did she look familiar in any way? Did she remind me of anybody? I just shrugged my shoulders, said goodnight to my friends and left Cell Six.

Days went by. The newcomers were not that new any more. Names had been put to faces and physical descriptions. The girl with straight black hair was Bita. She was considerably smaller and shorter than me, but the toughness of her features made up for her small stature. She looked invincible, unreachable, and detached. There was a certain kind of seriousness in her face that attracted attention, not only mine, but that of several other prisoners as well. I heard her name come up in a number of conversations. My friend and cellmate, Sanaz, talked about Bita a lot. Bita had a close friend; they had arrived at our ward at the same time. They ate together, walked together, and washed their clothes together; strangely enough, they looked alike to a great degree. There was one unconventional fact about their friendship that attracted gossip and in my case, admiration. Bita's friend, Homa, was a communist. Despite their different ideologies and values, Bita and Homa seemed to get along well, and this was a major part of Bita's appeal for me.

One morning, before breakfast, Sanaz came to me excited. "I had a strange dream last night. I dreamt of Bita. I should go tell her."

"But what are you going to tell her? You don't even say hi to her. Are you just going to go to her and say, 'I saw you in my dream,' out of the blue?"

"What's wrong with that? I should start saying hi to her someday. That could be today." She walked away from me, towards Cell Six.

For a second, I doubted that Sanaz had actually had the dream, and wondered if this was just an excuse to make friends with Bita. Sanaz was always attracted to unconventional people. If there was someone we were forbidden to talk to, who was badly beaten and tortured, or who boldly spoke her mind, Sanaz would start spending most of her time with that person. She wouldn't pay attention to all the warnings and threatening looks of *tavvab*s because she believed that hers was a politically insignificant case herself, and that there was no need to worry. She did not support any opposition group in any way. She had been arrested only because she had a friend who was connected to *Mojahedin*, and that friend had used Sanaz's office phone for her organization's business a couple of times. Sanaz believed her innocence gave her freedom to behave as she wanted. This was hardly true, though. The *tavvab*s were always on the watch, waiting for the right time to strike.

I saw Sanaz disappear at the threshold of Cell Six, and ran after her. I couldn't let her keep up her pattern of behaviour. I caught her elbow and pulled her back forcefully. "What do you think you are doing? Please don't do this again, Sanaz. You are still under the close surveillance of the *tavvab*s because of your friendship with Mana." Mana was another *mojahed*[70] who was in very bad shape as a result of massive torture. Her kidneys had stopped working and she had to be taken out of the prison regularly for dialysis. The *tavvab*s were on her case all the time, and anyone who spoke to Mana put herself in great danger. Sanaz visited her frequently and recited poems to her. When the *tavvab*s warned Sanaz, she said, "But she is very sick. I just go visit her, that's all!"

Sanaz ignored what I said and pulled my hand, taking me with her, and in no time, there I was, standing right in front of Bita, while Sanaz babbled about her dream. Bita smiled. If she was surprised, she managed to hide it very well. Sanaz had walked into the private space Bita had built around herself since her arrival. I felt embarrassed to be part of the scheme. I had always respected people's privacy, and I felt bad to be breaking into hers uninvited. I just wanted the awkward moment to end. When it did, I walked out of Cell Six as fast as I could; Sanaz trailed happily behind me. She was thrilled that she had opened up an opportunity to talk to Bita, that she'd broken the barrier between stranger and acquaintance.

In the days that followed, whenever I saw Bita in the hallways or

---

70 A *mojahed* is a member of the *Mojahedin-e Khalq* Organization. The *Mojahedin* were an Islamic opposition group during the Shah's time and at first supported the Islamic revolution. The organization was sidelined when the religious clergy took over the revolution and gradually began to limit freedom of expression and the activities of all political opponents.

the yard, we acknowledged each other with a smile and a quick hello. For some strange reason, I was conscious of her when she was around. When she was not, I caught myself looking for her. I, too, had become curious to get to know Bita. She was with Homa all the time, so the idea of taking a walk with her was out of the question, and I couldn't think of any other way to start a conversation with her.

One day, however, I was lining up for the washroom and I saw Bita a few places ahead of me. Being far along in the washroom queue was a big advantage. We had six washrooms for about three hundred prisoners, and there was always a long wait time. Despite the advantage of being at least half an hour ahead of me in the queue, Bita left her place and came towards me.

I couldn't hide my surprise and said, "What did you do that for? You just lost at least half an hour."

She shrugged nonchalantly. "Not in a hurry! How are you doing?"

"I'm fine. Getting by, really. How are you?" I didn't know what to say, and the awkwardness showed itself in my clumsy response.

She didn't let me suffer for long. She began asking me questions, one after the other, about how I spent my days, what I liked to do, whether I enjoyed walking, and so on. There was no particular point, she was just attempting to make conversation. I truly appreciated her effort that day. She started a different kind of communication between us. Before then, there had been something between us that neither of us could identify: curiosity, affinity, some kind of chemistry. After Bita's initial attempt, we began to talk and try to understand this feeling better. We did not, however, discuss it directly – far from it. In fact, it wasn't until we were out of prison seven years later that the feeling and what happened between was discussed openly. But when we talked about ordinary things, each of us – alone – began to question, analyze, and examine the nagging feeling more seriously.

That day marked a new era in the friendship that followed: we were seen together in the yard more often, and we often sat down in a corner in the hallway and had long conversations. We came to enjoy each other's company a lot. For me, Bita was a stark opposite to my own personality, especially emotionally. Most of the time, she was deep inside herself. Even when it was obvious that she was making a great effort to express herself, it took a lot of work to get it out clearly. I, on the other hand, have always found it natural and easy to express my innermost feelings and thoughts. To me, self-expression often feels like pouring a liquid into a different container, giving it enough flexibility so it can flow easily into this new space and make itself at home. I rarely worry about the consequences of such self-disclosures, and see them as efforts to relate and reach out to other souls.

For Bita, it was a totally different story. It was as if she didn't even let herself feel her feelings freely, let alone talk about them.

After more careful consideration, I know now what Bita's major attraction was for me back then. As a nineteen-year-old, I, like many others in my generation, had a huge amount of passion and energy to bestow on life. I had embraced a national – or more accurately, universal – cause with all my being, and would not let a single drop of my energy dissipate. Life in prison had little stimulation or variety, and could hardly accommodate such power and passion. Therefore, when a challenge presented itself, even in the most unfathomable shape, instead of running away from it, I felt strangely drawn to it. Bita offered me such a challenge. I also liked the fact that her best friend was a communist, and now she was making friends with me, another supporter of a communist group. She seemed to be very dedicated to her religious beliefs and practices; however, she had chosen to spend most of her time with non-religious people, and that puzzled and attracted me.

I am not sure what attracted Bita to me, but at the time, I had worked out an explanation for myself. She apparently enjoyed my expressiveness, my openness, the easy way I talked about myself. She also seemed to enjoy my love of poetry and writing. She would ask me to recite poems to her, amazed that I knew so many by heart. I used to write a lot, most of the time in my head since paper and pen were forbidden for long stretches of time in prison. To her, I may have appeared a decoration, something shiny that was not necessarily useful and practical, but had a strange appeal. Our relationship offered aspects of life that she had never before experienced and up until this point, had thought of as useless. It was something she didn't know what to do with, yet was unable to let go of.

So we became friends. After awhile, Bita spent a good chunk of her time with me. I had difficulty placing Homa in the picture. She was distant and never engaged herself in our walks or conversations. It was as if Bita had to be either with me or her; a trio was simply out of the question for Homa. She didn't even acknowledge me with a nod when she saw me. I came to accept this, not because I saw any sense in it, but because I felt more comfortable that way, as well. Bita did not disclose anything about her friendship with Homa and gradually, I lost interest in it, too, since I got a good portion of time with Bita. If Bita didn't mind splitting herself in that way, I didn't either.

As I mentioned earlier, our friendship formed at the time when my belief system was in crisis. I didn't feel comfortable talking about it with anyone, including Bita, at first. But as time went by, our conversations became more intense and serious. Though I was tempted to talk about my struggles, I stopped myself each time. We were in prison because of our political and ideological beliefs. For us, our belief system was our entire identity, the reason for our existence. If that was questioned or doubted, we would have little to live by or fight for. Since I was a supporter of a leftist opposition group, even if I questioned a few of my organization's political positions, I was, in the very least, expected to believe in its Marxist-Leninist ideological framework. During my crisis, however, I had begun to question the root of my beliefs, and even consider the question of God. When *I* was censoring my thinking, how could I share it with someone else? Sharing could end in my fellow inmates stigmatizing me as a *tavvab* or an opportunist who wanted an easier life in prison.

With Bita, however, I somehow felt more comfortable with my questions. She firmly believed in God and Islam. But she also had an interesting ability to keep an open mind to other ideas and possibilities. She didn't judge me. I soon opened up to her about my crisis, and she listened. We started to ask each other fundamental questions and try to reach convincing responses. Whether we reached conclusions or not was not the point; it was that I'd found a safe space to place my burden, take a deep breath, and feel all right.

This made me feel especially close to Bita. She had become the embodiment of my internal thought process. I looked at her and saw where I had left off in my train of thought. I sat beside her and managed to summon up the courage to face my challenge, and take up where I'd left off. This demonstrated itself in the strangest ways. One night, during the Iran-Iraq war air bombings, we had a lights-out after a bomb alert. When it happened, I was sitting in front of Bita, talking to her in the hallway. In total darkness, enveloped in fear, worry and sorrow, I gently put my head on her knee and closed my eyes. For a single moment, a thought flashed in my head: that I would be happy to die there and then, to make the moment last forever. I didn't say anything about this to Bita but after that night, I looked at her in a different light: she had become my haven, the source of my survival during that period of my life.

My happiness – our happiness – didn't last long. If we'd know what was to come, maybe we'd have kept a tighter hold of each other. As I mentioned before, prison officials did not see close friendships as favourable. They liked to see friendships form, so that they could separate the two parties, striking yet a further blow to both prisoners. We knew this well, so we expected something to happen to set us apart. What we hadn't expected was the reaction we got from our fellow inmates.

Soon after we became closer and started to spend more time together, several of my friends came to me to "talk." They were curious about my relationship with Bita. They wondered what we talked about during all those long hours. How could we have a lot to say to each other despite our totally opposite ideologies? Was I converting to Islam or was Bita becoming a communist? Which one of us was turning our back on our beliefs and political convictions? It was hard to say which of these scenarios was more dangerous for us potentially: if I had become religious or if she had become a communist. At the time, I thought that in the eyes of the prison officials, Bita would be in a worse situation than me.

These visits became more frequent and they brought with them a heavy air of insecurity. My haven had been violated; it wasn't safe anymore. Later, I learned that Bita was being approached with similar inquiries from her *Mojahedin* friends. At first, I tried to ignore these incidents. In response to my so-called visitors, I said that Bita and I talked about things unrelated to our beliefs and political opinions. They did not accept this. The pressure on us to separate began to increase, and we each bore it alone, while we continued to get together and keep our friendship as alive as best we could.

The last blow came one day when Bita was called for interrogation. While she was away, I was moved to a room at the other end of the hallway. It was late in the afternoon when she came back to the ward, and she deliberately avoided me. In the yard, I watched her walking alone. She seemed to be in her own world, cut off from others. I took a few steps towards her but she didn't seem to notice. When I finally worked up the nerve to go to her and try to fall into step beside her, she just whispered softly, "Please don't…" and moved away from me. A huge tiredness came over me, a lethargy in the face of the big obstacle in front of me. I knew I had to do something, but I didn't have the energy to take even one step. So I let it go that day.

A few days later, I found out that Homa had reported Bita to the prison officials. She had informed them that Bita was developing socialist ideas and losing her interest in Islam, and that they could easily observe this from her friendship patterns, including her friendship with Homa herself. This was beyond belief. I was sure that Homa was not a *tavvab*, so how could she have done this to her friend? What were her motives? How had she rationalized it? This incident, as devastating as it was, did not stop our friendship altogether. We still got together and talked, but as days went by, it happened less and less often. There were powerful tides pulling us apart. In vain, I struggled against them.

I learned more about Homa's intentions later. Homa and her group were not *tavvab*s. She and some other prisoners from communist parties had formed a group that believed most *Mojahedin* prisoners reported communists to prison officials to shift their attention from *Mojahedin* to communists. They had decided to retaliate by reporting any suspicious activity in which a *mojahed* participated. Bita had been the first victim of this plan. Homa and her crew approached me with the "advice" that I stay away from Bita, because if I didn't, they would see and treat me as one of the *Mojahedin*.

All of this was very hard on me. My friendship with Bita had made me more optimistic and contented. For a while, I had ceased to feel lost, confused and hopeless. It had given me a purpose. When I look back, it was a kind of informal therapy for me. So when this blow came, I didn't know what to make of it. At first, I tried to reason with Homa and her supporters. I didn't approve of their strategy. How could we rationalize our betraying of one another? *Mojahedin* weren't our enemy; they were on our side of the bars, suffering and fighting on our war front. What would we gain by breaking that solidarity? But then I stopped. My line of argument was going nowhere. They were adamant about their mission, and would not listen to anybody's reasoning. So I gave up, and went to Bita instead.

Naturally, as a result of these events, our being together had lost its spontaneity. Our lively conversations about the meaning of life and the nature of our ideological outlook stopped. Whenever we were together, we felt many eyes on us, and that made us uncomfortable. Stubbornly, I fought this process. After so long in prison, I had found something meaningful and I wasn't ready to let it go that easily. But it was like death: it had to happen, and no matter how strongly I wanted to prevent it, I couldn't. I didn't know then that the toughest part of this friendship was yet to come, from where I least expected.

I woke up one morning, earlier than usual. It was a Tuesday, and Bita and I washed our clothes together on Tuesdays. We got up early in the morning since the bathroom was less crowded at that time. I got my laundry ready and looked through the doorway, ready to go whenever Bita showed up. When twenty minutes passed and she didn't show up, I went to check her cell. She wasn't there. She wasn't in the bathroom either. I hurried to the yard. There she was, walking. Before I could go to her and say anything, I saw her already-washed clothes hanging on the clothesline. I stopped short. This was unusual. "Bita, you've washed your clothes already. How come?"

She continued to walk at a fast pace and with a shrug of her shoulder said, "The bathroom was empty, and I just did it."

Her cold and emotionless face froze any words I was about to speak. I felt so left out and let down, and suddenly so out of energy that I stopped walking. Bita continued on her way while I stood, frozen.

Similar incidents followed, each a further blow to my trust, self-esteem, and security. It was as if someone was stabbing me with a knife to stop me from moving. Just when I had survived a blow and finally adjusted, another one came along. Then, one day, without any explanation, Bita stopped talking to me altogether. When our paths crossed, she would immediately take her eyes away from the direction of my inquiring gaze, and walk away. A few times, I went to her and asked for an explanation. She responded in the most neutral of ways, with as few words as possible, saying things like: "It's better this way. It's hard to explain, but it's better for both of us." Later on, I didn't even get that. Bita would just take a deep, sad look at me, sigh, and walk away. She never initiated a conversation with me again.

This was unbearable for me. I entertained several thoughts in my mind: maybe she wanted a safe life in prison, or maybe staying away from me provided her with a break from the tough time she'd had recently – but then again, Bita was not that type. Under no circumstances could I picture her turning away from someone or something out of fear or a desire to play it safe. Then I wondered whether she was considering the new trend – not mingling with prisoners of different ideologies; maybe she had grown to believe in some *Mojahedin*'s strategy of siding against the communists. This was hard to believe, too, since I knew in my heart that Bita would never sit at the same table as the prison officials, no matter how convincing the argument. So, what was the problem? What was she thinking? Had she begun to dislike me and our friendship for some reason? I could even live with that, if only she offered me an explanation. What devastated me was that I felt like a helpless child being harshly punished by an adult, and I had no idea why or what would come next. I wondered if Bita had not believed in my ability to understand her points of view. I expected at least that much from our friendship – for her to trust me and discuss with me any change of heart or ideas – but what I got was a vacuum of absolute silence.

What I remember most about that period of time is restlessness and deep pain. I couldn't sit still or stay involved in one activity for long. I had to just *go* – to the yard, to my cell, to her cell, to the washroom, anywhere – to be somewhere else. Coming and going soothed me. I wanted to be nowhere, to forget everything. Even death seemed sweet, the only solution to my problems. Unfortunately, I couldn't go anywhere. I was forced to watch the ties between Bita and myself be cut, one by one – by her hands. I began to avoid Bita. Before I went anywhere, I first had to take a quick glance to see if she was in the vicinity. Seeing her had become too painful.

Little by little, I became a solitary figure. I preferred to be by myself and do everything alone. If someone in the yard attempted to walk with me, I said a few words and continued on my own. This gave others the signal that I didn't want to be disturbed. I carried a deep, fresh wound with me at all times. I watched Bita. She spent a few days alone like me, and then made friends with a *mojahed* known to be a *sar-e moze'-i*. This contradicted my theory that Bita had severed our friendship out of fear for the safety of her life in prison, because making friends with Tina was anything but safe. It was ridiculous, the way they talked together and did everything in each other's company – everything that Bita had once done with me. It was like a bad dream. I grew more distant, from Bita, other prisoners, nature, daily life, and myself. If someone mentioned a quote about friendship or trust, I caught myself cynically laughing out loud.

Embroidered notebook given to Shadi by Bita.

Meanwhile, the work I had managed to start on – changing my be-lief system – stopped altogether. The thought of what happened be-tween myself and Bita overshadowed everything. This aggravated my situation because I was doubly suffering, for the loss of both my friend and my beliefs. Bita had betrayed me and so had my beliefs. There was no rescue from the outside. If there were ever to be any salvation, it had to be from within, or I would lose my sanity. There were times when I saw, very clearly, how easily one could go insane – brief moments when

I said to myself, "You are losing it. This is how people go out of their minds, to escape, to forget. It could happen to you right now," then yanked myself back with a jolt. During the long hours I spent alone, I had extensive conversations with myself, my inner being, or God – whatever one may call it. These internal dialogues offered me a source of strength. Because I didn't see much strength and resilience in myself, I didn't believe I was the source of this respite. It calmed and encour-

In prison, Shadi spoke a lot about writing her prison memoirs when she was released. This embroidered pen was made for her by Bita to symbolize this promise.

aged me, wiped away my tears, kept me company, and when things were beyond tolerance, took me out of my prison. When I slept, something stayed wide awake to oversee my dreams and nightmares. When I woke up in the middle of the night in a cold sweat, it put me back to sleep. And this was how I didn't go insane.

Sometimes, the line between sanity and insanity is very thin. When I saw that line, I began to take baby steps in the direction of sanity. The change was barely noticeable at first, but now when I walked in the yard, I weakly looked around at the faces of other prisoners. In the mirror, I saw a resemblance to those patients slowly recovering from tough chronic illness. The hours of loneliness became shorter and shorter, and I began to talk to others, first small talk, then daily conversation, and before long, discussions. Gradually, I found myself searching for a new friend. I looked at Bita but I didn't see her anymore. I felt safer that way. I went back to writing – at this time, notebooks weren't forbidden – and produced some of the best pieces of writing I have ever accomplished. I dug deep into my mind to remember the poems I had memorized, and whispered them to myself over and over. The words washed over me, cleansed me, and made me stronger. They also brought me a new friend: Sousan, another soul that loved poetry and words. This new friend became the shore for my wandering boat. I had docked; the cycle had completed itself.

Many years later, outside of prison, when I found Bita – or rather, when Bita found me – we talked things over, and I finally found out what had gone through her mind during those days.

"Why did you do this to me, Bita? Why?" I asked. This time, I had no patience for her silent treatment.

She kept her eyes averted. "I didn't do this only to you; I first did it to me."

"But why?"

"I would have done it differently if I was who I am now, but at the time, I needed to prove to myself and others that my beliefs were still unshaken and strong."

"But what did that have to do with our friendship? Was it taking away your strength or your beliefs? Weren't we strong together?" I cried out.

She sighed. "I got scared of our friendship. I'd never experienced such closeness, such intimacy. It was taking control of me, and I was afraid to let that happen. I had to be in control, otherwise I risked losing the firm ground underfoot, and without that, how was I to go on fighting?"

"Bita, I can relate to all of that. I was going through the same process myself. But our friendship wasn't blocking me; it was making me stronger. It was when you cut the ties that I started to go down. I –"

Impatiently, Bita cut me off: "Don't you see? You confused me. You represented a different way of being that attracted me, tempted me. That wasn't easy. To change and try new things you have to doubt and make mistakes, and I couldn't afford that. I had just enough energy to go back to my safe, defined, secure self."

"Why didn't you tell me all that then? You owed me that much!"

This time, she looked straight into my eyes: "If I had, would you have given up and let me do it?"

She had a point there. I would have argued with her relentlessly. Nonetheless, I still believed I should have been a part of this decision-making process. "So you accomplished what you wanted. Now what? Why did you come to find me after all these years?"

She smiled bitterly. "When you and I made friends, a small window opened up in my life. I underestimated it at the time. But then I realized, as small as the window was, it had let in too much light for me to ignore. I wanted more. So I had to find you."

The long-desired explanation came late, but not too late. We managed to rebuild our friendship bit by bit, this time under more normal circumstances. We were among the fortunate ones, though. Prison friendships didn't always turn out well. Some were lost and never found again.

That Day and the Days After

For over an hour, I had been sitting on a stool – an empty, upturned feta cheese pail – in front of our small but beautiful garden in the prison yard. With my back to the other prisoners, I faced the flowers. I could see more beauty and meaning in the existence of flowers than in myself or the other prisoners. The flowers were more resilient than us, too. They grew and bloomed continuously, and if a flower got picked, the others just kept blooming, never giving up. But what about us? How long could we go on existing when we were aching, being cut and beaten? This wasn't the first time in prison that I longed to be something other than human. What a burden being human had become!

A few days before, my name had been called out. In a way, I was expecting it. It had been a little over five years and my sentence had come to an end. I knew that any day, I could expect to be summoned and taken to the so-called *Otagh-e Azadi*. The time had finally come.

The *pasdar* asked me some questions about my change of heart and mind. He didn't want too many details; he wanted an overall review.

I told him that I had changed, and would not be involved in *any* activity, Islamic, socialist, or otherwise. I wanted to experience life, to study, work, and spend time with my family.

"And marry, have children," the *pasdar* finished my speech.

"I wasn't thinking of that," I hurriedly said, mortified.

"Why not?" the *pasdar* asked. "After all, this is an essential goal of your life, which you have missed for five years."

I decided to remain silent. What good was it to argue with him? How could he possibly begin to understand my frame of mind?

He went on to lecture me about life outside prison: how I would need to keep praying to God to forgive me, and hope that my people would also forgive me for the heinous act that I had committed in fighting against the Islamic Republic, the regime chosen by Allah and the people. "You will have to be careful around people. They will hate your guts. If you tell them you were a political prisoner of the regime of Allah, they won't even want to talk to you. Explain that you've changed and are not fighting the regime any more."

I was very close to bursting out in laughter, but I stopped myself. I had to keep quiet and resist the urge to expose the stupidity of the idea he was espousing. Who were "the people" to whom he was referring? Was he really this deceived? Did he really believe the majority of people still believed in the regime? Then again, what if there was some truth in what he said?

When I returned to the public ward after my interview, I was a different person. Something had disturbed the calm and quiet of my prison days. I couldn't go about my daily routine with the same ease. I began to feel torn between what I had grown to love and what was waiting for me outside: my family, ordinary life, freedom, reading, studying, talking freely. Why didn't that make me happy? I looked at my fellow inmates and my heart ached. How could I eat normal food in freedom when I knew the gross details of the meals they were having in prison each day of the week? On Saturdays, lunch was rice with "lost chicken" – nicknamed such because there was only a hint of chicken – and, for dinner, chicken soup made with uncooked split peas that gave us stomach aches for days. Sundays, we were given *ghormeh sabzi*[71] or *gheimeh*[72] stew for lunch – two delicious Iranian dishes that the prison cooks managed to make utterly tasteless – and sour yoghurt and cucumbers for dinner. Mondays, lunch was lentils and rice – the prison's most unappetizing food, it tasted like warm water on rice with a few raisins here and there. Dinner was soup with traces of lunch: lentils, rice, and tomato paste. On Tuesdays, we were served *abgousht* for lunch – now and then, we'd find various odd objects in the dish: a T-shirt sleeve, a pair of scissors, a used band-aid. We were disgusted, but it made us laugh so hard that we forgot the issue altogether. For dinner, we had beans. On Wednesdays, we ate rice and broad beans for lunch, and bread, cheese and cucumbers for dinner. Thursdays offered rice with tomato paste for lunch. Dinner was the "weekly report," a dish with traces of several dishes we had been given throughout the week. There was also a TV program under that name, and we laughed about it every Thursday night, and every time the show was on. On Fridays, we had *aash-e reshteh* for lunch, and butter, eggs and potatoes for dinner. I would remember the order of meals for

---

71 *Ghormeh sabzi* is a stew with certain kinds of sautéed herbs, red kidney beans and meat.

72 *Gheimeh* is a stew containing little cubes of meat and yellow split peas. It is often served with French fries on top.

the rest of my life, even the irregularities that happened every now and then. How could I eat, feel free to go out for a walk, take my mother in my arms, or read a book?

On the other hand, I couldn't imagine how to fill in the five-year gap that stretched between my family and myself. It seemed like an impossible task. I had changed so much. Certainly they had too, each in their own way. Was it possible to build any relationship upon foundations I no longer knew? Could I trust them again? Could I live a normal life?

During those days, the atmosphere of the ward had undergone some changes. A new group of *sar-emoze'-i* prisoners that had recently arrived had started to do things that were at odds with our usual ways. They read the newspaper together as a group and discussed it openly in the yard. They kept their food gathered in one place and washed their clothes as a group. They played volleyball noisily in the yard, and paid no attention to the office warnings. Once, when they felt that our dinner of feta cheese and cucumbers was not sufficient, they lined up all their plates behind the ward's barred entrance, and shouted that they were returning their food because it was not enough. They slept on an empty stomach that night. In response, the prison officials stopped serving us lunch and dinner. For two days, we were only given tea and breakfast.

Like many other prisoners, I didn't agree with their actions and points of view. I saw this kind of resistance as pointless. Every few days, new diseases broke out and spread, prisoners committed or attempted suicide, and other prisoners lost their sanity and mental balance. Did the regime care? Many of us had come to the conclusion that we had to get out decent, good human beings. We refused to betray our friends and family. We were trying to stay loyal to our essence of humanity. We also did not want to commit any openly confrontational acts. There are times when keeping this balance might not be possible, but this was not yet such a time.

This group talked to other prisoners who, like me, had adapted a seemingly neutral lifestyle, and were unwilling to get involved in any overtly political or confrontational act. They called us *bi-taraf*s[73] – the indifferent ones – and openly said that they found us more dangerous than the *tavvab*s. Each room had naturally been divided into two sections: the *sar-e moze'-i* sat on the left, and the *tavvab*s on the right. People like

---

73 A *bi-taraf* is a person who does not take sides.

me, who were struggling to keep an independent position, didn't know where in the room to sit. I had made a small desk for myself out of a wooden fruit crate and I'd also made a tablecloth. At it, I sat, and read or wrote. At this point in time, prisoners were allowed to study. Those who had not finished high school could study and take the exam to get their diploma. We all took turns teaching others whatever we were good at. I used to teach English. One day, I took my small wooden crate to the middle of the room under the TV, and just sat there. The *sar-e moze'-i* threw daggers at me. Even up until the day of my release, I refused to sit on either the right or the left side of the room.

Recently, I had somewhat recovered from the blow of my break-up with Bita, and had made new friends. There was Sousan, who shared my love for poetry and words. We exchanged poems and short pieces of writing. She understood my feelings about Bita – our friendship and the emotional crisis I experienced after its demise. The day I went to *Otagh-e Azadi,* I began to feel this strong urge to express everything I was thinking in a poem. A poem I wanted my friends to read after I had left. Above all, I wanted Bita to read it when I was no longer there. I had to portray the complex range of my contradictory feelings on paper, give them a picture that they would all understand. I needed to bare everything in front of their eyes, but only *after* I was gone. I started to write the poem, and added to it each day. The poem became symbolic of my wrenching of myself from Evin, my home for the last five years. It became a tool to explain and understand the two opposing forces that were pulling at me and causing me such pain. I named it *The Five Seasons.* On the one hand, there were the five years of my imprisonment. On the other, the four seasons were my life and experience in prison. The fifth season was the life that awaited me, my life after release.

Before long, my day came. It was about a week later, and we had emptied our cells to do a total cleanup – even the carpets were out in the yard, being swept and cleaned. The day's workers were washing the floor, walls and ceiling. We did this once a month.[74] I was sitting on a rolled-up carpet in the yard, resting after sweeping, when they called my name. I was to go to the office with all my belongings. For a few seconds, everyone who knew me stopped what they were doing, and began

---

74 The prisoners formed themselves into work groups that took turns doing the daily tasks in the prison: washrooms, hallways, cells and the yard.

to search for me in the yard. Questions were asked: "Is she a worker today? Is she inside or out in the yard?"

I simply got up so they could see me. I felt their warm presences crowding around me, saw their smiling faces wishing me well, their teary eyes. A sack containing my clothes appeared in the yard doorway. The workers had brought my belongings. None of the clothes in my sack were my own. I had traded my clothes with my friends. Because the guards wouldn't let prisoners take out any prison crafts, we exchanged pieces of clothing to remember each other. Each item was a reminder of a friend and held hundreds of memories.

They started to hug me and say goodbye. Each prisoner had something to tell me: a piece of advice, a reminder for me to call her family (I'd already memorized the phone numbers I had been given). There were good wishes, or just hugs and tears, which could be more expressive than words. In the sea of faces, I was looking for Bita. I hated myself for it, but I badly wanted her to say goodbye to me, to have tears in her eyes, to tell me she'd miss me. I finally saw her, teary-eyed and quiet, patiently waiting her turn. In the middle of the chaos, the prisoners around me gave way suddenly, as if they clearly saw what I felt. It was as if everyone, having closely watched the rise and fall of our friendship, was now waiting to observe our farewell, too. They needed closure, as did I.

To break the awkwardness of the moment, we both rushed into each other's arms. It had been a year since our separation. I didn't know what to say or do, or even what to feel.

She whispered in my ear, "I'm so glad you're getting out. So glad. Take care of yourself, and don't forget me. I really want to be remembered by you. Do you think you can do that?"

Between tears, I managed to say, "I'm *sure* I will do that. Do you still want me to go visit your family?"

She held my shoulders firmly with her hands, and nodded.

Sousan was next. She had been close by me the whole time, watching everything patiently. I stretched my arms towards her. In the tightness of our embrace, I said to her, "What am I going to do outside?"

With the wise hesitation that was always in her voice and everything else she did, she said, "Read the book I told you about. I'm sure it will help."

She was referring to Dr. Victor Frankl's *Man's Search for Meaning*, a book about the years he had spent in a Nazi concentration camp. She had recommended that I read that book after my freedom. And that was what I was going to do. "The poem," I said to her, my voice breaking in my throat.

"Don't worry about it. It's done."

We all moved to the bottom of the stairs together. I climbed a few steps and stood there for awhile, looking at everyone, trying to take in the totality of their existence. I wanted to freeze the moment and somehow make it permanent, so that I would remember it in all its glory and sadness. Then I shook my head in disbelief and almost shouted, "How am I going to live without you? How can I leave you all here and just go?" Time stood still for a second, and then there were hands pushing me up, telling me to hurry. I am sure in their hearts of hearts, they were afraid for me; they wanted me to go quickly so as not to lose my opportunity. It was as if they were saying, "Nothing is certain in prison. Hurry up, we don't want any reversal of the decision to release you." It had happened before. We all remembered the story of a prisoner who took a long time to say goodbye to her friends at the time of her release, and by the time she was finished, the *pasdar*s told her she was too late and wouldn't be released that day. She was returned to the ward and released about ten days later. Remembering this, and hearing their unspoken concerns, I climbed those stairs.

The office door opened and closed behind me, shutting off the familiar sounds and voices of the world downstairs forever.

With sarcasm, the *pasdar* in the office said, "It took you a very long time. Don't you want to get out? Do you love staying in this place so much?"

I put my sack on the floor and simply said, "We had a cleaning day, so it took me a while to get my stuff and come up. Sorry."

She opened my sack and rudely started to rummage through it. Every small pocket and zipper was opened and searched. She found an embroidery that a friend had made me, as well as the paper that noted my official prison sentence of five years. "You are not allowed to take these out. Come here." Then she searched my body. When she found nothing, she sent me out to the big corridor.

After a wait and a minibus ride, I found myself in the interrogation building, five years later, with a different purpose. It was a dark remembrance of those early days of confusion, pain and shock. I was taken to a room and told to sit on one of those chairs with a desk flap where I had sat so many times during interrogations. A thick pile of stapled paper was put in front of me. "Fill everything out. Don't leave anything unanswered. You won't be released until you answer everything."

In that last interrogation, they did indeed, ask for "everything." It was a thorough review of my case, as well as information about my family, including cousins, aunts and uncles. They wanted the addresses and phone numbers of everyone – even those that lived abroad. They wanted to know first and last names, what everyone did for a living, and if I had any relatives in prison. It took me a very long time to finish answering those questions. Just when I thought it was all done and that I would soon see my family, a *pasdar* came in the room to talk to me. He explained to me that after my release, I would have to sign in at a *comité* once a month on a certain day and answer some questions. This would go on until further notice. So, it wasn't a real release after all. They would still keep a close eye on me, not letting me forget that absolute freedom from the boundaries and limitations of this regime would never happen. He asked me to take twelve four-by-six photos of myself to my first session. I had to stifle a laugh because I thought that even a famous actress wouldn't be asked for twelve photos all at once; what did they need twelve pictures of me for?

A few minutes later, my blindfold was taken off and I was taken outside the gates of Evin. Words cannot describe the way I felt; the same gates that had let me in five years ago were letting out a different person: older, wiser, and maybe sadder. I was put on yet another minibus that drove through the streets of the village of Evin, on our way to Luna Park, where my family was waiting. As I greedily took in all the details of my surroundings, my eyes became fixated on a group of people a little further ahead. There were others on the minibus with me, and naturally their families were in Luna Park as well. But when I saw the group from afar, something told me it was my family. Before they saw the minibus, they were distracted and looked tired. I saw them gather and get closer to one another, as if they wanted to face this moment together. And then they all turned their heads in the direction of the minibus. Now I could recognize familiar faces: my mom in the front of the crowd, then my sister and my aunt. My dad was further back. My heart began to jump with joy when I saw a group of my prison friends among them. They had all come to welcome me. They would ease my difficult transition: I wasn't alone.

The things that happened afterwards are still blurry: hugging and kissing everyone, going from one person to another, hopelessly trying to fill the five-year gap; the ride home; the moment I took my first step into my home and how everyone followed me wordlessly, to see if I still remembered where every room was. I remember going up the stairs to my room and looking around. Things were not as I had left them: my bookcase had new, unread books in it, my closet held clothes I didn't remember having, shelves had sweaters my mom had knitted over the years, my bedcover and sheets were new, even my carpet wasn't the same. In an attempt to make me feel welcome and special, they had removed every trace of "me" from my room, and it made me feel utterly lonely, a stranger to myself. Where was I supposed to find myself if not here?

I turned to my piano and approached it silently. The room was so quiet despite everyone in it. I opened the lid and ran my fingers over the keys softly, not making a sound. The feel of the keys made my heart ache; how long would it be before I realized the depth of what those years had done to me? What they had stolen from me? Could I live a normal life again? And suddenly my fingers began to play a song I apparently still remembered, *Fur Elise* by Beethoven. But I couldn't finish the song because of the sniffing and crying of the listeners. I ended the melodrama by asking, "What? Why are you all crying? I'm back; I'm still alive. We should all be happy. Shouldn't we?" as if I needed assurance.

My mom hugged me tight and said, "Yes, this is the happiest moment of our lives. Forgive us for crying. Let's go eat something."

Eating was not an escape, either. My mom had used the full scope of her artistry in cooking for that day's meal. There was so much food and so many varieties on the table, but I couldn't make myself eat much. Every spoonful of food that went down my throat tasted like bread and cheese, tasteless lentil rice, and camphored tea. I felt sick after a little eating, and my family decided that we had to take things slow and suggested that I go to bed and have some rest.

I was happy to have my prison friends there, around me. When night came, a few of them wanted to leave. I hung on to their sleeves, asking them to stay, to not leave me alone. This was so strange in the eyes of my family and relatives, and so embarrassing for me. I was asking my friends not to leave me alone in my own home, among my family members. I blushed, but hung on to my friends tighter. I felt the need to stick with them, or else I felt I would drown. Two of them changed their plans and stayed for the night.

It is strange how sleep can sometimes be so far from relaxing. My family decided that it would be better for me to sleep alone in my room to enjoy the new feeling of independence. Beds for my friends were made up in my sister's room, which was next to mine. I didn't want to object to everything they did, so I gave in. When I closed the door of my room behind me, fear overcame me. I was scared to turn the light off, and I was scared to leave it on. I got in bed and pressed my eyelids together, but kept opening my eyes, desperately looking for other warm bodies around me. After a few minutes, it became unbearable, and I got up, went to the other room and said out loud, "Can I have company? I haven't slept alone for five years. Can we do this gradually?" And my friends came to sleep in my room.

That night, I didn't sleep. It wasn't until the next afternoon that I finally closed my eyes and sleep brought me some peace. My friends had forced me to bed to rest. Each sat at one side of the bed and talked to me, answered my incessant questions. I kept looking from one to another, afraid to keep quiet. If I stopped talking, sleep would take me away from my friends into unknown territory. I fell asleep as I was seated in bed, with my friends still sitting there holding my hands.

Freedom was good, but at the same time, it brought issues that were difficult to deal with. It was like I had somehow acquired eyes that saw and noticed more than before, ears that heard everything, senses that were more open to everything. My antennae had simply become so sharp it hurt. I noticed my parents had aged; I traced every wrinkle on their faces and related it to the stress I'd caused them. I felt the cracks in our family life, cracks that were beyond remedy. Children had grown up. Everything was unrecognizable. I tried to find the excitement and youth and energy I had last experienced in my familiar environment, but I couldn't. No matter how hard I tried to relive that life and revive the feelings, it got further and further away from me. I was sinking, groping for a lifesaver, and missing every time. Day after day, it dawned on me that a lot had happened while I was away. I had changed, too. But something bothered me: I seemed to have lost five years of my life somewhere. I hadn't lived normally. I hadn't been a teenager, fallen in love, explored the madness of things, been difficult, had rows with my parents. I had to be rational and reasonable, to cope with the most un-usual circumstances, and just focus on staying alive and maintaining my decency. Had I grown up too quickly?

For a while, it was hard for me to take my scarf off. I kept it on in our family gatherings, and it both surprised and scared my family, be-cause I had never been particularly religious. We didn't have a tradition of covering our head in our family. Nobody addressed the scarf openly though, being afraid to trouble my already fragile state of mind. Only I knew why I did it: in a way, it was my prison identity. My efforts to re-build my former identity had failed, so by keeping this token of my life in prison, I was hanging on to the one secure thing I had. Removing the scarf happened one day, in one single act. It was like a fruit that, ripened, fell off the tree by itself. One day, I just felt I didn't need it anymore. I felt I could face my family without it. It ceased to be merely a reminder of my prison self, and began to bother me, a symbol of the prison limi-tations. Prisoner or free, they wanted me to have the veil, and something inside me rebelled. One day, when I was in my room getting ready to go downstairs and meet a group of relatives, I pulled the scarf off my head in an act of defiance. I brushed my hair and went down the stairs.

I ran my fingers over the edge of the row of books in my bookcase. It felt so good! I had dreamed of this moment a thousand times during the past five years – the moment when I would hold a novel in my hand, a book that I had chosen. What a joy to feel the texture of its cover, flip through the pages, peek at the beginning and guiltily at the end, read the back cover, reflect on the title, flirt with the book for a while, and then start reading it, slowly and attentively, devouring every word and digesting every meaning. My fingers stopped on a four-volume novel on the shelf – Romain Rolland's *The Enchanted Soul*, and I picked up the first volume. I had heard about it a lot from my friends and now I could read it.

A few hours past midnight, I was still struggling with *The Enchanted Soul*. The feeling was driving me crazy. I hadn't been able to read past a few paragraphs. By the time I reached the end of the page, I realized I hadn't registered a single bit of its meaning. I had to read it over and over and still, all I got were scattered words and concepts here and there. I was unable to grasp anything. I had lost the ability to concentrate, settle down with characters, and get involved in the plot of a book. How was I to go on living like that? I, who devoured books, spent money on them, who stayed up all night greedily reading, how was I going to get used to this newly discovered aftermath of prison? One cannot begin to understand the depth of my frustration. I threw the book on the floor and burst into tears.

There were other attempts I made to get back to normal life and move on. I started to study for the comprehensive university entrance exam. In Iran, this entrance exam is a real nightmare for high school students. Everyone who wants a higher education takes this exam and picks a number of program choices in order of preference. First, scores and ranks are announced. Then, one day, names of all the accepted candidates appear in the newspaper. It's almost like a lottery, but it demands

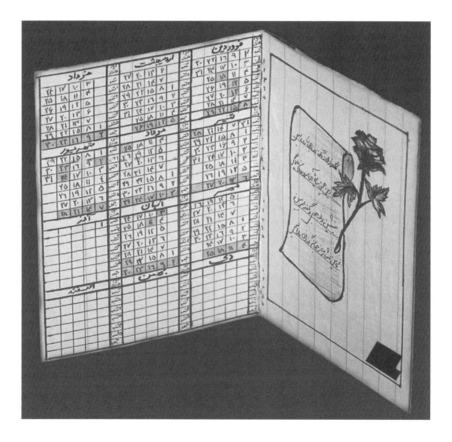

This is a handmade calendar that Bita made for Shadi. The days are only filled in up to Shadi's anticipated release date.

many nights of studying and hard work. The universities that had been closed during the Cultural Revolution had been reopened, so I could now try my luck at continuing my studies.

I made a plan, and with the help of friends and family, started to study. It wasn't any easier than reading a novel, that's for sure. Long sleepless nights were spent reading passages out loud several times in order to comprehend, working out mathematical problems, formulating biological concepts, and memorizing the fundamentals of Islam, which was a necessity for admission. I had to read all four Islamic Studies textbooks to brush up on my knowledge of Islam. There were times when I gave up the idea of taking my entrance exam. It was then that my mom tried to gather in all of my frustration and talk me into trying. She suggested that I only look at it as a test, and not worry about the outcome. It didn't matter if I was admitted or not – what mattered was that my studying abilities return. This was practice; next year I would try again. It was with this outlook that I got back on track. I stopped pushing myself over the edge. I took it step by step. Friends who had taken the exam before mentored and coached me. And my mother and sister fed me with love and care.

During this same period, I began to "drink in" my mom and sister. It was as if I had just begun to realize how much I had missed them and how much I needed them. Before then, my ability to love or even to be loved had somehow frozen. But time, meaning, work, and unconditional love thawed the ice. Now, I could absorb the love that was given to me. I began to realize that love comes in all shapes and forms, as does suffering. People who hadn't been in prison had suffered too; they had been in a larger prison. All the people of my country have been, and still are, in prison. Initially, I divided people into two groups: those who had been in prison and would understand me, and those who hadn't and therefore wouldn't. Now I could see that the formula was too simplistic. I began to see the scars on the souls of my family as well, and I began to bond with them in a new, strong way.

Life goes on, and sometimes that's a great consolation. It may have been deadly for me to stay in my initial post-release state of mind for too long. A stage had ended and a new one had begun, one in which I started to connect with life, people, and myself. Over time, the self develops into a newer self, and the past merges into the present into the future. Once a carefree child, I had developed into an energetic, revolutionary activist teenager; an idealistic, then disillusioned, realistic humanistic political prisoner; a released yet lost youth; and finally, a more mature individual with insight, the ability to adjust, and some hope. And maybe that's the secret of my survival.

The Five Seasons

It was five days
of rain
and loneliness was in the air.

Five days
in which time passed by
and the Earth didn't rotate.

Five days
with the length of five springs.
Five falls.
Five years…

When the bird died,
the cage laughed at its wounded presence
and the sky
grieved the absence of its flight.

The bird wanted to sing
but no song
matched the beauty of its voice.
The bird stopped singing.

Maybe the death of the bird
was the beginning of the fifth season; I don't know.

It was the season of the leaves rising up,
the season of the buds shooting forth,
and I,
standing at a crossing,
between the spell of the moon's lullaby
and the wise sleeplessness of the glowworm.

The bird
was the footstep of the moment
when clouds covered my blue sky.

The bird
was the hammer of death
on the anvil of life.

When the bird died
it bestowed the secret of its love
to the deprived heart in the clouds
so the thirsty trees
would believe in the drizzle of love.

Five years…
It was exactly five years
that daggers flew
and wounds bloomed.

Five blossomless springs
that spared no jasmine fragrance
for the desirous noses.

Five falls
In which we were the trees,
with the pieces of our hearts
for leaves.

Five frozen winters
in which humanity watched its ugly destruction
and the springs of conscience
dried up in the stone hearts of self-preservation.

Five dark years
in which failure roared
and growth glowered.

Five lively stages of Nature
that bore the death of trees and water and plants,
and we walked on five dead-end roads
like tired dust-covered pilgrims.

I must salute the road
at the threshold of the fifth season of the year
beyond the bars.
I won't believe in a fifth season
because "time" is here.

Maybe these stone walls
are eyelids
covering eyes that see.

And none of you could know
how brutally tomorrow's daybreak
would cut my body loose from my birthplace
but never my heart…

No, you wouldn't know
what an endless dark
tonight is for me.

Believe me
I haven't left.

I am present
in the loneliness
that claws at your hearts every sunset.

Believe me
I will turn my fingers into a pen
to record our mutual pain
on the blankness of every page
and ruffle the untroubled peace of every pond.

I have packed my suitcase.
I've filled it
with your smiles,
the fruitful sprouts of tears.

With your glances,
the mysterious depths of the seas.

I've filled my suitcase
solely with "YOU"
although I lived alone amongst you.
And tonight
am lonelier than ever.

Tomorrow,
is such a sad birthday.

The windows are waiting for me
with curious aimless eyes
and there will be tear-covered paths of emotion
that won't bear my wounded feet.

And the raindrops of honesty
that haven't yet realized
they've lost their way in the desert of my heart
five years ago.

And I will remember
that I was buried in your small garden last night!

How can I watch the sunset
without a star falling in the depths of my heart?
How can I step on the rustle of the fall leaves
without remembering the patient repetitious bustle of your steps
on this side of the bars?

Your faces
looking for the meaning of the moon
from beyond the barred windows.
That will be my moonlight
tomorrow night.

And my only friend
will be the sky
that covers your boredom everyday.

My sea
will be the tear
that rolls down your face
and my garden,
the cut chrysanthemums
in a glass of water in your cell.
Tokens of the fathomless beauty of Nature.

Hear me –
I'm the roll of the thunder,
I'm a cry of pain.
The only evidence of humanity left in me.

And tomorrow,
even the graveyards won't understand.
A thousand birds have died in me.

You familiar strangers
believe my mourning.
I'm mourning the bird that died
and my cry
is the same as the dead bird's cry:
"There's an unspoken word in my chest.
Behind the window
there's an eye
that's not asleep."

Glossary

Aash-e reshteh is a thick soup made with vegetables, noodles and dried beans.

Abgousht is thick soup resembling goulash.

Amuzeshgah literally means place of learning.

Ayatollah Ruhollah Khomeini was the first Supreme Leader of the Islamic Republic of Iran, December 1979-June 1989.

Azan is the call to prayer made over a loudspeaker. There are five daily prayers required by Islamic law. In the Shiite tradition, there are three daily calls to prayer: before sunrise, at noon and after sunset. The noon and afternoon prayers are combined, as are the evening and night prayers.

Azari is the language of the northwest province of Azarbaijan.

A **bi-taraf** is a person who does not take sides.

A **chador** is a large, shapeless, dark piece of cloth that covers a woman's body from head to foot. It can be held to permit the wearer to see. For all female prisoners, *chador*s were required attire, worn over the *manteau*, scarf and clothes. Prisoners wore navy blue *chador*s if they were taken out of prison to distinguish them from ordinary people, or if they did not come into prison with a *chador* of their own.

Chelo kabob is a dish favoured by Iranians but seldom served in prison. The prison variety used ground meat of some sort, served on rice.

The **comité** is the Revolutionary Guard station located in each neighbourhood in the city of Tehran, as well as in other cities. They were used for a variety of civic functions in the beginning of the revolution.

Evin is a large prison located in the village of Evin in the north of Tehran, close to the mountains. Originally built for political prisoners during the time of the last Shah, it was used primarily for political dissidents during the 1980s.

Gheimeh is a stew containing little cubes of meat and yellow split peas. It is often served with French fries on top.

Ghormeh sabzi is a stew with certain kinds of sautéed herbs, red kidney beans and meat.

Gilaki is the language spoken by Iranians living in the northern Iranian province of Gilan, on the Caspian Sea.

Gohardasht is a prison near Qezel Hessar.

Hawji Davood Rahmani was the notorious warden of Qezel Hessar Prison, known for his extreme cruelty towards prisoners.

Hezbollah literally means Party of God.

A **Hezbollahi** is a member of the *Hezbollah*, a loyal follower of Ayatollah Khomeini. *Hezbollahi* were armed, self-styled, unofficial defenders of the revolution that could be mobilized by the government at any time.

The **Hosseynieh** is a huge hall with high ceilings in a special building, on a hill in the Evin compound. It was used as a place of assembly when prison authorities wanted to gather all the prisoners together, for propaganda sessions, mass prayers and public "admissions of guilt" by prisoners (admission of guilt was a precondition for leaving the prison even after a sentence had run out). A divider in the hall separated the female and male prisoners.

Jadidi means newcomer (i.e. to the prison).

Kafar is the term for an infidel, or non-believer.

Asadolah Lajevardi was the Director of Prisons during this time. His office was in Evin Prison. A fanatic hardliner, his edicts and opinions carried weight beyond the jurisdiction of Director. He was later assassinated by a member of the *Mojahedin-e Khalq*.

Madar, meaning mother, is sometimes used by younger prisoners as a respectful prefix to the name of a woman who is a mother or an older woman.

A **manteau** is a long coat that covers all of the female body.

A **maqna'eh** is a long scarf that is slipped over the head to cover the neck, chest, chin, and part of the forehead. It is sewed tight at the front.

Mohammad Reza Pahlavi was the Shah of Iran from 1941 until the Islamic Revolution in 1979.

A **mojahed** is a member of the *Mojahedin-e Khalq* Organization. The Mojahedin-e were an Islamic opposition group during Shah Mohammad Reza Pahlavi's time, and at first supported the Islamic revolution. The organization was sidelined when the religious clergy took over the revolution and gradually began to limit freedom of expression and the activities of all political opponents.

The **Mojahedin-e Khalq Organization** was a guerrilla organization formed in the 1960s to fight the Shah's government. It continued its insurgency against the government of the Islamic Republic, as well. The *Mojahedin-e Khalq*'s mass demonstration against the Islamic regime initiated a government clamp-down on political activity and widespread arrests of government opponents. Older women in prison who were mothers were more often than not *mojahed*s, members of the *Mojahedin-e Khalq*.

Monafeq is the term for a hypocrite, someone who pretends to be a believer.

A **mullah** is a member of the Islamic clergy.

Najes means religiously impure.

Otagh-e Azadi means Freedom Room, which was as office in Evin where prisoners were taken before their release.

A **pasdar** is a member of the Revolutionary Guard. Prison *pasdar*s tend to be from religious families of the lower middle and lower classes, and fanatical supporters of the revolution. Not always well educated or well trained, they were in the pay of the Islamic government. In the beginning of the revolution, men from neighbourhoods would keep protective watches. Gradually, these men became a people's army. *Pasdar*s deal with matters of immorality and ideology and serve as guards in Evin Prison. The *pasdar*s refer to each other as *baradar* (brother) followed by the last name. Neither *pasdar*s nor members of the *bassiji* were part of the military.

Qapan was a form of torture in prisons. The prisoner's hands are tied behind their back in an awkward manner for long periods of time. It is very painful to return the hands back to a normal position, and there is usually numbness, which may or may not disappear.

Qezel Hessar is a prison situated in fields near the city of Karaj, a short drive west of Tehran.

Qur'an (Koran) is the Holy Book of Islam.

A **sar-e moze'-i** is a person who openly stands their ground.

Sharbat is water with something added to make it sweet.

The **Shari'a** is the Islamic law which regulates all aspects of life.

Ta'zir is religious punishment. Flogging the soles of the feet was the most frequently used method of *ta'zir*.

Taftoon is a type of traditional bread made in a special oven called a *tanoor*.

Tavvab is a religious term meaning repentant sinner. Dissidents who renounced their ideological beliefs were used to inform on other prisoners and to perform duties for the prison authorities. By repenting and cooperating, the *tavvab*s could escape death and torture, and receive shorter sentences, as well as preferential treatment in prison.

The **zir-e hasht** is the area in the ward where the ward captains lived while on prison duty. This area was opposite the Prison Library or *Mosque*. A second *zir-e hasht*, outside the wards, was used for torturing and interrogating prisoners.

About the Authors

Azadeh Agah

Azadeh was born in Iran into a politically active family: very early on in life she learned about totalitarianism and oppression. She witnessed the harassment and imprisonment of several members of her extended family, and heard amazing stories of courage and resistance from the adult members of her family. By the time she reached high school, she was already an advocate of women's emancipation, and human rights in general.

After secondary school, she began studying sociology, with a side interest in politics. She was active in student protests which opposed the dictatorial regime of the Shah, and was harassed, questioned and temporarily detained as a consequence. She finished her undergraduate studies and spent a few years working at a private institution before attending graduate school, where she received an advanced degree in Women's Studies and politics. Upon graduation, she began teaching at the university and did so until the Islamic Revolution of 1979. Azadeh's optimism turned into despair when the post-revolutionary regime brought no change for the better and women's rights became even more restricted. She continued advocating democracy and human rights issues up until her 1982 arrest. Azadeh spent four years in the Islamic Republic's prison system, going from one jail to the next, where she observed and experienced the conditions described in part two of this book.

Azadeh is married with two children and lives in Canada. She is still active in promoting human rights issues in general, and the rights of political prisoners in particular.

Sousan Mehr

Sousan Mehr studied languages in Iran and France. A twenty-five-year old teacher in 1983, she was arrested and confined to the Iranian political prison of Evin. Sousan loves to write poems, and literature has always been a main part of her life. In prison, however, she did not have access to pen and paper. Sousan remained in prison for approximately five years; after her release, she was forbidden to leave the country for twelve years. She married, and continued to teach and write poems and short stories. By writing and publishing her memoirs, Sousan hopes to portray the life and times of her generation for her child. Sousan currently lives in Canada. This is her first published work.

Shadi Parsi

When Shadi Parsi was arrested by the guards of the Islamic Republic of Iran in 1981 – almost three years after the Iranian Revolution of February 11, 1979 – she was eighteen years old and had just finished high school. At the time, due to the so-called Cultural Revolution, the universities were closed and as such, higher learning was not an option.

In high school, Shadi had developed sympathy for an opposition organization. Political activity was not yet illegal, thanks to the revolution and the relatively open political atmosphere it had created. On June 20, 1981, however, following a series of simultaneous demonstrations coordinated by an opposition organization, the regime began to frantically arrest, en masse, anyone who had been connected to the opposition groups in any way. Shadi's arrest happened about six months after this event. Because of her political beliefs and affiliation, she remained in prison for five years. Her five-year sentence was served in Tehran's infamous Evin Prison, which, built expressly for political prisoners during Shah's regime, was later expanded upon and utilized by the Islamic regime.

Shadi started to write poems and her prison memoirs while in Evin – because pen and paper were forbidden tools, however, she wrote in her mind. Upon her release, she began to reconstruct her experiences on paper, first in Farsi, and in English a few years later, when she left Iran. In *The Five Seasons*, Shadi narrates parts of her experience as a political prisoner in Evin.

Shadi has a Masters Degree in English Literature, and is currently working on a full-length prison memoir. She lives in Canada.

Authors' Acknowledgements

This book is not a work of fiction. Every character described in these pieces existed, in flesh and blood, in the prisons we experienced in the Islamic Republic of Iran. The three of us have thought at one time or another that if we were lucky enough to leave the prison alive, we would write about what we witnessed there. We wrote these short pieces to keep that promise.

We don't look upon the people who are the subjects of this book as heroes or villains. We see them as people caught up in a web of unforeseen and tragic circumstances, trying to cope with their situation as logically as they could. Depending on their level of commitment and personality types, they reacted to the very unusual and unprecedented circumstances in very different and imaginative ways. Whatever their reactions, they were all victims of the theocratic and dictatorial regime of The Islamic Republic of Iran.

In an attempt to respect the women's privacy and security, we have changed the names, and in some cases, unimportant facts that were irrelevant to the authenticity of these stories. We are sure many prison mates reading this book will be able to recognize the characters portrayed in the events.

We believe that the more you distance yourself from an experience, the better you are able to judge the individuals involved in that experience. By looking back at our years in prison, we hope to be more objective about the characters and events. We are no longer the exact replicas of ourselves at the time these events unfolded, and we are sure the same is true for many of the characters portrayed here. We no longer feel the anger that once prevented us from seeing clearly what created the chaos in which such atrocities could be committed by a certain group of individuals. Many factors contributed to those circumstances culminating in the mass executions of 1988. Among them, people's apathy both inside and outside Iran, played a leading role. It's important to write these memoirs as widely and in as many languages as possible, to prevent these events from happening again.

The authors of this book would like to thank a number of people without whose encouragement, support, and hard work, the accomplishment of this book would have been impossible.

Our heartiest thanks go to Ann Decter, our publisher and developmental editor. From the day she took an interest in our stories to the end of the project, she was our ongoing source of guidance and support. Ann, we can't thank you enough for helping bring our untold stories to life.

Many sincere thanks to our editor, Rivanne Sandler, for her sharp eye, insightful suggestions, and genuine interest in our work. Rivanne, you made it possible for us to communicate our most unusual, hard-to-express experiences with ease and clarity, never letting the true meaning be lost in the process. Thank you.

Our grateful thanks also go to Shahrzad Mojab, for writing the introduction to our book and helping to put it in perspective for readers. Even as ex-prisoners who experienced these events first hand, we had a hard time digesting and coping with them. In reaching out to a different audience, we continuously faced the challenge of explaining why things happened the way they did. Shahrzad, thank you for creating the context for a better understanding of our stories.

We would also like to extend our thanks and appreciation to all the individuals who have made this book a reality: Lisa Foad, Schuster Gindin and Heather Guylar.

The authors' special note of thanks goes to the one individual who took the initiative to bring us together, and mentor us through the painstaking process of writing. If it weren't for her, we would still be merely entertaining the idea of someday unravelling our stories. You will remain anonymous, as you wished. Thank you for your true mentorship, and for believing in us.

Finally, we would like to express our deep appreciation and gratitude to all the parents, siblings, and other family members who selflessly fought their way to every visiting session during those very difficult times. Many thanks to those who raised grandchildren, nieces and nephews in their parents' absence, and to those who offered their unconditional love to us. Without their constant support, our lives would have been far more unbearable.